ANTO

Dismantling the
3rd Dimension

Transforming Our Trauma
on the Road from Tribe to Collective

ISBN Paperback: 978-1-7389815-0-2
ISBN Electronic: 978-1-7389815-1-9
ISBN Audio: 978-1-7389815-2-6

Portions of this book are works of nonfiction. Certain names and identifying characteristics have been changed.

Printed in the United States of America.

Antonia
TribeToCollective.com

This book is dedicated to all my clients.
Each and every one has propelled me
forward on my/our journey into love.
I am overflowing with gratitude.

The teacher is the student.
The healer is the patient.

Preface

Many years ago, when I began writing about my experiences, I was motivated by a desperate urge to be seen. While terrified of being shamed and rejected, I longed to be acknowledged: I wanted someone, anyone, to witness and validate the magic and, in particular, the agony I was experiencing in isolation. But as I continued to integrate more darkness into more light, more pain into love—as I increased my capacity to *see myself*, with acceptance, without expectations—the egoic motives attached to the writing dissolved, and in their place was the pure desire to share. To connect. To show up. To be.

We, as individual human beings, have become our own teachers, our own gurus. We don't need others to tell us our way. It is all within us. We have enough energy right now to access the wisdom we could never access before; to penetrate the darker parts of our humanity and reveal our truths within. That doesn't mean we don't seek support or information. When we are ready to see it in ourselves, we bring in the specific energy, the support, the frequency that we need in that moment.

Allow the space and silence you generate on this journey to help you absorb these inarticulable concepts into your subtle body and into your intuitive Self. Often, the mind doesn't quite know what to do with the new information, feelings, energies. Let go of time, deadlines, expectations, and goals. All those things will need to be released anyway. The mind has its own time signature, which is connected to your egoic expectations, connected to your pain. By letting go of your mind's expectations, you connect to your internal clock and the goals of your metaphysical Self. To release ourselves from pain defining our path, we unleash the magic within and reveal the magic without.

Table of Contents

Acknowledgments

I thank each of my healers, teachers, and guides,
both seen and unseen.

I am deeply grateful to my partner.
He is my foundation, my home, tethering me to safety
while I soar with the cosmos.

And big thanks to my editor, Michael Ireland. The first to
really see me and give me the confidence to be seen.

Note to Reader

In this book, you'll find that I repeat words and ideas throughout. Our 3D minds don't absorb abstract, intuitive material as easily as linear concepts; so, I create a deepening familiarity with the subject through repetition. In addition, I have created chapters and sub-chapters as stand-alone reflections so you can refer to them out of the context of the entire book.

These are just drops in an ocean of magnificence that is there for us, that is within us, and that is within you. Because I communicate with you through the limiting reality of this 3rd dimension, the words I share with you are going to be limiting. How could they not be? And I am still on this journey, so I too am still expanding my awareness and my language. My desire is to point your heart toward a feeling, a notion, and an essence of a reality that you must then explore for yourself.

While I refer to North America as the example of and leader of a fast-paced, pain-avoidant culture, that reality has, in fact, permeated many continents, countries, and cities. The use of North America as the example is not meant to exclude the existence of other "modern" cultures but to provide a singular term for convenience. This is also my home continent, so it is the most familiar point of reference.

When I write "fear, shame, and rage," it is a shortened version of the articulation of the complete range of uncomfortable feelings that include fear, shame, rage, anxiety, grief, jealousy, guilt, and disgust.

Throughout the text, some names have been changed to protect privacy.

For your convenience, a Glossary has been included to assist you with any unfamiliar concepts. You can find it on page 246.

At the end of the book, you will also find a link to Chapter VIII. This addendum is available on my website. In this chapter, I share many of the struggles I faced in releasing 3D toxicity from my body over the last 16 years. I include many recommendations on how to take care of yourself during this challenging process. You will find tips and tricks on how to manage the energy, the toxicity, especially in places where, geographically, energies are denser and therefore can be a bit more challenging to the body as we detox. I suggest things you can do to keep yourself as healthy as possible during a time that is challenging to the physical, emotional, and energetic body. When there is a lot of energy, we want to give it room to move, to flow. Therefore, working with the body is essential.

When pain and love occupy the same space-time,
transformation occurs.

Chapter I

Landing in the 3rd Dimension

For thirty-five years, my perception and experience of the planet under our human stewardship had been a constant source of rage, fear, and grief. Since the age of sweet sixteen, I felt compelled to spend my life fixing it. Before 2006, I was hell-bent on getting as many university degrees as I could and being as useful and right as I could—all to save the world from itself. In later years, I came to see that in a reality below my conscious mind, my need to rescue the world was part of a clandestine operation to stave off the waves of the inarticulable shame, fear, and self-loathing I'd felt all my life. I've never done anything too terrible…certainly nothing that would have justified that kind of inner pain. Both my parents abandoned me at different times in childhood, and more than once. For most people, that would be enough of an emotional maelstrom to kick off many inner crises. I spent many years trying to prove myself in academia, attempting to place myself beyond the scrutiny of anyone and everyone, and willing myself into self-acceptance and praiseworthiness. I received the praise, but it was never enough. I started out my early life and career trying to be a justice-serving, crime-fighting, social-political animal committed to being on the side of right. I was planted in the heartland of an evidence-based reality. I needed to see it to believe it. I was curious and accepting of unseen worlds and their possibilities, but that magic was not part of my reality, and it didn't serve my need for mainstream acceptance: *Be seen as smart and successful.*

In my childhood home, the topic of God never arose, and religion was the object of social and political critique. Beyond the basic rituals of our ancestry, we didn't entertain religious topics. The ivory towers of higher learning became my God, and I looked to those towers for validation. I always kept an open, respectful mind toward things outside the realm of evidence-based living—I had a mild curiosity even—but my dignity would not allow me to engage (with any seriousness) the mystical arts (even though looking back I can see there were indicators that I had one foot through the woo-woo door). I rejected most of it as something very rejectable.

Then, in 2006, all my political and economic and academic acumen were for naught. My entire world turned upside down, inside out, and to be honest, I still haven't landed. Things beyond my imagination popped into my life. My body did, felt, and knew things I didn't know were possible. And my external world seemed to match my inner bedlam. There was no apparent reason for this. No crisis of faith, no near-death experience, no clear trauma, no influencing person. Nothing. A switch went on. No reasoning or rationale the hallowed halls of higher learning had fed me for years could help me.

A blend of confusion and knowing was precipitated by four months of bliss. But I lived with constant inner tension, as I felt a knowing that I'd spent years doubting, distrusting, even fearing. And I was alone in this bliss/terror. No one else could see it, sense it, let alone explain it or believe it. I had nothing, no one to turn to for answers, and no point of reference. Yet the answers served themselves up daily, in cryptic handfuls. New ideas, books, and people came into my life, my dreams, and my thoughts. Bursts of understanding came through in meditation (something I suddenly felt compelled to do). I expected things before they happened and knew when I was supposed to read something, see something, meet someone. I was led by the nose down a scary magical path—but who was doing the leading? In an instant, I was on a new trajectory, and when I looked back, I wondered, *How did I get here?*

The academic and political worlds I had looked to for meaning and purpose were no longer a source of validation. Instead, they were a source of shame and rejection. I couldn't imagine my friends, colleagues, or academic associates believing what was happening to me, let alone respecting it. Of course, before 2006, I'd taken part in naturopathic medicine and yoga for years, which already put me on the fringe, but collecting evidence on intuition, energy bodies, consciousness, synchronicity, spiritual emergence, and past lives was not on the agenda of any academic or public institution of which I was a part. Almost overnight, I was dramatically and effortlessly led from a social, political career into counseling psychology and alternative healing. Everything had turned on its head spontaneously and independently, and it was as if I was standing outside, looking in, managing absolute terror, an exploding understanding, and an inability to trust what was happening within my mind/body.

I found myself in the company of new people: energy healers, astrologers, intuitives, mediums, and traditional medicine practitioners. I had my first foray into setting up real boundaries. I knew I needed to let people go who had been close to me. I turned to people I'd held at a respectful distance for shreds of explanation and validation. They told me about things I never knew existed, using terms like *kundalini awakening*, *accelerated awakening*, and *spontaneous awakening*. In 2009, in my second psychotherapy session with Matthew Remski, he told me, after having read my Vedic Astrological Chart, "You are a shaman! You are very porous and you bubble with fire." I had no idea what he was talking about. My thought was "Astrology? Really?" A healer told me, "Toni, you will heal yourself and others at the level of DNA." Many people told me I was a "big energy," "a bright light," and that I have been hanging around this planet for hundreds of thousands of years. "This is your last lifetime," a seer told me, "and then you're getting out." I laughed at that one because the idea of past lives was something out of philosophy class or fairy tales, neither of which were credible sources of wisdom for defining my life. "And *DNA*? Are you kidding me? Show me the science!" I yelled inside my head with disdain and judgment. Sure, I tried on a new concept occasionally—meridians, chakras, channeling—but each one was always accompanied by a hint of shame. *What are they all talking about?* For a while, I laughed at it all, rejected it, threw it out, or made light of it, and rarely repeated it to anyone in my circle, for fear of being laughed out of the room. For years, I sought credible, grounded, "reasonable" individuals and plied them for scraps of evidence and explanations of what was happening to me. I would go looking for validation in cautious ways, afraid of saying too much, worried that I would tip them over the edge and be cast out as a fringe lunatic.

This new metaphysical path became painful, distressing, and isolating, because after the scary bliss came the scary pain. Almost overnight, pain was coming out of me all the time, at all levels.

It jarred my body like an earthquake, or it got stuck, leaving me shaken, contorted, and exhausted from a body energetically and physically struggling to release so much toxicity. I could sometimes connect to the essence of the pain, like a desperate, childlike cry for my mother or the shame-filled ache of rejection. But there was a sense that while some of it was attached to childhood experiences in this life, it was also ancient, surfacing from an age-old drama, playing itself out, over and over and over again. The narcissistic parents, the raging mothers, the abandoning fathers. Yes, this was all my life, but it has all been done, repeatedly, in hundreds of lifetimes, centuries of humanity. And it was all coming out. I had moments where I glimpsed the story of the pain that was coming. I could feel and see battles I'd never fought, wounds of family dramas I'd never lived, illnesses I'd never had. And these were often verified and validated by others who were better able to access and explain imprints and experiences of other lives, other realities.

But what took up most of the space was suffering moving through my body that was too big for my mind to grasp, to make sense of. I got hints of being tortured, imprisoned, and buried alive. It made me scream, wail, even pass out as the unimaginable agony worked its way out of my body. I became intimate with a crippling spectrum of fear, shame, grief, and rage that made itself known to every crevice and corner of my being. For the first few years, I kept looking for answers: "Why is this happening? How can I manage it?" No one could tell me. Surely, I could find a person or a book that could explain what my life had become. But no one could provide me with an answer, a comprehensive explanation. They told me how powerful I was, and how lucky I was, but I didn't care. I was often so exhausted; all I wanted was for it to ease off, to take a break, or cease. My life became about finding ways of moving pain easily or rapidly...or stopping it altogether. I was flooded with doubt. How could I not be? Pain tells us when something is going wrong, right? Well...I learned later that the pain had been telling me I was doing something *right*.

The first year of this transition was a Wizard of Oz kind of year. Scary, but magical. Within seconds or minutes of writhing in excruciating pain, I would feel a subtle energy flowing through me. Ease and compassion flooded my mind and body. I felt big shifts from the perpetual anxiety I had lived in but had never realized, similar to the many clients who arrive at my office unaware they have been living for decades in the haze of depression.

The magic kept coming in weird ways. Things happened that I had never imagined for myself, and I hardly believed them when others discussed them. Through the very first (and last) instructional dream, I was propelled into learning from the most ancient healing modality. A woman with long brown hair sitting among others in a circle of office chairs swiveled to face me as I stood outside this circle, looking in. She said, very matter-of-factly, "Ayruveda."

"What?" I said.

"Ayurveda," she said again.

I shrugged and responded with simply, "OK."

I woke up and burst into uncontrollable tears. With suspicion, still not trusting myself, I went to the computer, plugged in the word, spelling it wrong since I had never heard it before that dream. Up popped the site for the only Ayurvedic school in Canada, four subway stops away. Cautiously, I enrolled as a student in the Ayurvedic counseling program. For the next three years, the ancient wisdom cracked me open, laying bare all my intellectual assumptions about human beings and what it means to be healthy. Years later, I understood that Ayurvedic healing is the ultimate companion for the spiritual journey, the kundalini awakening, the spiritual emergence, the journey out of this reality and into a higher vibration. But with each new high vibration, each new herb, treatment, or meditation, more pain and more energy moved through my body. I was releasing terror, nightmares, agonies, but in an accepting, healing space. I felt vulnerable and overwhelmed with the shame of it all, but here I could be seen, if only for a glimpse. It was my magical, dirty, painful secret, this overwhelming, unexplained, unexplainable process of moving terror, torment, and agony through this body.

At an intuitive level, I understood I was releasing pain. But why did it need to be so painful? Nearly every day for years, I navigated agony. Fear, shame, rage, and grief hijacked my mind, thoughts, and perceptions and messed with my body, my nervous system, my strength, my sleep, my biochemistry. But thankfully, each release impacted my perception of myself and my life. Each change was a movement toward greater ease—less fear and anger, grief and shame, followed by more joy and love, and greater feelings of connection. For the first time, I felt I was not alone. There was something beyond me accompanying me. The impact was profound. The results were simple. I hurt less, loved more. I wondered: *If pain can be fleeting, here one second and gone the next, is it real? Does it exist? Can the pain mean anything? Is anything real?*

In the seconds after a big pain release, I was struck by sudden insights. Insights I dared not trust kept coming and getting clearer. It felt like I was being rewarded with a new, magical chapter of awareness. It dawned on me that I was integrating a new reality. I was beginning to know. To see. To get it. To get IT. And as I got it, it seeped into other avenues of my life. My work with my clients evolved, and I saw that this process, this magic, this energy, was not a secret. It was available to everyone. But it was in hiding, underneath mountains of pain.

Through this process, I felt more connected in one way but alone and terrified in another. It was to be this way for years. To move things along, I began to use plant medicine. The more I released, the more I felt a new energy move within my body. My senses heightened. I tuned into my inner world. I realized I was not just moving my own feelings but feeling the energies of everyone else. The energies were all around me, moving through me—and all too often, sticking to me. It took years to figure out how to clear them out.

In sessions with clients, I saw that just by bringing non-judgmental awareness to the emotional source of the pain—not the story around the pain, but the source of the pain in the body—that the process of transforming and releasing pain could be activated. I saw people experiencing new life coming into stuck places. I saw choice where there had been fear. I saw love where there had been self-loathing. I saw people's own wild and magical paths ignited. But I could also see that this only happened if they stepped into the role of observer of the dramas within their own beings, if even for a moment. If they could sidestep the stories their mind had been telling them and see the pain separate from the goals and motivations their minds fed to them, things dislodged. Energy moved. If they returned to their minds, the energy stopped flowing. I saw that facilitating inner quiet was an essential element on everyone's path through pain. As I worked more with my clients and they experienced a lightening, I saw my own journey progress. My journey became connected to everyone with whom I walked, whether clients, family, or the grocery clerk.

On my jaunts to new and interesting places, people looked at me and spoke to me in ways I had never experienced. Each new group gave me a different name, a different label. Countless labels. In the beginning I was called a lightworker. What the hell did that mean? I was called a healer, a shaman, a witch (endearingly, I believe). I was called a star seed and an alien. I was told I could do magic. A couple of times I was called an angel—and once I allowed someone to adjust my wings, because I was both curious and didn't want to offend. A few years ago, during a painful plant medicine session, a shaman called me a "transmuter." (Still woo-woo, but clearer on the function!) But none of it meant anything—just more stuff to put in the vault—because to say any of it out loud was to invite shame and banishment from my professional community.

And... We've Landed

Pain I had never encountered in this lifetime was filtering through me. I felt the many colorful ways I had experienced torture and death; my throat cut, being disemboweled in battle. Were these past lives? Memories? Other people's memories? I still didn't know. I felt many of my children die, my village wiped out, followed by a white-hot, burning desire for revenge. In the throes of one altered state, I called out for my mommy. In others, I felt the deep, familiar longing to escape "here," to get the hell out. What "here" was came into sharp focus one morning when I underwent a horrific remembering while doing my exercise routine on the elliptical in my basement. I was reflecting on a YouTube video a friend had sent of Christian Sundberg, wherein he describes his arrival into this reality as the farthest place from God. The thought churned and churned in my mind. And then it hit me: *This is the farthest place from God, the farthest place from God…. The farthest place from God is…hell?! I am in hell!* A deep, lonely, isolating, suffocating terror swept through my body. In a flash of energy, clarity, and big feeling, I remembered landing here. I was squeezed into this dark, heavy, dense, far-away place. I felt overwhelmed, crushed, and terrified. Seconds later, my thought was, *What kind of idiot must I be to have signed up for this?!* And the next… *I gotta get everyone off this boat!* Then I went into shock.

An hour or so later, I walked by the fridge in a dazed state, and a small note I placed under a magnet caught my eye. It arrived the day before, attached to some flowers sent by a client in gratitude. The note simply said, "A Message from the Universe."

Later that day, I tried to put words to the feeling. The analogy that came was being buried twelve feet underground. Throw in the feeling of everyone I knew and loved being ripped away in a moment. Add to that, flashes of landing in the jungles of Vietnam in 1969, at night, bullets flying overhead. For weeks I couldn't go back into that memory without weeping instantly. It was touching a giant, raw wound.

You can listen to this recollection in greater detail in my podcast: *Dismantling the 3rd Dimension.*
Episode: "Look Right Into the Eye of the Storm."
https://podcasts.apple.com/ca/podcast/dismantling-the-3rd-dimension-the-journey-out-of/id1588908885?i=1000537616749

Here's a truth I accessed about the 3rd dimension: *This may not be hell, but I'm in one big trauma-filled reality. No wonder I hurt all the time! I've been moving a mountain of pain.* However, the prize for all my efforts was incomprehensibly enormous. It was an expansion of energy that both revealed and created a compassion-filled connection to self, to others, and to things beyond the seen world. It was the explosion of creative potential within my own being. This was the mystery unfolding before me. So, this was all for something—something big. These gifts of growing awareness and ease gave me a goal, a purpose, and a promise of a life outside of this reality. I know that while this mind/body's experience is limited to a few years, there is something boundless and mystical surrounding me and coming into focus. While I began to understand I was undertaking a giant purge at all levels to access this bigger reality, it took years to grasp the extent of it, and to trust it, even if I was still unclear as to all the how's and why's.

The Body Is a Step Behind

About seven years into this releasing process, in December 2013, I awoke to a pain that radiated from my knees to my neck. I couldn't move. A golf-ball-sized lump was sticking out of my spine. I lost the use of my left arm for six weeks. I had to sleep on my back for three months because my rotator cuffs were shredded. My massage therapist said the muscles in my back looked like cooked spaghetti tossed on the floor. I had turned into a Picasso painting overnight. I had a vague knowing that my body was trying to purge but was ill-equipped for the process. Years later, I began to understand how much energy I'd been moving through, how much trauma/karma I'd moved through, and how my body had always been a few steps behind the expanding energies. My physical body couldn't keep up with my growing energy body and it was being challenged—and damaged—in the process. I signed up for yoga teacher training, figuring that I should exercise like a madwoman to *metabolize* the toxins. For every energetic shift there is a release of toxins—emotional, energetic, and physical—that correspond with the lower energy. To metabolize is to burn them off so that they don't stick around any longer than necessary. For years, boxing, hot yoga, saunas, kayaking, and elliptical, each multiple times a week, became my survival strategy.

As the energy grew, so did the symptoms. My skin would repeatedly burn during a large transmutation and release. My spine would torque with the force of the energy trying to move through. I eventually realized that the energy was there to take pain out of the body. But if my spine wasn't in alignment, toxins would jettison into the rest of my body, causing inflammation, swelling, stiffness, brain fog, often instantly. Things got stuck, transmitting an accompanying emotional pain signal to my mind, temporarily, and often severely, distorting my mood and my worldview. Depression, rage, fear, and grief were constantly cycling through. My closest companions became my chiropractors, osteopaths, acupuncturists, and massage therapists, all trying to unstick the debris from my body.

I struggled with an egoic story: "You're doing something wrong." Had I failed somehow? Missed the point? Was I being punished? As the years went on, the detoxing and expansion increased. I expanded my seeing, my knowing, my abilities, my energies—and eventually I came to see this was as it was supposed to be. With a few key people seeing and validating my experience, telling me I was on the right path, an accelerated path, a miraculous path, I accepted what was happening. I was part of a giant transformation that was opening up around the globe. We are on the precipice of a mind-shattering shift toward a new world. It may not be as dramatic as the one I have been living through—not yet anyway—but it shows up in the rainbow of trajectories that reflect the uniqueness of each human being on this planet. Through our unique paths, we are each zooming out. Stepping back. Shedding what no longer serves us. Together we are transforming a mountain of pain. And sometimes the physical body is the last to catch up.

Let's Begin

All my life, I have been labeled "brutally honest." True to form, I am here to share an uncomfortable and confronting reflection in the hope of shattering delusions we maintain about our human experience—delusions that distract us from moving into the next phase of our evolution. I suggest the essence of our reality is constructed primarily of pain, suffering, and discomfort. Yes, our reality peddles pain. Human history suggests I am correct. The Buddha himself said, "Life is suffering." For most people, this concept is not too shocking. Some of us have been living, studying, and witnessing human discomfort all our lives, desperately trying to figure it out or fix it. Others may accept it at a philosophical level or find the concept fascinating when they see it portrayed in a documentary or in a university textbook. However, the exploration of this concept rarely goes beyond academia or rigorous religious practice.

Many people have a vision of where humanity is heading and who we are under all this heavy reality. They see lightness and life beyond our hard existence, and they inspire us to move forward in our evolution and healing. I, however, am delivering a parallel and hopefully complementary message: *To myth-bust our current reality and reveal the light beyond, we need to see pain for what it is, for the myths it retells, and for the delusions it perpetuates. To dismantle pain, we need to see pain.*

The fascinating (and I believe necessary) thing to observe is that while our existence is painful, we live in denial. We pretend it is otherwise. We walk around it, talk around it, making do, pretending all that pain is not there. We repress and suppress. Our pretending has gone on for so many thousands of years, we can't see it. The pretending along with the pain has faded into the background and become part of our hard wiring. Countless people walk into my office, informing me with confidence that their childhood was great, a wonderful experience, only to find out in later sessions that they were abused, neglected, or violated. Often our denial runs around trying to fix the horror and badness out in the world, but it can't or won't see what is happening in our own life, our own body, or our own home.

To crack this open, we need to explore what I see as one of the biggest (if not *the* biggest) and most widespread pains we suffer in this dense reality. *Aloneness.* We feel abandoned, isolated, rejected, and misunderstood. At all levels of self—physical, mental, emotional, energetic—we feel this pain. For most (if not all) of our lives, many of us have felt unseen, unheard, and unloved. The multitude of experiences of feeling alone are the building blocks of our uncomfortable collective reality. When we experience rejection—when we are dumped, fired, or betrayed— our rage surges. We are blinded by the pain of our own wounds, so we lash out at the other. When we hurt, so many of us hear the story of aloneness whispering into our ears, telling us, "Everyone's abandoned me. Only I have this pain. No one understands me."

Human beings also recognize we have lived with, accepted, and normalized an unimaginable amount of pain in this reality. We have turned pain into an art form. Our history is a history of pain and a study of how we've created and moved through varying expressions and experiences of suffering. Much of our lives have been about surviving that pain, avoiding that pain, all the while believing there is no other way we can exist. Or believing we have escaped it, but really, we have just stuffed it in a closet.

I suggest this heavy, trapped, pain-filled existence is the primary characteristic of the *3rd dimension*, our present reality. It is an existence built on the scaffolding of uncomfortable, low-vibration human feelings, the king of which is fear. Shame, anger, guilt, grief, jealousy, and disgust emerge out of fear. These feelings, stuck in our bodies (as trauma) and in our collective memory banks (our collective programming), make up our reality. We have been cycling around this dimension, sharing these low-vibrational energy fields of pain for thousands of years. The culmination of all this stuck trauma? *Separation.*

The pain of aloneness and separation has little to do with how many people surround you, how many people understand you, or how often you feel betrayed by others who seem to behave badly all the time. Aloneness isn't about what is happening in our external lives. We can have dozens, hundreds, thousands of people clamoring to see us, to know us, and to understand us, yet still we feel alone. We can live in a house filled with people and feel alone. The pain of aloneness lives within you and your perceptions. It's not about others.

Many of us came here to experience the myth of separation. We bought into it. We wear it like a smelly old coat passed down through generations. Aloneness is a central characteristic of this pain-filled reality. Our grand project is to figure out how to transform ourselves and transform our reality, by creating a million paths to connectedness. I believe there is enough evidence to suggest that a time of transformation and healing of separation is upon us—and it is accelerating rapidly.

Tribe to Collective

Many of us believe, feel, or understand that we have chosen to dive into this 3D experience. We signed up for this. We volunteered to come down here for a little while, or a long while, to walk an uncomfortable path, but with a purpose. We may sense that we are in this painful, heavy, exhausting existence—with all its exquisiteness—for a reason. If you accept that we are (or might be) eternal beings and we come here to experience the deep pain of death, there must be some payoff, right? Sometimes the purpose eludes us, but when things are not so crazy and we experience moments when our hearts are open, we can connect to a reality beyond the pain.

Many of us are living at the perimeter of that other reality. This is the frontier. We are sitting on the outskirts of this pain-filled 3D space. But this is not a physical border. This is the frontier between density and light. It is the line between asleep and awake. It is the space between eyes slammed shut and seeing with eyes wide open. *We are living on the edge of awareness.* From that awareness the next dimensional reality will emerge.

We have come here to this density accepting that we will crawl on our knees through the dark to bring light into our beings. The sticky quality of this frontier makes that task challenging, almost beyond comprehension. We often feel subsumed by pain, a pain telling us we are stuck. The dark tells us our pain is real. We think it can't be different, that it's someone else's fault, or that we're bad. The dark convinces us our source of power is in the hands of others.

How our pain shows up is through a bazillion expressions of the story of separation. We feel alone, unloved, not good enough, rejected, and abandoned. This pain is held in our bodies and is suspended in the contract between us. We share an agreed-upon reality that is perceived through ancient lenses constructed out of pain. Our pain is the central pillar of our organizational structures. We see and assess each other through these lenses of the social organization of pain. *How does that person or group alleviate my sense of aloneness? How do they serve my need for validation and keep me safe? Who sees me? Who doesn't? Who threatens me? Who doesn't?* We gather near people who validate us; we push out those who don't.

We construct enemies, camps, differences, threats, and the other, and we live in that us-versus-them reality. That is tribal existence. The social, economic, political, and religious organization of human beings is tribal. The tribe is how our social organization manifests. And the tribe is organized around pain.

Currently and in great numbers, we have signed up to bring light into the darkness of perceived difference. Into the darkness of enemies and "others." I see in my private practice that so many people make that their mission. Many are part of a project to transform the dark/density into light and expand the limits of that light. We are here to see the pain, to bring it out of the dark and into awareness, and then to drown it in love. Then we can find the next dark thing, bring it into awareness, and bring it into the light. Then the next and the next. And thus, we expand the light, our reality, and ourselves. In doing so we dissolve the tribe, the "us versus them," and we reveal the *Collective*. We connect to the Whole. Awareness reveals there is no Them. There is only We. Without the pain and the trauma of separation, we are One.

Our Physical and Metaphysical Inheritance

We live in the perpetual frequencies of fear, shame, and rage, but we are rarely aware of it. Just as children can normalize horrific and painful conditions in the home, human beings have normalized the painful lens through which we see each other and ourselves. Parents and caregivers pass down hidden perceptions of fear, shame, and rage to their children; the same ones they learned from the behaviors of their parents. They absorbed their parents' perspectives and beliefs, or they incurred wounds trying to cope with parental behaviors, perceptions, and beliefs. We build our relationships on, and experience them through, the filter of trauma. We rarely see it when it's trauma from our childhoods, and we see it even less if it's inherited from our family lineage or human history. When we do see it, rarely do we want to do anything about it. In my practice, I commonly witness at least one person in any relationship who doesn't want to talk about it, doesn't want to change it, and sure as hell doesn't want to go to counseling, no matter how painful things get.

Since 1886, when psychoanalyst Sigmund Freud launched the great therapy experiment, psychotherapeutics has brought the impact of family dynamics on our sense of wellbeing and safety in the world into focus. Concepts such as attachment, abuse, neglect, and abandonment have solidified in the therapeutic zeitgeist of the twentieth and twenty-first centuries.

Not only do we carry trauma from our family dynamic; we also hold traumas from our family line in our genetic makeup. There is a growing body of research demonstrating how behaviors and environment affect genetic behaviors in offspring.[1]/[2] We carry the collective record of our ancestors' unresolved fear, shame, rage, and guilt in our bodies. Our great, great, great grandparents' offspring inherited their parents' unresolved fear/shame/rage imprints. Each generation wears the echoes of alarm bells from thousands of years of trauma. Sometimes these echoes are strong, sometimes they are subtle, but our egos are managing imprints all the time and assessing the world through the lens of this pain. Without recognizing it, we are responding to and believing most of the signals these imprints send out. They become *reflexes*. Nearly involuntary.

There are billions of people who connect to the "spiritual" or "metaphysical" model, which holds a deep knowing of our increasing connection to the unseen worlds and unseen parts of ourselves. They reveal that we exist as eternal beings, learning and expanding through the experience of many lifetimes. Many faiths know this framework as reincarnation. The journey that is a

[1] Richard Frances, *Epigenetics: How Environment Shapes Our Genes* (New York: WW Norton, 2012).
[2] Galit Atlas, *Emotional Inheritance: A Therapist, Her Patients, and the Legacy of Trauma* (Boston: Little, Brown, Spark, 2022).

life here is not just about my singular goals to achieve or evolve. It is connected to the whole, and when we are born into a body, our souls commit to adopting all its inherited trauma. We contribute to the collective healing, the collective expansion, by taking on the healing and intergenerational pain imprinted on the body we inhabit at any given time. We experience the trauma imprints in the subtle layers of the energy bodies we carry from one life to another, separate from the physically inherited traumas. These imprints impact our worldview, and we are here to transform them into light as part of our individual and collective evolution.

This model for evolution and the role of human suffering within it comes from the merging of an evidence-based framework (intergenerational trauma and epigenetics) with a metaphysical framework (reincarnation). Our evolutionary path plays itself out in both our bodies and our souls. We expand our energetic/soul self as well as heal the trauma imprints within the body.

I believe higher frequencies are affecting our DNA directly, as energies of change and healing come in at this time. This energy contains information that our bodies, souls, and energy systems need to thrive, and there is a rise in energy on this planet that is not only allowing us to heal the pain we have suffered in this lifetime, but it is healing generations of trauma. This energy is *consciousness*. I have accessed this information about this growing healing potential while in altered states as well and have also learned about it from varied and distinct sources (such as Richard Rudd).

A Tidal Wave of Denial and Avoidance

You don't have to look far to see how much time we spend escaping pain, rationalizing pain, and looking for someone or something to take our discomfort away. Religions promise millions of people compensation for suffering, in this life and the next. We suffocate ourselves with addictions to help deny (or find temporary reprieve from) pain. To make sense of all this discomfort, philosophies from all corners of the globe and all eras have struggled by compartmentalizing, organizing, classifying, and recording our pain. But most of them failed to look at it head on. We have a subconscious aversion to looking at our own stuff. When we glimpse pain, we feel victimized and trapped by it, and we can't see it for what it is. We don't realize being a victim to our pain is how we have kept it entrenched. Being pain's victim is believing the power it holds and the stories it tells.

But what if I told you we are in the process ("we" being some, many, more than usual, and an increasing number) of no longer needing to avoid, ignore, or deny this pain? That we no longer need to engage in a battle with this suffering? What if I told you that now, more than at any other time, we are engaging in the work (consciously or not) of dissolving this pain? We are dismantling the infrastructures of suffering we have been holding in our bodies for thousands of years. To dismantle this reality, we need only look at ourselves. *We* hold that infrastructure within our beings.

Fortunately, you also hold the power to *transform it* within your body. The old infrastructure and the new are in your body. Within our individual, physical, emotional, energetic bodies and in our human coding, we host a system of low-frequency goo that we experience as pain, as suffering, as chaos, as torment. The campaign now underway is for a critical mass of human beings to look inward, to find out how to see their own host, their own vessel of pain, in a new way, and to transmute it, integrate it, and transform it into light. The large number of people engaging in this campaign represents a migration out of the tribe and back into the Collective. Or more accurately, back into *feeling* the Collective. It has always been there. We just didn't feel it. We haven't felt our connection to it.

We Are Skillful Distractors

It all seems so convenient, right? We have the problem. We are the solution. What a perfect problem to have. What we also have is a sophisticated, robust, finely tuned system of self-sabotage—that crafty ability to distract ourselves from our discomfort. In North America, we have turned distraction into a high-tech fine art.

For thousands of years, many of us have lived in distraction and denial. We are so immersed in suffering; it is impossible to consider any reality but one wherein we survive by thinking about and feeling something other than our pain. We can't imagine it could look any different. We have been so attached to this infrastructure of pain, aloneness, and separation; it hasn't been possible to recognize it. We've tried to make sense of pain in creative ways. We've classified it as good guys and bad guys, right and wrong, predator and prey, oppressor and survivor. The good guys thought, *If we can just vanquish the bad guys, all will be well. If we can just make everyone see how to be good, we can stop all the suffering.* It kept us going; fighting the good fight; fighting for justice, liberation, cooperation, and a better world. But even we so-called good guys can't see that when we battle pain, we construct pain. With our righteous warring, moralizations, shamings, prisons, and stomping out evil, we perpetuate the story of suffering.

Until now, when we thought we were looking at pain, we weren't. Pain has become so much of our reality, camouflaged in our group psyches, we could be fast asleep in the 3D and believe we are acting out of love and light. I witness our sophisticated systems of denial and avoidance every day with my clients, and I see them every day with myself. We have honed our ability to rationalize our ongoing regurgitation of pain. Our favorite method of denial? *Oppression.* It's one of the many ways we try to offload our pain onto others. Of course, we want to avoid pain—it's painful! We have constructed a plethora of systems we believe will save us, heal us, and keep us safe. In fact, they maintain, if not deepen, our wounds.

But I want to suggest that all of this is as it should be. Accepting a reality that is (by default) painful is an incomprehensible pill to swallow for many people. But I suggest we choose to come here, to this deep, beautiful dungeon, to crawl around in the dark, to beat each other over the head with clubs for a few thousand years to find out that it doesn't work. What we do find, after exhausting and tormenting ourselves for so long, is how powerful we are! Without the club. We are powerful enough to create a whole new reality.

With a culture, economy, and politics built on distraction, this method of bringing awareness is inconvenient and incongruent. We in North America have been perfecting the skill of escaping, denying, and avoiding. Crafting it into a fine art, in fact. Distraction is how many of us have built our life's meaning and purpose. We have constructed jobs and relationships, entire economies, to serve our desire to distract. We've needed to see how far our distractions could take us. But now, we are reversing course. If you are on this journey, now may be the time to build a practice, a purpose, of doing and being the opposite of distraction. Dive right in the middle of the thing you are avoiding. Find your way into discomfort and pain. Close your eyes, plug your nose, and free-fall. Fall deeply into the eye of the hundreds and thousands of pain storms we carry around in our individual bodies. Fall in... and take consciousness with you.

What Is Consciousness?

Throughout history and around the world, philosophical, theological, and scientific pursuits have explored, defined, and sensed consciousness. Some people equate consciousness with intelligence, and some with awareness. Some link it to the mind, others to everything outside the mind. Some connect it to being human, others suppose that all living things have consciousness. Some people describe it as a behavior, others as an experiential phenomenon. At this point in our understanding, it is unlikely we could come to an agreed-upon definition for something that is, essentially, unmeasurable (or at least the instruments our dominant institutions use cannot measure it). Anecdotal "evidence" that arises from altered states can "prove" that consciousness exists, but, of course, this evidence has no credibility in the mainstream.

So, what is this consciousness thing? My awareness is limited, and I await the rest of the story. However, for this reflection and our work, we can draw on Dr. David R. Hawkins' mapping of consciousness in his book *Power versus Force*. His brilliant, pragmatic work on consciousness helps us to understand our journey out of suffering.

Dr. Fran Grace, Hawkins' editor, sums up his definition of consciousness as the energy that connects us to everything. It flows through everything and is everything. However, there are measurable levels of consciousness, or "energy fields" that are:

> *...calibrated to measurable effect. With each progressive rise in the level of consciousness, the 'frequency' or 'vibration' of the energy increases. Thus, higher consciousness radiates a beneficial and healing effect on the world, verifiable in the human muscle response, which stays strong in the presence of love and truth.*[3]

And conversely, as described by Dr. Hawkins, we experience negative energy fields in emotional states such as shame, fear, and guilt. These have a detrimental effect on our lifeforce and body.

Consciousness flows here in this dimension, but it must squeeze its way into this density; push its way down into these lower frequencies. It has difficulty moving through us because of the calcification of pain in our bodies at group and individual levels. Where the energy of consciousness does not flow well (in lower frequencies) is where we experience the denser feelings of shame, rage, fear, guilt, etc. In those low vibrations, we are cut off from experiencing the intelligence of higher energies. The flow of consciousness has slowed to a crawl while we hold

---

[3] Fran Grace, ed. in David R. Hawkins' *Power vs. Force: The Hidden Determinants of Human Behavior* (Carlsbad: Hay House, 2012), xxxvii.

on to the ancient traumas of our ancestors' millennia-long murderous rampages.

But now we are shifting into a place where significant little drops of high-frequency consciousness are making their way into and penetrating our dense 3D beings and our lower frequencies of suffering. Many of us are getting a ping from our souls, a ping from the universe: "It's time to pay attention." Something is coming in that has many interesting things to say.

As we open and expand, and as consciousness flows, we discover that it has the power to take away our agendas of pain, replacing them with the agendas of love. When consciousness takes over, we give up wanting, we give up needing, and we give up controlling. We give up process, evolution, and active manifesting. We see these as constructs of our minds and history, and that all are attached to the densities of the physical plane. We see that these continue to keep us engaged in the pain stories of this physical self. They are 3D details. Once we get lost in the details of a desire, a judgment, or an analysis, we have most likely returned to mind, and are in physical self and the 3D personality once again. When we invite a drop of consciousness in, we experience it as a knowing; a knowing of something outside of our low-frequency individual perceptions. A bigger drop of consciousness interacts with our emotional body. We feel the knowing as love, joy, or gratitude. When we enter a wave or flow of consciousness, we transform. As the higher energy works on the denser, it transmutes those denser vibrations into the higher energy of itself. We explode—consciousness consumes us. We transform, piece by piece, burning off the pain and density of this space, until we shift into something else, something in greater alignment with unity consciousness, the singularity of everything.

Consciousness is that energy that takes us beyond this current physical container. In fact, I would argue that what we know in medical or physical terms to be "conscious" is actually state-limiting consciousness. When we break out of the dense state of this dimension, we experience consciousness. Pure awareness. The mind, most of the time, limits or prohibits this experience because it is focused on the survival of the sleeping vehicle; the individual who is not aware but is instead lost in the stories and dramas of pain and survival. It is, for example, during a near-death experience (NDE), when many people experience brain death, that they have their first conscious experience of consciousness, experiencing an awareness beyond this limited reality. The more we invite consciousness in, the more we allow intelligent energy to break down the densities within all layers of our being and transform us from a lower vibration to a higher vibration.

On my journey of expansion, on a daily basis, as I increasingly transmute fear from this being, I experience the contracting effects of low-frequency pain as it moves through my body. I have been dissolving a large density in the sacrum for years. Each time I integrate a layer of the deep, ancestral coding, or maybe a past-life imprint, my physiology loosens. Energy opens and moves. But before I feel the full effect of the expansion, I experience a contraction as the body detoxes emotional, energetic, and physical debris. Toxins are released. My hips and psoas muscles turn into concrete, solidifying from the dense nature of the painful toxins as they move through. These toxins, the leftovers of the lower energies that have inhabited my body in this dimension, are being eliminated, sometimes multiple times a day, through yoga and meditation, sauna, walking…and sometimes just through our shifting collective energies and the passage of time.

As we transform and release the lower frequencies we have been holding, we free ourselves from the painful reality of living in a 3D human body. We awaken, expand the Self, and experience states of awareness in greater numbers. We are bringing in higher frequencies, the increased flow of that ordered, higher state of being, and experiencing our liberation from the painful vibrations we have been regurgitating in this dimension for thousands of years. But it is those low frequencies—ancient, accumulated low frequencies—that are the fuel for the metabolic process of awakening and transcendence.

A Surge in Energy

We are crossing the threshold into a space and time of great potential. Authors and mystics Richard Rudd, Eckhart Tolle, and Penny Pierce have all written of the imminent launch of this profound era of change, propelled by an increase in energy; an increase in frequency, vibration, healing, evolving, *consciousness*, which alters the very nature of existence and even how we understand ourselves as human beings.[4]/[5]/[6] The healing experiences of things like meditation, plant medicine, and energetics have revealed that our deep healing involves a release of energy within our own bodies. We transform a dense, heavy story of pain through the infusion of healing energies (we can source this energy from within our bodies or from elsewhere). We transmute the density of pain into something higher and lighter. That new site of light releases even more energy—energy that has been trapped in our dense pain stories in our bodies. There have been millions, maybe billions, of people engaging in high-frequency healing activities in the last few decades, and each one of these seekers has the potential (and increasing potential) to exude higher energies. I see evidence of this energetic surge in "real world" manifestations such as the increase in meditation (as a viable healing practice), the increase in yoga studios, the growing popularity of healing/meditation retreats,

---

[4] Richard Rudd, *The Gene Keys: Embracing Your Higher Purpose* (London: Gene Keys Publishing, 2015).

[5] Eckhart Tolle, *A New Earth: Awakening to Your Life's Purpose* (New York: Penguin Group Publishing, 2006).

[6] Penny Pierce, *Frequency: The Power of Personal Vibration (Transformation Series)* (New York: Atria Books, 2009).

and the use of plant medicine at a global level. Over the last few decades, I have noticed that all of my healers—osteopath, massage therapist, naturopath—are familiar and work with subtle energies, something rarely experienced just twenty to thirty years ago. There is room for subtle energies to move when densities are healed and transformed into something lighter. That lightness is entering all corners of the lives of so many of us. And with this energy comes the experiences of peace, safety, love, and connection.

For our mind's sake, we can look toward quantum physics to explore our increasing understanding (and how little we understand) of the nature of energy in this reality and elsewhere. Research in quantum field theory explores energy coming from vacuum states, and more recently, explores how fusion reaction puts 1 part energy in and gets 1.5 parts energy out. I have taken a one-ounce dose of plant medicine and a few hours later felt like I was going to burn up from the power of the energy flowing through me. That was not energy from the plant medicine; that was intelligence from the plant medicine that released consciousness from my body, trapped in pain, through transmutation. Energy comes from places we are only beginning to understand. There are many authors, healers, and wellness practitioners who discuss how the planet and the cosmos are facilitating or contributing to this energy surge. I am able to share how I see *human beings* increasing, releasing, and sharing higher frequencies on their healing journeys, which I believe not only heals us but works in tandem with the planet to move us to another reality.

I find it a fascinating coincidence that we have the largest population on this planet who have inherited thousands of years of suppressed pain at a time when energies are surging and pain is the fuel for the greatest transformation, possibly ever. Or is it a coincidence at all?

Beyond the 3rd Dimension

Over the last few decades, many of us have witnessed or developed an increasing curiosity about the unseen world. We are exploring what happens beyond our five senses, and topics like the occult, spirituality, NDEs, channeling, psychic phenomena, angels and guides, the law of attraction, manifestation, and more are mainstream communications. We use words like energy, intuition, ascension, and awakening more than ever. We want to plug in, to connect, to access something bigger, both within and without. We want to know more, reveal more, love more, and we long to connect to a force that is both outside of us and a part of us.

Some people who are in tune with subtle energies are seeing this new reality as it comes in. New worlds, new universes, new earths. Visionary Penny Pierce refers to these phenomena as "evidence of a higher frequency," and says the so-called 4th dimension is percolating through our reality. She describes how in the future, we "...won't be interested in linear cause-and-effect thinking or angular shapes. You'll think in spirals, and life will move in oscillating waves."[7] The surge, the expansion, is happening. It's not without its challenges or its egoic influences, of course, but it is there, and it shows our hunger for the frequencies of love and awareness—and our shift into the next dimension.

On my own magical journey, I recognized there is something required of us. We must activate our journey and move it along. I realized when working with my clients that it is hard for them to see where they are going without knowing where they are. We are curious, excited, and hungry to touch the next reality, but first we need to bring awareness to who we think and believe we are now. What is our current 3D reality? What are we here to let go of? What doesn't work? What no longer makes sense? To see it

---

[7] Ibid., 4.

allows us to direct the energy of change and transcendence into it, and in order to direct energy, we need to know the answers to questions like, "Where are we directing it? What does it look like? What does it feel like? How does it operate? How will I know when I am lost in it? How will I recognize when it changes?"

Penny Pierce describes this reality we are stepping out of as a world that:

> ...*contains time, space, and matter: finite objects and empty space; an inside and an outside world; a past, present and future; and an idea of self based on what reflects back to you from other beings.* [8]

The 3D world we are stepping out of is a state with little awareness. We only see ourselves in relation to others. The density of it, its stickiness and heaviness, gives us little room to move or to see. To expand, we need to make room and bring in energy of awareness to these heavy, unseen places. Where we can see ourselves. That remolds our reality so we can elevate to the next one.

Through my uncomfortable journey unpacking the 3rd dimension in myself and my clients, I have had glimpses, visions, and a profound sense of how and why we are on this journey. To get where we are going, we need to dislodge ourselves from where we are. Where we are is like a plug in a drain. Pain is dense. The pain we are holding in our bodies shows up in goopy blobs. To shift ourselves into the next space, we need to target those blobs, alter them, and lighten them, so we can experience the flow of energy. Shame, anger, and fear are thick—they stop us from moving through the doorway.

On our walk out of the 3rd dimension, we are adding the metabolic power of awareness; consciousness to transform our thick pain into lightness and fluidity. When we apply awareness

---

[8] Ibid.

to pain, it transforms into compassion, love, and gratitude. Those beautiful energies can walk through any door.

Energy Plus Pain

But with profound change comes profound discomfort. While we have romanticized human history somewhat through our movies and fictional accounts, recorded history is a history of suffering. All of that is coming to the surface as we ready ourselves to shift to the next dimension, so…we might want to talk about it.

Millions of people around the world are getting primed to evolve into the next existence, the next reality. This reality is not about the deep levels of suffering and pain we've been accustomed to on this planet. It's about love, connection, and creativity. In this next reality, there's an energy of connection that flows. We are standing at the threshold of this new reality—but how do we walk through that doorway to the other side? The blueprint for transcendence is unfolding before us.

A multitude of changemakers are contributing to this evolutionary process, and we each have a role to play in our migration to the next reality. We each contribute an energy, a frequency, on this human journey into the next higher vibrational existence. Some of us are here to reveal a vision. Some of us are here to foster silence. Some are helping you heal your body and some your mind. Some are revealing other realities and showing you the way there. Mooji,[9] a spiritual Master aiding people in their path to self-realization, directs you straight into you, to show you who you are, your eternal Self, underneath your stories and pain, and helps light a fire underneath your 3D scaffolding.

I want to reveal to you what you are by showing you *what you are not*. You can't see the forest for the trees. I want to show you the jungle, and how to take a machete into that jungle and hack

---

[9] https://mooji.org/.

away, with love, at that which is not you. I want to help show you how to release the pain, release the energy you hold within, so you can reveal the real you. I am here to assist you in activating your inner alchemy, to share with you an awareness—a seeing of Self—and to enable you to let go of what no longer serves you, of what you no longer are and no longer need. I want to direct you to the denial, the darkness, and the fear (of this lifetime and many other lifetimes) that your mind has always thought you were. I will try to show you how to see the pain and suffering of this reality that is no longer yours to hold.

You need to see that pain, intimately, deeply, lovingly. You need to heal the separation right out of your body. You need to become limitless and acquire the ability to morph right out of this reality. Right out of your history. The even bigger magic? A deep awareness has the power to transform your pain into a high-frequency version of your Self. It feeds the purpose of your journey here—which is your expansion out of here.

This deep seeing has not been available to most human beings for the last many thousands of years. We have been lost in the heaviness of our pain and the density of our reality. But with the rise in energy, more of us are willing, wanting, and able to receive that energy for our healing and evolution. We can raise it to a place where we can see the pain infrastructure of this reality sitting in our bodies. And we are getting ready to transform it, because, well, we can't take it with us. What we do take with us (or what takes us to the next reality) are the higher frequencies of consciousness: compassion, gratitude, and love. Conveniently, it is those frequencies that transform fear, shame, and rage, and that transformational process launches us. Through metabolizing pain with consciousness, we explode, expand, create, and move into the next realities.

Awareness is the beginning, middle, and end of this process as we facilitate our inner alchemical transformation, transmutation,[10]

---

[10] Pierce, *Frequency*, 3.

and expansion, out of the 3rd dimension into the next one. But first we need to ask, "Where are we coming from?" Where we are going will unfold from that. We are coming from suffering. Our systems of resistance and avoidance have kept us (and keep us) from seeing that suffering. I invite you to see; to increase the energy and raise your awareness to facilitate our transformation into the next reality.

None of This Is Real

Not everyone is going to like what I am going to discuss, transmit, and activate in this book. What I am saying is not pretty. It is not positivism, at least not at the start. It is not sugar-coated or dressed up. Many people may find it confronting or feel I'm not making sense or that I've lost the plot. That's okay. We are all on distinct journeys, and they should not look the same. This process is not for everyone. If you haven't felt that intuitive click, if there's no emotional or intellectual pull, this book may not be for you. That is perfect.

So, if you are still here, I'm going to keep asking you to deepen your focus on the thing you are trained not to look at—that mountain of pain you are in. An evening of local or international news alone is enough to lead us to a bottle of vodka or antidepressants, let alone the threats of war and poverty, not to mention our twenty-first-century players—a pandemic, global recession, and a looming war. Family trauma and drama deserve special mention, as does humankind's tragic relationship with our environment. Since the advent of the internet, evidence of our disconnected selves abounds. If we see all our bad behavior as simply a manifestation of pain, it may be easier to get an idea of how much pain is floating around. And maybe we can get better at seeing it versus avoiding it, judging it, or denying it.

I help my clients bring their pain into focus, become aware of it, and love it. I help people see pain's density and sense the discomfort of it so they can transform it into light. The deeper they see, the deeper consciousness flows. It flows into tissue, into bodily fluids, into cells, into energy channels, and right into their genetic coding. And then out comes pain. Poof! It vanishes. It dissolves. A new energy moves in in its place.

Does something here resonate with you? Do you feel a sense of curiosity, relief, or validation? That's because there is a part of you that is ready to look at your pain and not look away. Maybe you have been feeling the pain (maybe a lot of pain), which is often a part of this journey, but you have not allowed yourself to acknowledge it. Or you've acknowledged it but not known what to do with it, which can lead to pervasive avoidance. Avoidance is easy, especially here in North America, where so many acceptable forms of addiction exist: our phones, our wine, our blaming, our righteousness, our rage.

The seeing needs to happen. Full ownership needs to happen. Then consciousness is available to do the work, the healing, the dismantling, so you can shift realities. Because what we are seeing on this path is that this reality, this 3D existence...well... it's not real. Our minds and our nervous systems may tell us it is real, but that must go because it is all unreal. What is real? Love. Compassion. Gratitude. The rest we leave behind. As we connect to the energies of our next reality, our 3D delusions fade.

You can explore this concept in great depth in my podcast: *Dismantling the 3rd Dimension*.
Episode: "There is Nothing Going on"
https://podcasts.apple.com/ca/podcast/dismantling-the-3rd-dimension-the-journey-out-of/id1588908885?i=1000539213478

We Live in a Dream

While we do not yet understand our sleeping dream states fully, I refer to our current reality as a dream. We exist in the echoes of ancient terror and torment that human beings have been inflicting upon each other for thousands of years. That suffering that is held within each of our bodies constructs most of this reality, a reality lost in the haze of history, filtered through old imprints of pain held in our beings, and disconnected from the present. That is being asleep. To be asleep is to be unaware of the reality around you because it is suppressed by the reality before you. That is what we are. We are seeing through a lens of pain, unaware that this is a construct, not an immutable truth, and we are unaware that we create it (as opposed to being its victim). Our lack of awareness is our dream.

Not everyone is here to let go of the dream, so for them, it may be real. The more pain we feel, the more real it feels, and the more our egos tell us, "It's real!" But the pain is only an anchor to a reality we are dissolving this very second. Everything in your being is going to fight it, argue with it, or contradict it (especially when you feel uncomfortable). But as we move through, we ask ourselves, to what reality we are connecting? From what reality we are disconnecting?

Dismantling Project. Healing Process.

I am here to share a seeing of the 3rd dimension. You might not see it all or understand everything, not all at once, at least. My progress came in bite-sized pieces. What follows might not feel like your truth, now or ever. You may not agree with, like, or be comfortable with everything you hear or how you hear it. Take it all in. Spit out what doesn't work. I hope to provide hundreds of concepts and inspirations to ignite and encourage your unique experience, your own journey inward. You may be familiar with all, some, or none of these concepts. If you are familiar with them, sit and absorb them. An idea can run around in your head for years and then, at the right moment, under the right conditions, the idea drops, and you absorb its meaning in a new, expansive way.

You might also use the tools provided here as reminders. Know that when you are uncomfortable (especially when you are uncomfortable), something incredible might just be happening—you might be coming out of a story, releasing a trauma, or deepening your journey into Self. Use all the reminders you can get. When you are in the pain, the pain will tell you the bigger reality is not real, that it is the only thing that is real, and you are trapped in it. Your job is to keep your eye on the ball. Use whatever techniques you can (including re-reading sections of this book) to remind yourself and get past your historic, low-density "victim" story. You can integrate and release that pain.

The beautiful thing I realized through my personal and professional work is that many of the tools we use to heal ourselves of this reality and bring the dream state into focus are some of the same tools we use in psychotherapy. For example, examining our core beliefs, turning into our pain, developing boundaries and self-compassion, and creating safety are all instruments of transformation. In a quasi-systematic way, I combine the tools of psychotherapy with metaphysical tools and frameworks that have emerged out of my process. While we step out of one reality and into another, it is the resolution of old pain stories we carry in our bodies that facilitates that step.

Your Own Unique Breadcrumb Trail

I find an increasing number of people describe how they experience synchronicities, signs, and messages. They get what they need for the next step. Sometimes this message delivery is rapid, and sometimes it feels slower. It can deliver books and people and inspirations and concepts in your language. Not just linguistic language but mental language, emotional language, or cultural language. However, in the first years of the process, I was flooded with doubt and terror. Even while bombarded with undeniable daily guidance, it took a while for me to trust the information and experiences that were coming to me. For example, I would walk into a room and know that I was supposed to talk to someone, and they would approach me out of nowhere to start a conversation about dreams or destiny or awakening or healing, or about anything I was experiencing in the moment. Once, I was walking through a book fair and felt drawn to a table selling a book on kundalini. I bought the book without knowing what kundalini meant. A week later, I had my first appointment with my Ayurvedic doctor. While struggling to explain to her what my life had become, she calmly told me that I was experiencing a rise in kundalini. After I got back from a five-day hike, my feet were bleeding—I could hardly walk— yet I still felt compelled to get out of bed at 6:00 a.m. and go for a two-hour walk in my local park where I began to connect to magic, experiencing the process of daily releases, felt subtle energy for the first time, and launched a process of learning and healing that continues today, where I am connected to a piece of a puzzle, an insight after a release. My mind and body would feel the clarity and lightness of a new understanding. Lessons came on the nature of compassion, how human pain existed, the function of thought versus feeling, and forgiveness. Lessons came from the inside more so than anything on the outside telling me where to go, what to do, and who I am. Skeptical, I scrutinized everything. I had to triangulate information to compile enough evidence to begin to believe that what I was experiencing was not a delusion. I spoke to a friend or two, hesitantly; friends I knew would call me out if I was fooling myself, falling for something. I laid out my experiences, step by step. They couldn't deny, but they had no explanation, because, of course, they came from the same "rational/logical/evidence-based" reality I came from. Now, years later, I believe. Doubting is just part of the process. We need to get past the Cerberus that is the mind, which is trying to make sure we are not being duped. And if you are already convinced, then your process may be about learning discernment. Whatever way this journey crashes down or creeps up on you is right for you.

It's all perfect. I'm not taking you anywhere, leading you anywhere, or giving you anything that's not already yours. If you walk away from this book with only one thing, that's the thing you came for. I'm serving up what you've already selected for this adventure. Your job is to see that you're the creator of your reality on this magnificent adventure. Releasing yourself from this dimension is the journey you are on. Take care of yourself, be kind to yourself, and be patient. Get quiet. Be curious, generous, and tender while you are on the road to finding you.

I have three goals in mind in sharing this book with you:

○ First, I want people on this journey to know that we must get more comfortable with being uncomfortable. The pain that's been cycling around this reality for so long is going to come out through our bodies—and that's uncomfortable. Many people are getting ready for this with plant medicine journeys, but uncomfortable experiences are going to happen outside of the plant medicine arena, too.

○ Second, I'm here:

  a) to nudge you to launch the process of disconnection from this dimension. This *activation* is about seeing the 3D as it lives within you. It sets you on the path beyond your delusion of separation, beyond the veil, and connects you to the multidimensional magnificence that you are.

  b) to *enable* you to find and follow your inner capacity to heal and to expand.

  c) to help you *expedite* your journey along the path if you're already on the way to your expanded reality beyond your pain, fear, and suffering of the 3rd dimension.

○ And third, I want to tell those that have been living in the world of the mind, as I was, that we are so, so much bigger than our minds tell us we are. I wish for those sitting on the precipice to take the leap and explore the magnificence below our thinking world.

Some people come to this dimension to figure out how to have a good time. They are here to step out of the battle. Spending years processing ancestral pain won't serve them. Some people are here to stir the pot and invest in creating the discomfort. They won't want to, or need to, expand their awareness. All of it is perfect. We stay in our journey and let others be in theirs, regardless of what our judgments tell us. This journey is about you. In knowing that, you serve the Collective.

The transmissions are flying around our Collective, coming from all directions, and are here to support the big change. This is my offering to the flow of higher frequencies and to the collective evolution.

Raising the Frequency

This is a collective story. It is about Us. My clients follow me into the energy where their mind/body wakes up, awareness enters, and a new reality opens. We are seeing a tidal wave of consciousness that is asking us to let go of the infrastructures of fear, shame, and rage we hold in place when we look outward for validation and meaning. This new reality is asking us to look at our belief in pain's story of separateness, to use pain to feed our awareness and our expansion, and to let go of the wells of suffering we carry around, in, and between us.

I now understand this healing, this evolving, this expanding is raising people's frequencies—in their physical, emotional, and energy bodies, and in the electromagnetic programming of their bodies. It raises the frequency of others and of the world around us. As energy rises over the coming years and decades, it will penetrate the pain and suffering of human history and genetic memories that are recorded in our bodies, elevate us out of pain and out of the contracted states of suffering, and expand us into the next lighter, more conscious, more connected reality.

All the labels—lightworker, angel, healer—are 3D labels for methods of delivering high energy and raising frequency. There is so much more energy available now than when I started on my journey. There is more wisdom, and it is easier to access. Things are different now. A much bigger community has plugged into The Field.[11] There are more safe spaces to talk about our woo-woo world, and we are making giant leaps forward in consciousness. We are on the leading edge of a global awakening.

As the energies continue to rise, I believe more pain will surface to be metabolized. I want to encourage more loving discussion on how to embrace it and help each other see it so we can transform it. We are changing our relationship to pain, and with that change comes consciousness. Our pain is not something to avoid, but something to bring into awareness, into the light. If we don't see our old pain stories—ancestral, past life, childhood—we will continue to recreate this reality of suffering.

The more of this life I live, the more I know I know nothing. That truth wraps around me, comforts me. My knowledge is disappearing like a white circle on a black screen, shrinking into a speck, until... Poof! From that profound existential unlearning trust emerges—a trust that the journey out of pain is a letting go of everything we thought we knew. I am a speck, but I am also exploding like a supernova, bigger and brighter than all my learning.

I want to know even more about nothing. Because in that nothing, everything appears. My heart opens to the universe, and I see myself. This is why I am here. To share. To assist you in raising your energies and to direct you in receiving the healing of deep awareness. To enable you to find your Self through transforming pain. To turn pain—that which is not you—into something bigger, wiser, more loving, something that serves you, becomes you, expands you. To connect you to the healer within and to your own process of expansion.

---

[11] Lynne McTaggart, *The Field: The Quest for the Secret Force of the Universe* (New York: Harper Collins, 2008).

As we continue our exploration into the 3rd dimension, we'll look at how pain has unfolded in historic and global societies, exploring two common globally shared pain patterns. We'll continue by bringing the nature of the 3rd dimension into focus, unpacking some of the major players as they pertain to our expanding journey, including Trauma, Ego, Mind, and what it means to be asleep. Once we have our sights on the density, we'll examine the healing journey out of our dense reality, creating a new framework, process, and a new narrative for the next reality. Out of this new narrative comes five key elements I found to be the building blocks for shifting realities; these are the 5 Pillars of our process. They are pivotal practices of silence and presence that move us along this path, and we will look at them in detail. Finally, we will look at our To Do list and discover what those practices that deliver the healing energies of consciousness and facilitate our shift into the higher realms are.

These writings may speak to those who are on the "spiritual path." The seekers and journeyers. I believe there are many routes into our metaphysical realities and these reflections may contribute to your path of expanding awareness, connection to Self, and connection to the Whole. We are also managing pain and trauma, so these writings may serve people who are trying to make sense of their own pain and who may benefit from exploring a different relationship with it. It may also serve present and future healers and therapists who, in the coming years and decades, I suspect will assist people moving through pain in a new, possibly more rapid, way.

For all those who serve others, already creating light (which most of you are), being able to see our stuff means we are less likely to throw it up all over others. If we keep displacing our fear and anger, we stay stuck in 3D density and we do the opposite of what we believe we are doing. That's the trick of our pain stories, our ego. Your ego can tell you that you are doing good, that you are spreading love and light, when in fact you are still emitting

3D pain. That's what most of us are doing, most of the time—emitting pain stories in disguise. To learn to see our *own* pain so we can detect when it has taken over the show is to live in service of love and consciousness. It is to wake up from the dream.

When big pain stories of divisiveness, of "us versus them," are front and center at a global level, this will be a loving, conscious gift to the world. Seeing and being aware of the pain and what's on this side of the veil heals you, and therefore, it heals the whole.

We are burning off thousands of years of pain from our bodies and unleashing the next reality. The energy is flowing, and the next generation of healers is coming. Our frequency rises, and we discover and unleash our power to transmute pain. Let's open not only our eyes, but the truth within our hearts, so we can turn into the potential within us and assist each other in our collective transformation.

Recommendations

This is trauma work. We are healing pain. With our ancestral and past life traumas surfacing, it happens to be a lot of work, so it is good to prepare. We are going into the caves of our being, into the dark places that hold the density of our human experience. Our nervous systems, and our physical and mental bodies, have trained for thousands of years to shut down or run or fight in the face of pain. Now we are asking them to sit still. The egoic mind and the nervous system are resistant to pain. The body does some weird, uncomfortable things when the debris of those trauma codes oozes from our body. So, to help us feel safe and supported, we need to prepare.

I recommend that you explore incorporating some or all of these supports into your life. You will want to create a support system; a group of people with whom you feel safe, who can deliver the message that you are cared for and not alone. This list might include your:

○ massage therapist/osteopath/chiropractor, etc.

○ naturopathic doctor. (Mine was a lifesaver when things started to derail.)

○ yoga classes/Tai Chi, or other meditative movement groups.

○ meditation group. (In person is preferable. Online is great, too.)

○ psychotherapist—whom we will discuss in greater detail later.

○ spiritual counselor/mentor.

It could also include:

○ friend(s) who are also going through this or who can be empathetic.

○ books that support this journey. I have created a Reading List at the end of the book.

○ places and things that soothe you, calm you, ground you: favorite spots, baths, candles, music, altars, writing, walking in nature.

○ exercise. We are processing a lot through this journey, detoxing lifetimes of density. The more you experience ancestral transformations, the more physical the experience might be. Physical metabolism is linked to energetic/emotional and mental metabolism. We need to move when we are in the thick of it.

○ good nutrition. We need to support the body with good building blocks (i.e., live, digestible food).

If you have found (or can find) a therapist who is empathetic with this path, I recommend doing so. As you move into the process, you will understand what you need in a therapist. Any support getting into the energy body is a bonus on this journey. A therapist can assist and encourage you to look at the places your ego will want to avoid and deny.

If you have experienced painful life events (in childhood or adulthood), and it's difficult for you to sit in uncomfortable feelings, I strongly advise you to seek a good therapist before you start, to help you create a safe foundation. During challenging times, we need good support. If we don't feel safe, the ego will resist, and we can do damage if we force ourselves to look at our traumas before there is a soft place to land.

It is important to find someone with whom you resonate, so shop around for a good fit. You may not click with your first therapist, so keep looking until you feel that connection. Some psychotherapeutic modalities that are compatible and support this inner journey include Internal Family Systems and Somatic Experiencing.

Chapter II

Examples of Big Stories—Seeing the Tribal State

Introduction

My intention is to bring awareness into how we hold old pain stories in our bodies unknowingly and pass them forward into future generations. In the past, when we have attempted to examine, explore, and expose protected stories, we have invoked a lot of rage. When we first began to discuss the frequent occurrence of abuse in the Church, abuse in com-

petitive sports, family rape, or spousal violence, there was, and
often still is, public backlash. But over the last few decades, there
has been an increasing amount of room to shine more light on
how we have been perpetuating 3D pain in these places. We are
willing to see it. I am inviting you beyond your resistance, to look
at deposits of density that keep themselves hidden with 3D mechanisms of denial and fear.

Bringing the Tribe into Focus

The tribal state—the social organizational manifestation of our
pain—is held together by, and organized around, suffering. That
is the principle of "us versus them." The tribe is the social space,
the interactive space, wherein our individual pain stories play
themselves out within and among groups. Whether a group of
two or a group of two million, the tribe holds and perpetuates
pain stories in this dimension. But to see those patterns (meaning
bringing awareness to those patterns we have perceived as
normal) is to free ourselves from those tribal stories and move
ourselves into the *Collective*, a community of love, consciousness,
and connectivity.

We have been passing time in this space where, historically, we
have depended on the tribe. The Merriam-Webster definition of
tribe is "a social group composed chiefly of numerous families,
clans, or generations having a shared ancestry and language."[12] It
is a historically defined and recognized affiliation among human
beings—we are defined by, shaped by, and seek safety in the tribe.
We seek safety because, according to Thomas Hobbes, for most
of recorded history, life has been "…continual fear, and danger
of violent death; (….) solitary, poor, nasty, brutish, and short."[13]
He says, "Hereby it is manifest that during the time men live

---

[12] "Tribe," *Merriam-Webster.com Dictionary*, Merriam-Webster, https://www.merriam-webster.
com/dictionary/tribe, Accessed 3 Aug. 2022.
[13] Thomas Hobbes, *Leviathan* (New York: McMillan Publishing Company, 1962), 100.

without a common power to keep them all in awe, they are in the condition which is called war; and such a war, as it is every man, against every man."[14]

The hostile and adversarial nature of much of human interaction has been constant. I think we've needed that fear, shame, and rage to survive, to date. While in this pain-filled reality, shame and fear have made us better neighbors and maybe even prevented crime. We have been driven by shame-based impulses: "What would they think?" or "I want people to see me as a good person." More often than not, we are driven by the impulse to curb behavior so as not to face rejection and abandonment. That pain has regulated the behaviors of a world in pain. We have connected through threat versus love.

We long to feel safe with others and we seek that safety, so every act that has led to pain feels like a betrayal. Within us, we hold thousands of years of fear that has been generated by the many ways we have betrayed each other. Each betrayal is experienced deeply, at a childlike level, as abandonment. In our social system, in which we continue to seek safety, we perpetuate this fear of abandonment.

Five hundred years ago, five thousand years ago, we needed tribal approval to survive. Often, if we did not get that approval, we were ostracized, violated, or killed. We feel the threat of disconnection in infancy when Mum is not there, and our tiny bodies go on alert, becoming distressed at the possibility of abandonment. We feel threat when there is disruption or the absence of a secure, loving attachment between ourselves and a parent, which leads to cycles of harmful or dysfunctional behaviors.

In order to not feel so powerless in this desperate, combative existence, many people have sought and clung to oppressive power structures. This can be an abusive parent, a gang, a toxic spouse, a toxic boss, or a larger-than-life presidential figure.

---

[14] Ibid.

Or we feel protected when we are at the top of the hill—being that parent, that gang leader, that powerful spouse, boss, or president—hoping to escape the discomfort of abandonment.

So, we cling to that power for safety, or we assert that power aggressively for safety. That is how we relate to each other and what we have expected from each other for thousands of years. There is rarely a choice. We believe the tribe "out there" is going to be more hostile than the one we are already in. We stay in our groups to protect ourselves from attackers, predators, and the unknown.

We have a painful history of trying to survive each other, and that history is marked in our shared, deep terror of our fellow human beings. This makes sense, because we have been terrorizing each other for thousands of years, and that fear is imprinted in our bodies, wired into our 3D beings, and handed down from one generation to the next. We hold the memory of terror and enslavement to the tribe over thousands of years in our emotional, energetic, and physical bodies.

But now, with a densely populated world and in this interconnected and mobile existence—most particularly here in North America—we can confront some of the imprints. We have more choices than ever before. At present, we can choose from eight billion people to make up our tribe. As adults, we can experience a level of genuine freedom like never before. We can choose to understand that abandonment—as a threat to our survival—no longer exists for many of us. And even though we may feel the terrorizing pain of it, in practical terms, the life-and-death threat of abandonment no longer demands so much of our attention. We can entertain such notions as: "If someone does not like me, I can go find someone who does." "If this boss sucks, I can seek another." "If my partner behaves like an ass, I can go find someone else."

The gap between these two polarities (between the truth that we are safe from abandonment and the feeling that it is dangerous to not be liked or to be rejected) is where the healing potential sits. That is where the potential for change, for evolution, and for love can move in. In that delta, we can both release the tribe and open up to the Collective.

For most of us, throughout most of history, we have looked toward "the other" for our sense of safety. We have felt trapped in our relationships and our circumstances. We have lived in a feeling—conscious or not—of emotional enslavement to those nearest to us. Our tribe has represented a source of safety, but just as often (if not more often), it can be a source of imprisonment. When we say "No" or someone perceives us as different or not good enough, we fear backlash or punishment. We can feel frozen or trapped in our existing relationships and family dynamics or can't imagine another way of being. Leaving is often not an option, and when it becomes an option, it comes with a special kind of torture for even considering it.

In my many years of practicing psychotherapy, the most common story I've witnessed is human beings' resistance to detachment. The idea of leaving or being left in intimate relationships invokes extreme fear, anxiety, shame, and rage, even when someone is trying to leave the most painful circumstances. There is an allergic response to letting go. Sometimes that resistance is so strong we'll forswear attachment altogether (for example, we resist committing in intimate relationships), or we create a nice, steady habit of detaching, so we never forget how to get out. That fear also tries to tell us—blatantly or clandestinely—that it is too risky to connect to others genuinely because they will find out we are not worth connecting to.

This fear is at the root of our feelings of aloneness, isolation, and separation, and not having the security of the tribe is the foundation of the pain infrastructure. This fear, encoded in our experience of ourselves and each other over millennia, has propelled the ego forward in its self-serving agenda: *never, ever face rejection/ abandonment/aloneness.* The ego wants to keep fear in place as the navigator of our reality and our perceptions, and it has determined our priorities and behaviors, how we select our relationships and our life purpose, and how we cope with discomfort. But that fear-based reality is gradually coming into focus.

We can see how our social systems have evolved over the last few hundred years and are evidence of a changing reality. We see that in the past, pain has driven us toward social systems defined by pain. What was a haven in the past is now a perpetrator of division and us-versus-them mythology—oppressive relationships, oppressive employers, oppressive regimes. And when we let go of the pain of the tribe, let go of thousands of years of fear that tells us, "You depend on another to survive," we find the Collective appears before us. We connect to the Whole. When consciousness flows, being a good neighbor isn't motivated by shame and fear; it's motivated by authentic compassion and empathy. Underneath this pain infrastructure, within your body, you will find the universal energy of consciousness that connects you to everything. It flows through you. It flows through everyone. That energy is our Collective. That is our home.

The Family – An Egoic Haven

We have built big and small social technologies to manage the terror and the deep, perpetual states of aloneness and isolation to which we are all born. When I refer to these as technologies, I mean processes that extend our abilities through repeated use, and in this case, processes that have assisted us in managing our fear.[15] The far-reaching, all-encompassing social network that mitigates, manages, or hides our devastating fear of abandonment is the tribe. At the heart of tribal culture is the family.

It is easy to argue that perceptions rooted in pain stand farther away from truth than non-pain states. They are far from

---

[15] https://en.wikipedia.org/wiki/Social_technology.

consciousness. We understand this at some level when we ask twelve "objective" jurors, not the victim or their family, to decide the fate of a person accused of a crime. As will be discussed throughout this book, the primary pain, the glue of tribal existence, is fear. The primary fear is abandonment, aloneness. But as we raise our energies, we become aware that pain has been cloaked. We couldn't and shouldn't have seen it. It needed to be camouflaged because we needed to experience it. We have needed it to play itself out and reveal to us, through the consequences of our choices, the unwanted, painful patterns in our lives. We haven't seen this dense fear of abandonment because it is in our very bodies. We experience it as who we are, not as an appendage or something distinct from ourselves. And we have felt powerless to change, soothe, or fix it.

This deep fear plays out in how we organize ourselves socially. In fact, we have organized ourselves to quell the terror of isolation and separation and vanquish the sense of disconnection we come here to experience. We have existed in the tribe to find "a safe alliance" in a reality defined by an us-versus-them framework. We *believe* we can find shelter here from the great terror we feel. Everything out there feels like a threat, and we perceive and experience the tribe as a haven in our perpetual state of aloneness.

The basic tribe we cling to—to this day, and almost universally—is the family. Now, I do not intend to disrespect the family, but instead to take an honest, compassionate look at the role the family has played in maintaining and camouflaging the 3D in human history. The family formed the tribal center; it is the root of "us versus them." We survived because we found acceptance in the family tribe, and by extension, the clans. Today, as always, infant children are at the mercy of their caregivers. More than any other species, to survive we depended entirely on the beneficence of our parents. Women have been at the mercy of male leaders. As adults, we have been at the mercy of our tribal chiefs. We have needed to gain and maintain the approval of the heads of our tribal structures. We have *relied* on their approval. To do otherwise was to risk death at the hands of the tribal leader, at the hands of another tribe, even at the hands of a father, husband, mother, or brother. To survive, we needed approval. Approval was our protection. Tribal leaders were our protection. And this belief has been handed down through the generations through fear.

Those who gain power (who dispense approval versus seeking approval) within the tribe minimize the risk of abandonment. "I don't need you; you need me" is the logic. To manage their own fear (fear they may not be aware of), to *ensure* they are neither alone nor abandoned, they use the technologies of oppression. That strategy is applied at the global, national, municipal, cultural, and economic levels, but it is also a part of the family dynamic. That pain story has been handed down over thousands of years and hundreds of generations. For money, politics, and power, in order to harness that subconscious, fear-filled attachment to the family, North American ruling systems have wielded "family values" and "family first" political, religious, and economic rhetoric.

A Hidden Space

I believe this drive to either gain approval or to oppress for the purpose of safety is operating well below awareness most of the time, and in particular, within the family unit. Why? Well, the family has been a sacrosanct institution, sheltered from collective scrutiny. In that protected space, pain is handed down, generation to generation, in a contained unit, safe from challenges from outside the family and outside the tribe.

Because we have not yet found constructive ways to manage all our discomfort and fear of abandonment (and we'll talk a lot about this later), we have found destructive methods of managing it. For example, a long-standing strategy to deal with our fear is to make other people responsible for it. Because we feel powerless to soothe ourselves, change our circumstances, or manage our overwhelm, we hurl our fear onto other people. Tight, tribal units such as the family become sanctioned repositories of pain/fear for whomever has the power in the unit. The family unit is the safe place, the unscrutinized place, for the family head to take their uncomfortable feelings and make the rest of the family responsible for it. And if you are lower down on the family power structure, you are going to make someone even lower on the ladder responsible for your pain. You are going to throw your discomfort all over a person who does not have the power to say "No." This manifests both as violent abuse and as emotional abuse (such as gaslighting). Making someone responsible for your uncomfortable feelings is the definition of abuse. Is the very nature of oppression. The family has, for most of history and throughout most of the world, been a haven for patriarchal family structures to protect heads of household (which are typically male) in their conscious or unconscious displacing of 3D pain to other family members. The other family members (such as children, women, and the elderly) are held hostage, their survival threatened should they leave.

The delusion is that this tribal system still works; that it serves us, protects us, and assuages our terror of aloneness and separation. At a visceral level, we seek approval from our heads of family—and rarely recognize we do it. Through our need for approval, through rage and through our feelings of inadequacy, we cling to our patriarchs and matriarchs, or we cling to our hopes and expectations of them.

However, in seeking approval and requiring others to see us to feel safe and accepted, we perpetuate an ancient system of oppression through fear. It ensures that the primary bond in our social structures continues to be fear. We keep playing it out, looking toward "the other" to remove our fear, thus ensuring our survival. That keeps us from looking within, where the fear of separation actually exists.

Our programming looks to the family for a sense of safety through approval, which we experience as affection, attentiveness, being seen, and belonging. Belonging is the essence of safety. When we belong, we relax the fight-or-flight reflex. We let go of some of the shame, and we keep the dreadful feelings of rejection and abandonment at bay.

In adulthood, we crave this feeling of belonging from the family. Without boundaries, without the capacity to freely say no or to disagree with shaming and rejection, the family becomes a haven for our dense, protected pain stories. We want to be seen, need to be seen, fight to be seen, or we surrender to the agony that we will never be seen. The family unit can be the place where we are least seen, where it is the most dangerous to say no or to have a different worldview. Entire professions have emerged to address the wounds that occur when we do not feel seen by our heads of family, including psychiatry, psychology, and psychotherapy. These careers materialized in recent years when a tiny crack in the family armor permitted people to go to counselors and therapists to discuss their family pain—but only within the safety of a professional sworn to secrecy. We hold a visceral intra-family terror of experiencing abandonment. And we can compromise ourselves in painful ways to fulfill the aim of that pain.

It is our relationships with our primary family caregivers that model our relationships with the world. From the moment we're born, through what we learn in our families, we're taught what to expect from women, from men, and from intimacy. These road maps are etched into our bodies, into our subconscious minds, from an early age. And no matter how uncomfortable that road map is, we follow it and normalize it.

An Illusion of Safety

We have a reflexive need to make the family safe. As children, we blame ourselves for our parents' abusive or neglectful behavior because we feel vulnerable, and even though we may believe that our caretakers are dangerous, we may also believe that our safety doesn't matter, or that we are safer with them than we would be without them. To support that belief, our egos make up an alternate reality. We make abuse normal because the alternative—that the people who are our source of safety and love are also our source of pain—is unbearably painful. And in that reality, there is a part of us convincing us we are safe. But the experiences of being unseen, unheard, or being violated continue to land on our body, and make an imprint, an implicit memory. This is the function of the ancient technology of denial. This suppressed and repressed trauma affects our perceptions, our decision-making processes, and the foundations of our perceptions of self and of others.

It can take years to feel safe enough to look at the impact of our relationships with our primary caregivers on our lives. We expend a lot of energy protecting ourselves from the truth. But if/when we're ready to confront the dysfunction, abuse, or oppression (or even subtle oppressive inter-relational patterns), we can dismantle those stories and release them from our bodies and from our realities. When we heal ourselves from being a victim and own every experience, every pain, and every perception, we release the shackles of slavery. When people see themselves (and therefore their family), they can reach a point where they say, "Whoa! I can't do that anymore. I don't want to take that anymore. I don't want to carry that pain. I don't want to live that way, behave that way, or support another person who behaves that way. I can't be held hostage, threatened, ignored, or have a family member throw their pain on me, telling me they may do so because blood is thicker than water. Not anymore." They find creative, albeit uncomfortable, ways of creating space between themselves and the tribe, of distancing themselves from the pain stories of the tribe, and sometimes even walking away from the tribe. They walk away from the pain and the system that holds that pain.

When we walk away or try to walk away from the tribe, we can activate an ancient, terrorizing pain story. It can shake us to the core, ripple throughout the *pain body*,[16] and threaten us with Armageddon. It tells us we won't survive. Our families and our bodies tell us we are bad, disloyal, and betraying the most important people, or they tell us that by walking away, we are committing a sin or risking our immortal souls. I tell clients that when they choose to put up a boundary or create distance, it can be like leaving a cult. They are walking away from a social system that told them they needed the family to survive.

Bringing Awareness to the Family

Now, I am not suggesting that everyone on this journey get up and leave their family. Not at all. What I am saying is that examining yourself and the uncomfortable stuff that shows up in a family can help reveal how we have institutionalized pain. We can see with fresh eyes and not take for granted that the way our family operates is the way it is supposed to be. If you are uncomfortable or in pain, examine the infrastructure you are in. If that infrastructure is your family, you may need some help in bringing it into awareness, because when it comes to family drama, we all walk around with bags over our heads.

When we allow ourselves to see the pain stories in our families—without judgment but with boundaries—we elevate the frequency. By seeing the pain we inherit from our family and working to release it from our body, we release ourselves from the powerful pain infrastructure of this planet. Through generations, the family has held hidden deep pains within its structure that have allowed these ego stories to continue. For much of recorded history, the family has protected its secrets in many (if not most) nations around the world. Family has been touted as the sacred institution both political and economic systems of power consistently support—protect the family, encourage the family,

---

[16] Eckhart Tolle introduces us to the culture-shifting concept of the pain body in his works *The Power of Now* and *A New Earth*.

uphold the family. And, as noted, for most of history, men have held the systems of power. Supporting the family—which has been a patriarchal stronghold—makes good political and economic sense if you are trying to hang on to your power.

By allowing ourselves to challenge the pain stories that we (the family or otherwise) hold tight and protect, we break the bonds of pain. But at this stage, challenging is not about toppling, raging against, or manipulating. Because that feeds the story: it keeps the pain alive. Instead, we examine, explore, and release pain stories that have resisted examination. To bring in consciousness, to dismantle the 3D, you are open and willing to see places where the tribe has dictated terms that no longer suit you. When we let go of those patterns, no matter the source, through our process of healing and releasing, the energy of love and genuine connection can come through. We connect where there is love, with others who can live in that love. We discover we are safe and we can get our needs met by people who are outside of our traditional family nucleus. Belonging and safety are found with those who own their own pain and who meet us with authenticity and compassion.

So, while the family can be a place of entrenched pain and resistance, it also holds the greatest evolutionary opportunity for expansion. When we do the hard work of seeing the painful behaviors of our families, we not only face inherited stories of pain, but we look at the deep fears of rejection and abandonment that come when we choose to integrate these places of protected pain. We see pain stories that have been held in the dark, outside of scrutiny for so long, and we challenge that story that says, "But I need *you* to tell me I am okay; that I am worth loving." And this "seeing" is happening everywhere.

These days, it is common for people to arrive at my door wanting to talk about their family and what is not working. But they feel weighed down by guilt; afraid that to talk about their families is to betray them. But now I believe the drive to release the pain is becoming greater than the need to be seen by a toxic tribe. People are feeling greater support, safety, and validation outside of the family if they feel they must challenge the pain of their families. These are signs we're breaking the bonds of the tribe and moving into the Collective.

Summary: Out of the Tribe and Into Ourselves

We are integrating the creative power of knowing that we are in charge of whom we bring into our realities and whom we kick out. More than at any other time in history, we have the privilege of doing that. In disconnecting from systems of pain, in undertaking the courageous step of taking care of ourselves, by taking care of what we are creating, we are walking right into ourselves. Or, more accurately, we find creative ways of walking right into the pain we are holding within ourselves—not someone else's pain, or everyone else's pain—our pain, our stories, our delusions. We take ownership over the pain as it shows up in us, because we inherited it from our parents just as much as our parents inherited it from theirs. And once we are adults…well, who else is going to own it? So, we see it in ourselves, we own it, and we decide not to carry it forward…all of which is the evolutionary process.

I see the family as the platform upon which our wounds are made visible to us. In healing those wounds, we heal the physical human state of separation and move into the metaphysical state of oneness, arriving at a place where *everyone* is our family. We are not divided by the wounds in our cells and DNA. We are united by the universal field of consciousness.

The Dance Between Masculine and Feminine

I suggest there has been an historic and creative 3D dance between men and women, and the masculine and feminine, the active and passive, that we are now beginning to transcend. We see this dance in how men and women have reflected their ancestral/tribal pain back and forth for millennia. There are two dancers in this dance, each playing off the other to create a complete, globally relevant narrative. This narrative has taken center stage in service to our deep dive into pain and separation. It is a foundational story of separation we come here to overcome, to transform, and in so doing, it serves this episode of our great expansion. This story of masculine and feminine is the pervasive story of *oppressor/oppressed*, and it is a fundamental building block in our 3D reality. The dynamic between these opposing forces has laid the foundation for our experience of the state of aloneness. It is the ultimate representation of our experience of separation.

To oversimplify, the story of men has dictated that to survive they must stay hypervigilant and be ready to fight, use aggression, and dominate. The story of women has also created hypervigilance, wherein safety is about tuning into the needs of the other and altering or compromising their own needs to survive, thus gaining approval. Men's need for safety is met by making others meet their demands and agree with their worldview. Women's safety is gained when they heed the demands and worldview of men and masculine systems around them and being adaptable and malleable. Of course, these are not overriding truths for all women and all men throughout history, but I would argue that this dynamic of male as oppressor and female as oppressed has dominated the unfolding of our social, economic, and political arenas throughout the world for most of recorded history. Men haven't seen women beyond how they serve their vision of control. However, to ensure their protection, women haven't seen men beyond the need for approval. I would argue we haven't seen the other, nor does the other see us. We have only seen what we needed to feel to survive and to not feel fear. Dismantling this dimension requires that we see the other's prison to free ourselves from our own. Dismantling means we need to see the dance, see the pain, and stop—stop dancing and stop believing it.

I think women are one of many groups that have experienced the role of victim more than the role of perpetrator. Over millennia, women have lived in persistent states of poverty and enslavement—economic, sexual, and reproductive slavery. They have endured physical/mental/emotional/spiritual abuse, mistrust, et cetera. The echoes of this pain ripple through our DNA and exist in our collective emotional memory banks. Thousands of years of programming embedded in the coding of our bodies tells us (and the world) that women and the feminine are not valuable beyond how they serve power. And additional programming says that men are not valuable unless they are surrounded by people serving their power.

The key to cracking this one open, to dissolving this story of separation, comes with the awareness that whatever role you play in this dance, you are in the 3D suffering, disconnected from the whole, asleep in separation, and living in a pain-filled, limited reality. The only difference is that the oppressor has an ego whispering in its ear that it is the winner of this dance, and the ego tells the oppressed that it is the loser. This assessment and perception of winner/loser, right/wrong, good/bad emerges from the zoomed-in, disconnected reality of the 3rd dimension. A gauge for success is constrained, limited by the perceptions of the pain-filled infrastructure of the 3rd dimension. When we zoom out, we see this dance exists to reveal our disconnection, where we have allowed ourselves not to be seen, and where we have allowed ourselves not to see. Zooming out reveals reality as it is—as a state of pain—and shows us the path to healing, which is connection, awareness, seeing the other to see ourselves, and seeing ourselves to see the other. It is the most profound place to heal our wounds, our 3D imprints of separation.

A few years back, when the Me Too movement was gaining momentum, I listened to women clients expressing how they were mad—not about what was happening in the world or in their lives—about what they had "allowed" to happen when they were younger. Through a women-led global conversation, they had access to greater awareness and a new way of seeing themselves. They could see that, years before, they hadn't permitted themselves to be angry about things they never realized they could be angry about. They never considered saying "No" to the guy they were dating. They never pushed back when something didn't feel right. They never walked away when they felt that sensation in their gut telling them to go, or when they weren't spoken to with kindness, or when they were aware it wasn't okay. They didn't know what "safe" meant, let alone that they were allowed to feel safe, even if it meant inconveniencing someone else. I spoke to successful, educated, well-resourced women, now seeing how powerless they had felt and how unaware of that powerlessness they were.

When you walk this path, you experience a shift in knowing. Just when you think it can't go any deeper, you see another blind spot, more darkness, another hidden extension of fear or shame. I believe that what we assume is freedom for women at this moment is still barricaded oppression. We assume we are taking up space, asking to be seen, taking what is ours, but our freedom still contains depths of invisibility. Are we unwilling to see our fear of male disapproval, abandonment, or detachment?

But the rise in energy reveals our blind spots. Our journey must speak to—and bring awareness to—women's experiences of terror and the resulting (unconscious) perceptions we have of ourselves and the world. Our goal is to see the subtle ways in which these ancient wounds show up in our bodies, thoughts, and behaviors and how they ensnare us in our 3D perceptions and trap us in low-frequency realities. To transmute the trauma, we need to see its markers—and own them all.

Women, we have a story here. But this story is not one to tell, retell, or re-entrench. We let go of it. In doing so, we bring light into dark places. We have played the oppressed role for a long time, and it's time to buy out. But not in the way we have been trying to do this in recent decades. We're not here to fight the good fight, take what's ours, convince them of the error of their ways, or teach them a lesson. We're here to step out of the drama. We do that by healing the trauma within us and stepping out of this 3D dance.

By bringing the trauma into focus (both the trauma from this lifetime and the trauma we have carried and/or inherited), we can release the old stories and move into a higher vibrational truth—a truth that tells us there is nothing happening; that the pain story of the oppressed is no longer our reality and no longer our story. We back out of the trauma and own our drama.

The Story of Abandonment

Women have been crawling around in the story of abandonment forever. Of course, women are not the only group wearing it in their marrow. There is a story of abandonment through child abuse, ability abuse, indigenous abuse, people-of-colour abuse, labor abuse, financial abuse, faith abuse, et cetera. Many women hold a painful story of the terror of being left behind. Because often, to be left behind, to be marginalized, is life-threatening.

The history of women is riddled with abandonment, and the fear of it is encoded in our bodies. Women have been abandoned within most systems throughout the world—political, economic, social, and religious abandonment; abandonment during wartime; abandonment in family; abandonment in intimate relationships. And in the last 100 years, we have been challenging that story. We are uncovering the hidden (and not so hidden) abuses and neglects in our personal, economic, and political relationships. Challenging that story will lead us to the metaphysical stories of universal love and consciousness. We can free ourselves from that pain in the deepest parts of our human coding. But challenging that story means putting us at the center of our story. Much of the world does not really see women. But we are exploring what it means to be seen—not as our function, but as our Selves.

Because we fear each other, our view of love is limited, constrained by normalized fear, rage, and shame. We have a limited view of compassion too because it is founded upon, blurred by, and diminished by the all-pervasive need to survive. Most of us understand that love must show up within us before we can create it outside of us. But because our existence has been dominated by the need to survive, there has been little space in the density within our bodies to hold compassion, empathy, or authenticity, not in the way I believe we are capable of underneath our 3D agendas.

There is little to no sense of safety within us in this dimension, because not only do we not have it; we don't recognize we don't have it. We all live in pervasive fear. If we don't have an internal reference point, or if that reference point has been blocked or hidden by 3D pain for thousands of years, we can't know what it is. I often have clients come into my office who have been suffering from depression and anxiety for years, maybe decades, but had no idea. They had never felt anything different, so they were not familiar with the feelings that had been inhabiting their mind/body. And I suggest the opposite is true as well. If we have not lived a life infused with heartfelt kindness and compassion, how are we to know what it feels like? So, if we don't know how it feels, we are merely generating a *mental,* not authentic, construct of kindness, or respect, or non-violence. The pain of aloneness and abandonment is such a part of our existence here that many of us don't have access to an expanded reference point of profound kindness, compassion, connection. Pain is a current that runs beneath us. It is the norm. It's in the background, not available to our conscious mind. Love, on the other hand, is...nothing. In relation to our busy, contracted, 3D agendas, love is the energy of silence, presence, nothingness. It *is.* We can't access it through all our 3D abandonment noise.

Ancient layers of stories and violence are encoded in all our bodies. And that coding is the major architect for intimacy and relationship—with the other and with ourselves. The work, which brings in the feminine qualities, is to stop thinking we know what we are doing and to do the work of letting go of the delusions, and the pain of aloneness, so that we tap into consciousness. Historically, we haven't known what love is, what compassion is, or what seeing is. But we are at a spectacular time when we are finding out—and in great numbers. The beginning of finding out is in the project of unabandoning ourselves. We show up for ourselves.

Exercise:
Reflections on Showing Up for Self

Here are some questions to assist you in seeing your own capacity for love and compassion:

- How are we to know how another person needs to treat us or be with us when we have not discovered how to be with ourselves safely?
- How are we to ask for generosity when we are not generous with ourselves?
- How are we to ask for fairness when we are not fair to ourselves?
- How do we ask people to see us when we don't see ourselves?
- How do we ask others to validate us when we can't validate ourselves?
- How can we ask for kindness when we don't give kindness to ourselves?
- How do we recognize love coming in when we can't create it for ourselves?
- How do we see the higher vibrations without if they are not part of how we view ourselves?

The Story of Invisibility

For thousands of years, women have been carrying around a narrative of being neither heard nor seen. When one is invisible, it is easier to be the receptacle of violence, rage, or hate. In being that receptacle—knowingly or unknowingly—we keep the egoic artifacts of violence, rage, and hate alive. In the invisible feminine, we immerse the human psyche in an egoic epidemic of abandonment and rejection. This is the systemic infection we are trying to heal. We are not aware of how little we see each other. Ego believes it is doing its job by telling us, "Run and hide from pain." This ancient trauma is encoded in our beings—we allow ourselves to be invisible in our relationships; in particular, in the intimate ones. If we own that story, we can integrate it.

We must see how we perpetuate our own invisibility. It is not my job to make someone see me. If someone can't see me, my healing path is to negotiate a new reality, and if the other party is unwilling, for the sake of my healing, I may walk away. It may take a day or years, but I will create distance from that which does not see me and bring in that which does.

You are entitled to be seen and to be with those who see you. Don't fight it; just know it, believe it, and heal the part within you that doesn't believe it. Accept yourself and release people who don't see you. Most dominant societies have not taught men or male culture to see the other. They've been taught they are the only thing worth seeing, and that seeing is one-directional: from the other to them. To release ourselves from this 3D trap, we use higher-vibrational interventions. We don't fight it, oppress it, blame it, or shame it. We bring the story that lies in our own body/mind into focus and find those who share our vision. Don't allow yourself to play into the low-vibrational global victim trap. Create your own connections and reality.

In relationship, take up space. Ask for what you want. Nobody must give it to you, but you must ask for it; until you find someone who has what you want and who agrees to provide it. Women can feel victimized by men's distance and dismissiveness. We can ask ourselves, "Why do I bring in people who don't see me?" But then ask, "How am I not seeing myself?" From that place (instead of wrestling in an egoic victim state), we evolve, we move into the meta story, and onto our path to transcendence. If we keep looking to the other to provide what we are missing, we stand still. We remind ourselves that, *in this life, I'm here to see all my fears of disapproval, disappointment, and rejection; where they play out in my thoughts, show up in my feelings and emotions, and resonate in my body. I am here to own what is mine and to reclaim the power to heal myself.*

But I am also here to see all; to see past what ego says others do for me, what I get from them, or how they benefit my life. I am here to see whomever sits across from me. Not their stuff, not their stories, not their pain. To see them. This is a project of bringing all who have been buried deep in the 3D quagmire back into the light. We do that with the energy of awareness. Just seeing.

What Is the Feminine Principle?

When I talk about the feminine principle, I am not speaking of gender. I use the term to describe a set of qualities and energies. Each human being has both masculine and feminine principles within them. Masculine (active) qualities are those tied to an individual's physical reality...things like doing, acting, thinking. Moving, logic, structure, and linearity are masculine. Masculinity is driven to compete and accomplish, to check the box and to reach the finish line. Those qualities are a necessary part of our experience of this physical world, and, in a balanced state, they distinguish an individual's creative potential from the group's. They ask us to think for ourselves and challenge groupthink; to resist the enslavement that happens when we are too connected and reject an individual's unique creative expression. The masculine says "No" to being told what to think and how to behave. It advocates for itself and its tribe.

Each masculine quality is tied to how it wants to relate to, and be seen by, the tribe. The goal is to place yourself beside or above your fellow human beings, all of whom are to be bested in competition. We hold "the other" as our benchmark. Accomplishment and safety come with being better or having more. If that's not possible, it's about having enough or doing enough to get the approval of those whom we feel have what we want.

But masculine energy in more extreme forms becomes destructive to others and to itself. Historically, the pendulum has swung far toward a reality dominated by masculine principles. For a few thousand years, it has limited our experience to this physical world. The qualities we need to heal the pain of this world are not the masculine ones we have been ensconced in, nor are they the ones we are proficient in here in North America. We are invested in the qualities of action, performance, and accomplishment; in demonstrating intellectual intelligence and physical prowess; and in being efficient and effective. Our goal is that others will see us as being the best at one or all of them.

We don't need to look too closely to understand how these principles in excess can land us in both an aggressive existence (being aggressive with ourselves and with "the other") and an unsustainable existence. On a global scene, the dominance of this masculine project (led by North American cultural forces that reward accumulation, accomplishment, mental or physical supremacy, etc.) is one indicator of how out of balance we are and how far the pendulum has swung away from the qualities of silence and compassion. We are gathering momentum and energy to allow us to reverse course, to urge the pendulum to swing in the other direction. We are making more space for feminine energies. We are in the project of releasing, transcending, transforming, and healing, to dissolve masculine infrastructures that no longer feed a state of balance and connection.

There are many writers who offer descriptions of the qualities of the feminine (passive).[17]/[18]/[19] When we refer to the energies of the feminine, we are discussing the practices of acceptance, silence, compassion, intuition, and feeling. These qualities, practices, and expressions have a different feel, a different flow, from what has been dominant in North America and much of Europe for centuries, if not longer. The feminine contradicts and confronts what's been prioritized and valued in our economy, our culture, and our politics. To facilitate a dismantling of the masculine elements of our egoic densities, we invoke the feminine energies within ourselves. However, because of the dominance of male qualities in the power systems of our planet—from government to the family unit—the very things we need to heal and to evolve out of this 3D existence are those things the masculine egoic mind tells you are weak, invalid, and worthless.

The masculine has been keeping our gaze outside of ourselves, focused on the world. It directs us to focus "on the other" to assess where the threat is. It asks, "Where are you in relation to others? Can you evaluate what they are doing in relation to you? Do you have their approval? Are they disappointed? Are they toeing the line? Are you seen as you want to be seen? Do you need to apply force or aggression to keep yourself safe in the face of the other?" Our states of vigilance, with our attention drawn outward, perpetuate egoic densities. They keep the reality of fear and "us versus them" alive and well. They do so by believing in these thoughts and feelings and engaging with them.

Our current reality rewards skillful demonstrations of the masculine: being the fastest, strongest, smartest, and having the most. You don't win prizes for being the quietest, most patient,

[17] E.B. Weisstub, *J Anal Psychol*, Jul;42(3):425-52; discussion 453-8, doi: 10.1111/j.1465-5922.1997.

[18] Nurit Oren, *The Feminine Principle: The Key to Awakening for Men and Women* (Budapest: Gabor Arsanyi, 2018).

[19] https://www.nalandatranslation.org/offerings/translations-and-commentaries/the-wisdom-of-the-feminine/.

or the best emoter! Our dominant masculine culture keeps the feminine qualities from being legitimized, holding them at the margins of daily practices and attentions. We have been stuck in the masculine energies of doing, thinking, and problem-solving within the framework of power = oppression. This describes my reality for the first 35 years of my life.

The feminine asks us to journey inward, to unlock the inner universe. It explores the landscape of the psyche, the body, and the subtle world within. It draws the quiet to the center of our beings. And while the masculine mind would perceive our quiet efforts as invisible, without form or force, we find this inward gaze calls on a tremendous power (and a growing power) of transformation to aid us in the creative process of evolution and transcendence.

We currently live twenty-four hours a day in a masculine space. The mind thinks its job is to keep reminding us we're under threat. We have been existing in this punishing, busy, isolating, angry, fear-filled place (and continue to live in it), feeling a threat that's (usually) not there. Our economy, our government, and our relationships all live within this paradigm.

We are so far at the "doing" end of the pendulum swing, our mind tells us it's the only way to survive. To create momentum and reverse the swing, meditating for ten minutes, twice daily, may not be sufficient. That may just be another path to stay in forgetting; forgetting who we are and what we're doing. If we're looking to move into a balanced place, can you imagine living twelve hours in masculine energies/activities and twelve in feminine? It may not yet be possible, but such a thought experiment makes a point. It feels out of reach for many of us. If we're here to remember our Selves, who we are underneath and within this dense, masculine driven, egoic reality, we need to create a life of reminders—which reminds us of our reality outside of the 3D. We need to connect to our ambassadors for space, energy, presence, and surrender. However, our current lives don't yet facilitate that flow of energy.

By bringing in the feminine principle, we use that creative, powerful force to defuse those 3D artifacts that anchor us into this reality and burn them up; metabolize them. By bringing in the feminine, we sit in the space and energy of nothing, the energy of letting go. We invite in a nothingness and a spaciousness. We disconnect from and then transform the objectives of the doing and thinking of this reality. We detach from the goals and meaning that drive this reality. We loosen the masculine principles of accomplishing, competing, and thinking.

If you look closely, you will find that masculine principles are indeed activated and fed by fears—fears of failing, disappointing, not being enough—and that means fear of rejection and abandonment. By bringing in the feminine, we not only bring in balance, but through the energy of being and pure awareness, we free ourselves from, and dissolve, the inherent fear-driven goals of this dimension.

Summary: Women Healing the Story of Separation

We are waking up from a long nightmare in which the masculine part of ourselves has been telling us that suppressing, oppressing, weakening, dominating, or owning another serves us, and that to be oppressed is an unavoidable reality. We engage in disconnecting behaviors (such as blaming, shaming, rage, and deceit) as forms of protection. We use these tools of oppression to survive, and ego camouflages our actions as righteousness.

In recent decades, we're challenging the narrative that women have been living in: that we're not worth seeing/hearing. I'm inviting you to turn inward, and ask, "Where in my physical self am I hiding coding that tells me and the world that I am not worth it? That women are not worth it?" That coding sits below the surface of your awareness, and it has normalized a core belief that you don't matter. That coding enslaves you to individual and collective stories of powerlessness, victimhood, or martyrdom.

I witness women clients every day who are trying to see the deep story that says in order to have someone in their lives, they must compromise themselves and must agree to not be seen or heard, to own others' anger and shame, or to be dismissed or invisible. In order to not be "alone," they allow many behaviors that facilitate their own anger, resentment, and powerlessness. However, isn't that the greatest state of aloneness there is?

We have come into a world where the masculine has played the role of oppressor. Men have held their pain in the shape of shame and rage, have coped with that pain by displacing it upon women, and have raged, blamed, and shamed to manage their pain.

Those of us who have taken on a life as a woman have taken on the experience not only of absorbing shame and rage but of accepting responsibility for masculine pain in order to survive. We've agreed to be the holders of another's pain, and in doing so, we enable the pain infrastructure. When a man appears wearing the same old story (i.e., he wants to defend the status quo, believes himself to be a victim of women's choices, or refuses to see you or acknowledge you outside of his own needs), we see that if we reply in kind, with rage, blame, shame, or invisibility, we create that. We are creators. Our work is to dissolve the pain infrastructure. If we continue reflecting back the same pain-filled feelings (even if they have a righteous argument attached to them), we continue to maintain that low-frequency reality. We continue to feed the stories of pain. The story of separation. The story of victim/oppressor. The story of abandoner/abandoned. Using the masculine strategies of rage, shame, blame, or oppression to liberate ourselves is an ego trap. It's a difficult one, because we have some juicy arguments to keep our egoic minds feeling on top of the argument—feeling like there needs to be a reckoning or like we're winning, feeling righteous, or feeling safer in our rage. In fact, we're creating our own trap and feeding the pain machine. But the opposite is true as well. If we don't see how we are not seen, we hold male rage, shame, and blame, and we dance the same dance, holding the 3D in place.

The creative journey is a shift from separation—and all its forms and expressions—into connection. Throughout history, we have wrapped ourselves in the masculine to dive into the density. Now we are using the feminine to go into the light. We sprinkle in a little masculine to experience pain and pleasure, density and matter, separation and individualism. And now the energies are directing the global evolutionary trajectory toward feminine energy to create wholeness, connection, bliss, and consciousness. In this current direction that we call healing, we will bring in these elements, this medicine, until we no longer need it, and until we recognize and know how little there is between You and Me.

Now we bring in the energy of the mother to each painful, dense, abandoned part of ourselves. We bring in the energy of acceptance, patience, love, and care into each part that sits in the contracted space of pain. We are facilitating a decompression of pain by inserting the feminine energy of presence. To bring in the expanding feminine is to deliver space into the contracted masculine. Our consciousness-raising project loosens the grip of masculine, egoic agendas of this dense 3D reality and opens us up to the connecting, expanded state of our next reality.

Dismantling this dimension as a woman is to see our rage, guilt, grief, and fear but to no longer believe it. It is to acknowledge it's been a long path of pain but that we no longer feed that dense energy, that story of oppressor/oppressed. On the path out of the 3rd dimension, that reality no longer exists. It has served us in playing out the experience of being unseen, being invisible, being abandoned, being separate. Now, we women remind ourselves: *I no longer dance this dance. I no longer take part in the story. I see it for what it is. I am responsible for any part of me that wants to continue to stay in the density. Any part of me that continues to blame, shame, judge, or rage is where I am to direct love, acceptance, and awareness, not belief. I say "No" to invisibility, not with anger but with awareness, knowing that this path I walk as a woman is facilitating the greatest expansion.*

To move from the contracted state of the victim to the expanded state of the creator is an explosion in reality, filled with potential.

We need to see where this ancient story of separation is still hiding in the recesses of our bodies. But we also mustn't play victim to it. We may need to accept that many men are less willing to see the dance, to see where they are holding the ancient pain of the oppressor in their bodies. Their ego is telling them they've a lot to lose by stopping this dance. We must let go of owning their path and how it needs to unfold—and accept the possibility that this may be perfect for the healing of the Collective. Women may have an advantage in being able to, and being more willing to, see how the density of the 3rd dimension appears in our lives. We have more incentive to see it and to release it. I consider that a gift, one for which my gratitude grows daily. As I own my reality, my reality grows. As I take responsibility for all my pain, my healing grows. I see it all, integrate it all, and let go of it all. All but the love.

On this evolutionary adventure, I hypothesize we are moving toward the reality of there being neither man nor woman, male nor female, masculine nor feminine, active nor passive. I speculate that we came here in a great separation experiment, to find out how to pull these qualities apart to experience a deep state of isolation from the Whole—so we could find the creative energy to put them back together again. The manifestations of masculine and feminine have been the means—the bifurcation, the most obvious "us versus them"—to experience the division between men and women, male and female. Are the differences between man and woman a leading mechanism of the creative potential of this density? Have they been the dominating experience of the reality of separation? Has sexual desire, sexual ecstasy between men and women, been not only about the survival of a species but about how we have been trying to resolve our deep sense of division and separation?

From the discomfort of separation, we discover how to heal that pain, that story, and expand the energies into Oneness. Separation has moved us along this journey from density to light. Out of darkness everything emerges. We can see signs where that separation might be narrowing. I suggest it is the feminine principle that will allow the density of separation to fade, leading to a gradual erasing of such strong distinctions between genders and between the sexes.

Chapter III

Bringing the 3D into Focus

Introduction

Our goal is to disconnect, dissolve, and dismantle our 3D reality. But first we need to acknowledge the depth of our pain imprints in this grand bifurcation of human experience. By bringing 3D dramas of separation into awareness, we detach from the story and allow the healing consciousness to permeate our beings and flow into the drama. When we can see where density sits and what it's trying to accomplish, we know where to direct a new, higher frequency of consciousness. In this chapter we are unpacking the players in the 3D reality to create a lens through which we can see what is at work in this reality, what the dream state is, and how to detect it.

Trauma and the 3ʳᵈ Dimension

All human beings suffer. We all have some kind of trauma. They could be what we call small-t traumas, or they could be big-T traumas. Most people recall some event that left an echo or imprint in their psyches, leaving them shaken, wounded, tender, or slightly, if not incredibly, altered. For example, being afraid of spiders or having a gag reflex upon seeing tequila may be small-t traumas. Or maybe you mistrust people with green eyes or people who talk fast. These are imprints, most likely from an uncomfortable past event or even negative messaging, that leave a reflexive response but don't necessarily affect your functioning or your mood regulation. Often, we are not aware that imprints exist. A sweeping example is the fear that penetrates our psyches when we're exposed to racist or sexist content in the media.

Systematic childhood abuse and wartime violence can be classified as big-T trauma. Often daily functioning is hindered, moods are difficult to regulate, and we can experience flashbacks or states of hypervigilance, or feel trapped in the recurring feelings of a terrorizing event. Most often (but not always) big-T trauma results from a violation and/or betrayal at the hands of our trusted fellow human beings.

Our body produces a lot of adrenaline. Its function is to keep us safe. It helps us to fight or run from threats. However, if we are not being threatened, adrenaline doesn't serve us. Calm reasoning and grounded communication will allow us to accurately assess a situation and find an appropriate solution to a challenge. If there's no actual threat, the adrenaline firing through our body—racing heart, trembling, restlessness—is giving us a false alarm and a false cue. That false cue is prompting us to rely on old imprints of past threats stuck in our bodies that try to tell us a story we can equate with the present moment. They give us a false narrative about what is happening. That is trauma, both big and small. We are here to look at that trauma and those false signals in a new way so we can transform them into something astounding on our journey out of the 3rd dimension.

What Is Trauma?

Trauma is an emotional event or series of events that overwhelms a person. Their mind/body experienced such intense fear at the time of the event, they couldn't integrate it. The person couldn't experience the fear, make sense of the fear, or organize it in their mind as something in the past or that's no longer a threat. Fear got stuck in their body. Their mind and nervous system couldn't shift the meaning of the event so the individual could return to a feeling of safety.

Let's look at the classic example:

A two-year-old child experiences their first growling dog. If a dog growls when a parent is around, the child will have the regulating, soothing presence of that parent. That regulation allows room for the child's mind/body to assess the situation as their body's state moves from a sense of danger to a sense of safety. The body's experience of the dog shifts as their nervous system calms down, their breathing normalizes, and the fight-or-flight instinct has been reduced or eliminated. Through regulation, they transition from feeling imminent danger to integrating wisdom, learning: "I am safer when I don't go near dogs that I don't know or that I have not been invited to pet." Problem solved; the body/mind returns to feeling that safety is recovered.

However, a child who experiences the growling dog with no parent or adult to help them regulate will move into fight-or-flight, and that is the end of the story. Growling dog = run. Growling dog = freeze. No safety. No resolution. No meaning other than fear.

The signal for danger is stuck in the body and without regulation and meaning-making, it could remain an imprint through adulthood. That person may claim an identity/personality as someone who doesn't like dogs or who needs extra assurances before they go near a dog. That is, unless some other regulating force or energy can penetrate that imprint/stuck wound, bring it to safety, and thereby alter their perception of dogs.

So, when we cannot expel an emotional event, we store it. We hold it in ourselves, which affects how we view the world. The lens through which we view, experience, and perceive the world and ourselves now includes this unmetabolized emotional residue. Throughout our life, this residue will ping the central nervous system whenever a hint of this feeling surfaces. The brain gets the message and alerts the mind/body to a potential threat. Time to run. Or fight.

An imprint or wound is a perception of our past. While it exists, it interferes with how we experience the present. It is trying to draw our attention to the threats of the past. As a result, we disconnect from the present. This concept is easier to comprehend when we explore the experience of people who have undergone extreme violence. They may have a big startle reflex that goes off when there is a loud but benign noise. All phobias are the same...fear of heights, bugs, closed spaces, etc. *When we hold trauma, we cannot experience the world as it is. We experience the world through a lens of the past.* Maybe many pasts and many lenses of hypervigilance, suspicion, or deep-rooted terror. Whether big-T traumas or small-t traumas, they are cumulative. Each one is a smokescreen between you and pure awareness/consciousness/higher self/God/Goddess/Source/love/You.

Let's expand our understanding to emotional experiences that are recorded in the DNA we inherited from our ancestors. We carry a collective record of thousands of years and hundreds of lifetimes of violence in our bodies. Or more accurately, we carry imprints of the terror we have felt. We carry coping strategies that help us to live with all that terror. We store it and, as suggested by mystic and author Richard Rudd, it is most likely recorded in our junk DNA.[20]

Each repressed emotion (meaning each vigilant part contracted in a state of high alert) stands between me and the present moment. Each wound colors the lens through which I see the world. We can have the feelings of thousands of years of ancestors killing each other tainting the lens through which we see the world. And we will not see that horror for what it is because we come into our lives with the density of this human experience already in place—it is our current baseline. It is our normal. We know nothing different. We see nothing different. Few of us have access to anything different. Until recently.

Stored within each one of those contractions, each one of those wounds, is energy. Not only is it stuck energy from trauma, but it is also the potential energy of awareness, love, and compassion. It is the energy that was not accessed when the wound landed but remained trapped. It is the energy of resolution. If we can understand that the heart can see beyond space and time, then the wisdom—the intelligent flow that knows why an event needed to happen, and what the learning was all about—is also trapped within, stored as creative potential. Our current reality is layers and layers of pain. Underneath that pain is wisdom, which gets released when the pain begins to dissolve.

To date, evolution has been (in our minds) slow. But we can see it by how we've moved through pain. For example, consider someone who gets into a car accident on the highway because they are going twenty miles over the speed limit. Because of the accident, there are injuries, lots of fear, maybe even terror. If they're lucky, the driver will emerge from the experience with a good dose of healthy guilt, they'll review and reflect on their

---

[20] Rudd, *The Gene Keys,* 165.

speeding, they may have a good cry to release the store of fear/sadness/guilt, etc., and arrive at the realization that speeding puts themselves and others at risk. Perhaps they have a jarring realization after a week at a silent retreat. They can now *see* the part of themselves that's been careless with their life and the lives of others, has lacked empathy, and has been disconnected. They let go of that piece of imprinted pain and arrive at a new place in their evolution. Maybe forgiveness of self. Or maybe they have a greater understanding of why they were careless and what they needed to learn to connect more to the world around them. When a person arrives at such a resolution, a lightness, a new heart-centered knowing, comes. The trauma experienced with the accident moves through, and a greater awareness and wisdom follows. An "Aha! Now I understand!" follows the learning from the trauma. And if that person is lucky, they can continue to have another lesson, and another Aha, and another, and another. Can you see the potential for growth when we allow ourselves to see the pain?

Some brilliant seers and seekers have shared their clear, inspiring vision of our collective transformation. They see the shift we are undergoing and have offered high-vibrational wisdom and reflections to assist our process. Penny Pierce offers tools to help navigate the integration of fresh energies of the next dimension in her book *Frequency*. She outlines the nine stages of transformation, including a process of releasing anything that is not a reflection of love from within the body. In the process, she says, "...you typically become uncomfortable because you're looking at fear and what you've previously denied."[21]

Richard Rudd in *The Gene Keys* discusses the same process in Key 55, suggesting we are moving into a time where "what will

[21] Pierce, 7.

become more and more intense, is a process whereby ancient memories are being chemically released from our bodies. Heightened emotional awareness will gradually draw the toxic genetic memories out of the human form.[22]

Both authors refer to a transformative process that is almost upon us. They suggest we will soon experience a time of great intensity that is uncomfortable because we are working with, and releasing, the repressed fear we hold in our bodies.

What I have been experiencing in the last sixteen years of my journey and the work of my clients tells me we are crossing that threshold. The intensity of our process is increasing. The energy is rising and pushing through—burning up—our individual pain and the group trauma we have accumulated over the last many thousands of years. Trauma makes up our experience of this dimension and lives in the shared emotional matrix that has solidified in our DNA, in our genetic makeup. As the energies increase, and our willingness and capacity to see the pain increases, we will move through this process of learning and integration more quickly. Instead of decades or lifetimes, it may be days, hours, or minutes. We are at the threshold of a new reality. The old reality is flowing through. I suggest much of our work is getting out of our own way so that we can allow the discomfort of the 3rd dimension to transform us with the least resistance possible.

Contraction/Disconnection/Separation

Trauma is a state of disconnection. Trauma says that what's happening out there, outside my body, is dangerous, even if no actual threat exists. It contracts, clenches, and braces itself physically, emotionally, and mentally against expected harm. Trauma says, "To stay safe, I need to beat it down, run from it, play dead, shut down communication, or make the other guy like me even though they scare the crap out of me." These are

---

[22] Rudd, 443.

all common responses to fear. It is impossible to feel connected to anything when we are locked in vigilance, or fight-or-flight. Disconnecting from what is happening in the present distances us from others. We put space between us and anything or anyone that might distract us from protecting ourselves. Our traumas draw our attention and hijack our nervous systems, forcing us to direct our energy toward survival.

When we understand our bodies are storing not only painful memories from childhood but also collective ancestral memories and possibly past life traumas, we realize why we have felt isolated, unheard, misunderstood, and unsafe. Each story of pain believes it is all alone. All of our present, past, and ancestral pain is held in our bodies, as are the echoes of our forbearers' fears telling us constantly that everything is scary. Could this be part (or all) of the reason we have adrenaline flooding through our systems all the time? Some of us see our overwhelm when we are flooded with adrenaline because someone tells us we are wrong…or even when we feel someone might *think* we are wrong. We see it when we're told we have failed or when we make a mistake. We see it when we have to speak up and ask for what we need. None of these conditions are actually dangerous (for most of us), but they are alarm bells that say being rejected is dangerous. This is the state of separation at work in our bodies. On this metaphysical journey, we are releasing the trauma, the alarm bells between us and pure potential, between us and higher versions of us, between us and the Collective. Releasing the trauma frees us from abandonment and disconnection. When the disconnected state of the contraction decompresses and allows space and movement, what flows through? Unity consciousness. Love. Feelings of connection. We find out what a genuine connection is. We reconnect to the Collective.

Our bodies/minds are a collection of contracted nodules, pockets of density in which energy doesn't flow. How pain shows up in our bodies is a microcosm of our experience in this dimension. We can see it in our emotional responses to discomfort. We withdraw, we curl up, we hide, we limit ourselves to protect ourselves from more pain. When our bodies are in pain, we may become sluggish, with low energy. Spines curve, shoulders hunch. Digestion contracts. Breathing constricts. Muscles stiffen, and we swell with inflammation. Energetic contractions show up as calcified energies in the body that we experience as blockages.

We may experience the expansive qualities of healing when we get a massage or sit in a meditation or a sound bath. As we soften and decompress, the tensions in the body let go. We experience the same flow when we hug someone we trust or when we laugh with joy. When we heal, the mind/body/feeling/energies expand. They flow and move with greater ease. We breathe with ease. Blood flows with ease. Emotions move more freely. Thoughts flow easily. We sleep, eat, and poop with ease when we are not in contracted states of discomfort, pain, or trauma.

Can you imagine what might flow, what limits we might release, what ease we might introduce, what creativity we might express when we heal the ancient manifestations of the contraction of aloneness in our bodies? Imagine what reality might become when we transform thousands of years of the traumas of our ancestors. Imagine the expansion available to us when we heal all the invisible trauma of the 3rd dimension. With the rise in energies, that's what we are heading toward as we expand our seeing and our feeling and we gain access to those ancient contractions. We are bringing awareness to the contracted state of this dimension and, in doing so, we are releasing the energy trapped and calcified within us, allowing it to feed our healing and expansion. When we release stuck energy, we are not just releasing it from our bodies; we are releasing it from this reality. We are expanding into our shared world, into the Collective.

Healing Is Presence Is Awareness

Each trauma lives between me and the present, between me and my truth. Each trauma is still connected to, and trying to resolve, some event that happened in my past, where a part of me is being held in a contraction of fear. Letting go of trauma is about bringing presence and space to where there is pain and a density holding an agenda from the past. When I bring the light of presence in a contracted place, things begin to move.

The process for healing trauma while we experience this physical body is bringing in safety, the safety of the present moment. Safety is the energy of now. Because what is happening right now is usually…nothing. To bring in nothing is to bring in pure awareness. Pure awareness does not carry agendas, pain from the past, worry, apprehension, or rumination. It does not carry the objective of trauma—which is survival. Seeing the potential of pure awareness is critical in understanding why we want to deliver the energy of consciousness to our wounds. Pure awareness carries the higher frequency of safety that our traumas need to resolve layers of fear. Our goal is to integrate into our lives and lifestyles the creative ways in which we bring the healing potential of presence into our bodies. With the rise in energy around the world, we can deliver the energy of safety not just into our nervous systems but into our DNA and into the emotional matrix which holds the deep traumas and contracted agendas of our ancestors. The energy of safety is the healing energy of consciousness.

Ego and Mind

The most important commitment on this journey is stepping away from your beliefs about reality and what you are. If you just begin there, you will open up more potential than you can imagine. Opening up, loosening, your idea of what you believe you are leaves room to move, to ingest the notion that maybe your mind knows less than it wants you to think it does. To allow for the possibility that the mind is not the key source of wisdom is a fruitful reflection. There are many, many places the mind just can't grasp. For example, consider the idea of infinity. When I sit for a while with the idea of infinity, nausea wells up.

My mind/body rejects it. It's too threatening. Phenomena exist outside our assumptions about life and the nature of everything. To entertain the idea that your mind is extremely limited is to open yourself up mentally, emotionally, and physically to a reality beyond your current experience. So, suspend disbelief, at least for a little while.

The mind has always been a tool of the lower energies of this low-dimensional existence. It has been connecting to and reflecting the low frequencies of human pain out into the world. Just as our bodies have been stuck in the densities of pain, our minds have been stuck right along with them. We have been using the same methods to solve our problems and our pain for our entire lives, for generations. We have been using the same avoiding, denying, or oppressing tactics to resolve our discomfort. The ancient infrastructure many of us call "ego" keeps telling us, "This is the way it works; this anger is going to fix it for you." The shaming and blaming will fix my fear, my anxiety, my disappointment. The many forms of fleeing such as appeasing the other or denying myself will fix my problems with my boss, my colleague, my mother, my brother, my father, my neighbor, the system. Of course, we rarely find our way out of our pain. In fact, every time we try to solve a problem this way, we not only enforce the problem, but we also reinforce the idea/reality that there is a problem, a danger, a threat. Every time we "fix" pain, we validate that there is something to fix. Waking up is seeing that it's all a construct, and it's constructed by our egoic infrastructure.

What Is Ego?
Some people have nuanced descriptions and arguments about what the ego is. If you connect to them, great. I offer a humble psychological and a metaphysical framework for understanding the 3D phenomenon. But don't attach to it. My goal is to use this description as a tool for healing, not an anxiety-provoking intellectual exercise.

1. Ego is that part of us that is tied to our physical experience and that feels this experience as unique. It sees each human being as distinct from everyone and everything else. It is connected to the density of this dimension and this physicality, which, as noted earlier, is tied to feelings of separateness, isolation, and aloneness. Our egoic physical experience is at odds with the metaphysical reality of connectedness, unity, and Oneness. It feels both threatened by, and longs for, connectedness.

2. The human experience and the evolution of the individual is, to date, led primarily by pain, and we—our Selves—are hidden deep beneath this manufactured pain infrastructure. Ego creates a world based on how your pain needs it to be (as opposed to responding to what is happening).

3. The ego infrastructure asks human beings to record every fear they've experienced since they were in utero (and before) and to store it and recall it when needed. Sometimes it's recalled at the mere hint of a similar fear arising. Sometimes, it's recalled halfway through our life when something significant brings it to the forefront. We can pass these fears on to our offspring (intergenerational trauma and/or epigenetics).[23]/[24] As noted earlier, I speculate that unresolved traumas affect the genome (genetic mutation) or affect genetic expression or activity (epigenetics), but our modern scientific instruments are only starting to understand genes, our emotions (like fear), and their intergenerational impact.[25]

4. I refer to the egoic infrastructure as all things that contribute to the fear-based, separate perception of self. These

---

[23] Frances, *Epigenetics.*

[24] Mark Wolynn, *It Didn't Start with You: How Inherited Family Trauma Shapes Who We Are and How to End the Cycle* (London: Penguin Life, 2017).

[25] Pert, *Molecules of Emotion: The Science Behind Mind-Body Medicine* (University of Michigan: Scribner, 1997).

would include mind (most aspects of), the human nervous system (i.e., the fight-or-flight response), and fear-based feelings, behaviors, or genetic imprints or coding.

Let's have a look at how this might unfold. Remember the growling dog example I used earlier? If a child experiences the growling dog with no adults around to soothe them and make the dog a friend, that becomes a future reference point: dogs = danger. That signals adrenaline and cortisol release—the fear chemicals—followed by a flight response. That experience gets imprinted on the mind/body. In the future, our egoic minds and bodies interpret that imprint as truth. We take our fears as fact (or at least our nervous system does). Someone else who had the same growling dog experience may have had an adult help make them feel that dogs are safe, so their fact is that dogs are our best friends.

The fear trigger could be dogs, bugs…even avocados. People may have a distaste for food because of an unpleasant memory they had about being sick with that food. The body/mind remembers. But the body also remembers many things the mind can't recall. It leaves an impression—an implicit memory—that affects how we see the world and ourselves. We walk around with implicit memories of events that took place when we were two, and at twenty-two, the ego tells us the same thing is scary. We have a subterranean control panel we are not aware of, telling us what we should fear, be angry at, or feel guilty for, and most of these assessments of life and living jumped on board before we had the wisdom to talk or read a newspaper. In adulthood, how does the mind make sense out of these implicit memories? Well, we believe them. Implicitly. These are the records of our ancestors' unresolved fear, shame, rage, guilt, etc., that we carry around in our bodies. These are the imprints and alarm bells inherited by subsequent generations.[26]

---

[26] Richard Frances, in his book *Epigenetics*, discussed the impact of trauma on genes of unborn children during the Dutch Famine in WWII. *The New York Times* also reported on this research in

The root, the big kahuna, of many embedded fears emerges from the fear of rejection or abandonment by the tribe. Not feeling accepted by a primary caregiver (mom, dad, grandparent, or other loved one) when we are young can set off an alarm bell telling us that the threat of rejection or abandonment is close and dangerous. Depending on many things, ego will hear that alarm bell and try to make sense of the fear. It will try to organize the world—its beliefs and coping strategies—in a way it believes will protect its host from experiencing rejection or abandonment. The rationale it might create in such a case is that all people who get close (intimate relationships, family members) are threatening; people who get too close could be the source of significant pain and anguish. For example, if a parent is distant, neglectful, or self-absorbed when we are a child (a feeling that is often imprinted in pre-verbal stages), that establishes itself in our emotional/implicit memory and is responsible for a cascade of perceptions; about how we view the world and how we view ourselves.

We move into adulthood with a firm map already laid out about what to expect from our fellow human beings and ourselves. We are not aware of this map. We can't see it or describe it. We don't even know it's there. But at the center of this map is a terror of our tribe abandoning us. We have a base fear of being left in the woods to die while our tribe is dancing around the fire celebrating our departure. We also have deep within us old emotional technologies that use anger, oppression, shame, and fear to ensure we are not left out, rejected, or abandoned, or to make sure that if we are, it is someone else's fault. Or we get creative about keeping the *feelings* of rejection and abandonment at bay—typically using denial and avoidance.

If we pause and examine human fear, we can see that fear itself is not the problem. Fear can be rather useful if you are

---

this article: *https://www.nytimes.com/2018/01/31/science/dutch-famine-genes.html.*

being chased by a tiger or need to get out of the way of a moving vehicle. The problem is the egoic infrastructure that won't allow us to let go of fear. It sticks around well past its expiration date, which means ego won't let us see fears for what they are. Some professionals call this a virus.[27] They see it as a system that has taken over the host's reality and exists to perpetuate and justify its own existence. Ego feeds us a false reality so we don't see what's happening and can't change the trajectory. To maintain itself and the codes of emotional pain at the root of its existence, ego keeps us in a delusional state.

To add insult to injury, ego tells us, "You have to keep the pain." It sends us messages convincing us that if we give up our fears, we are going to die. Literally die—head pops off, eaten by tiger, die. It tells us we need to have all that fear and rage and shame coursing through us because if we let it go, we will be like vulnerable little kittens, at the mercy of that tiger. This fear of others and of potential rejection can infiltrate the most benign parts of our lives. We see it when our adrenaline spikes as we consider asking a restaurant server to replace our dinner because it is cold, or when we are trying to give up a bad habit, or change a self-sabotaging behavior (e.g., soften our temper, challenge our phobias, or exercise more). Common sense would tell us we can survive without the approval of our restaurant servers, yet adrenaline tells us that if we ask to return the food, we'll lose their approval, and then it's game over. Armageddon. Most of us will just eat the cold dinner.

Our ability to evolve, to let go of fears that no longer serve us, has been stalled for quite a while. We walk around feeling a sense of threat that no longer exists. For many of us in North America, the only threats are those we continue to believe are threats. These include collectively believed threats—threats that our family, our city, our nation, or the world also believe.

---

[27] Cesar de Morey, Bart Smit – plant medicine facilitators who teach ego-as-virus framework. First heard in Mexico, October 2018.

This system tells us that all these fears we've been collecting are necessary, and we need to live the rest of our lives in fear. Most of the time, we don't have the awareness to question it. It won't let us see that just because one dog growled, it doesn't mean all dogs are bad. So, we have this outdated survival system that is the main inter-relational tool for our society. These collected, repressed emotions (and therefore core beliefs and their ancient interpretations) are the things navigating our relationships. We pick from (or run from) partners, decide on careers, and declare war on other countries; all based on emotional lessons we learned at the age of two and from our ancestors (who thought that burning women alive was advantageous and pillaging a village was a good career move). Based on age-old records in our bodies, we are deciding about good guys and bad guys, right and wrong, who gets the rewards and who doesn't, whether we're worth loving or not, and what we spend our time thinking about, dreaming about, or worrying about.

The more fear we have in our bodies and the more we operate from our unchecked fears, the more we resort to fear-filled problem solving. Around and around we go, living in, believing in, and creating our fear-filled reality; resolving problems through fear; deciding what actions to take based on fear. Broadening this understanding to the family, national, and global levels, we can see why we are often stuck in social systems—economies, politics, and civil societies—that are founded on fear. To release ourselves from fear-based decision-making, we need to see the fear. We need to bring fear, and all its offshoots (rage, shame, jealousy, etc.) into awareness.

For many of you who are in therapy, this is not a new concept. But when we're talking about thousands of years of trauma radiating off our bodies, we want to open up another level of awareness, another energy of consciousness. We will continue to meander into that energy as this discussion unfolds.

What Does "Asleep" Mean?

To be asleep is to be stuck in thinking, feeling, or behaving as if your discomfort is you. It is believing all the stories you have told yourself about why you're in pain. It's believing the pain and trauma stories your mind engages in all the time. Contrary to what our minds tell us, because we are addicted to our 3D pain, our egos make us hold on to it, identify with it, and construct realities around it. We're asleep because we believe the stories our pain tells us and resist/fear challenging those stories. We believe we're trapped in those stories. When we wake up, it can feel like returning home after a war. We can see we are no longer in danger, yet we still feel like we are under attack. We can have the awareness that this is not real, but the body still holds the painful stories.

To be asleep is to stay in pain and to choose pain stories over your truth. To be asleep is to not yet be able to see the fullness of yourself. You are still hidden from yourself; in disguise. You can't yet connect to the enormity of who you are underneath that pain or see the Self beyond the limited experience in this physical world. It is our pain that tells us we are that limited. Now, I want to be clear. That disguise was/is necessary. I needed it. I am going to guess you needed it. It's still necessary for many people, maybe most. Those who are still in disguise, needing their disguise, won't be reading this book. Nor should they be.

To be asleep is to exist but to be unable to see yourself—to see your Self. And we can't see our Selves because of all the pain in the way. But we don't see that either. In not seeing your Self, it is difficult to see another person. The primary way we look at others is through our own pain-based constructs. If we do not see the magnificence in ourselves, how can we see it in another person? We don't see them; we don't see our Selves. We really can't see anything. Anything but pain; pain that we aren't even aware exists and is navigating our lives for us. That is being asleep.

Extreme forms of being fast asleep are, for example, addictions. An addiction is a need to distract, telling us that to feel pain, accept pain, is intolerable, and not an option. And there is no judgment in saying that. This is a painful reality. It makes sense to want to distract ourselves from pain. Another example of being asleep is to blame another person for the crap we do to ourselves. I used to argue with my partner about his defensiveness, for example. I tried to impress upon him how he was defensive in his approach to problem-solving in the relationship, but he refused to see it. We argued about it just before I left for a seven-day silent meditation retreat. Three days into the silence, after my mind calmed, my nervous system let go, the inner chatter subsided, and things became a little safer, I was clobbered by the awareness that *my* defensiveness had been doing a self-righteous dance with my partner's defensiveness. Seeing my little story of defensiveness, and bringing awareness to it, I woke up to a fresh stream of energy trapped in the hidden story. Alongside it flowed a new level of compassion—for him and for me. I felt gratitude to my partner for his role in assisting me in releasing a dark, invisible pain story in my body.

We are sidling up to a place where we see that distraction no longer serves us, and we have access to something far more powerful than distraction. Awareness. When you are waking up, you step out of your addiction to substances or other external distractions, and you realize the emotional addictions; because we are addicted to our shame, fear, jealousy, disgust, rage, and guilt.

For those of us who can, or have chosen to, surface now, we want to keep our eye on the ball. We want to see the moments we fall into slumber. In waking up, we're still deep in denial, avoidance, arrogance, fear, etc. It's going to be here. In our sleepy states, we follow the strange logic of the mind as it tries to divert, displace, avoid, and pretend pain doesn't exist. The egoic mind can create strange and convenient stories to stay away from the pain. The classic strategy is to blame. The entire world has a formidable habit of blaming everyone else for their pain. "I am uncomfortable. It must be your fault." "I am uncomfortable, so my 'bad' behavior is justified." We use it to justify stealing, hurting, punishing, and invading. If you are blaming, you are sleeping.

Another way of sleeping is shaming. "I am uncomfortable with what you are doing," you might say. "You must be bad. There is something wrong with you." These days, we're deep in that story in social media, news, and the internet. Yet another way of sleeping is creating big distractions. "I am going to stay super busy so I don't have time to sit in the pain." "Pain? What pain?" "I am so busy, and what I do is so important." Our 3D economy depends on this type of sleep state. And so does your ego.

Why We Choose to Stay in Pain

If someone were to approach me with an offer to rid me of my fear of rats, I would say, "Yay! Bring it on!" If they told me that to accomplish this, I needed to sit alone in a room with a rat for an hour, I would say "Nope, thank you very much. I will keep that fear where it is." That is pretty much how we approach most discomfort and pain in this dimension: "Thank you, but no thank you." Because I can avoid a life with rats. I currently have that privilege. And ego—which we will discuss in detail—has many creative ways to rearrange our psyches to convince us we can get along fine without having to get near our fears. And most of this decision-making is below conscious thinking. We are not yet aware that there is a comprehensive technology within us that is constructed to avoid and make our pain A-okay.

For now, let's reflect on the idea that human beings get stuck in some serious, pain-avoiding habits. These pain-avoiding habits land us in some painful places. Without even knowing it, we choose to stay in fear, shame, and rage. We are steeped in the fight, with family members, with neighbors, between nations. We fear ourselves; we fear others; we fear the past; we fear the future. We take medications by the tons to escape ourselves and spend billions on police and military services trying to contain our rage. In this big city I live in, every time I drive down a highway flowing with rage and frustration, it is clear something is not quite working.

However, human beings need incentive to change, and that usually shows up as a painful crisis. Living a life with too many martinis, credit card bills, and French fries. Or ulcerative colitis, heart attacks, or hepatitis. Being told off too many times, fired too many times, dumped too many times. Plagues, wars, pandemics—all great motivators for change. Our extensive, drawn-out discomfort has been the key to our evolution. So far. To move from point A to point B, B has to at least be a little more comfortable than A. In fact, it usually has to be a lot more comfortable than A, and often it has to be an obvious reward, or we sit still. Without a giant match under our butts, we are content to remain in pain-filled A. Big pain has pushed us to evolve, on both an individual and societal level. Devastated by war? Create a peace pact and develop additional levels of cooperation. Suffer a plague? Construct complex urban sewage systems. Have a fight with your partner? Deepen your communication skills. Pain allows us to generate the energy to move into learning, into consciousness.

Knowing that, we can see that our discomfort, our pain, and our challenges are both our bane and our boon for growth and evolution. It's rather inconvenient because pain is...well...painful. But throughout history, it has propelled us to new levels.

By bringing pain into focus, we might see that pain lies. It tells us to run from it. But we are lost and stuck in discomfort because we can't see another way of being. We can't see we aren't in our truth. Or we see it, but we can't see the exit. Ego tells us there is no other way. The mind and ego are great influencing forces. They don't want us to evolve—they want us to stay the same. They take up all our time and space, telling us, "It's someone else's fault, you're not good enough, nothing will ever work out, and you can never change." In that fog, we can't see alternatives. We get stuck in our loops and don't take advantage of the opportunities for growth pain gives us. We believe the pain-filled voice coming from inside of us is some universal truth.

We require a different perspective and approach to our pain. And a big one is being gifted to us right now. But first, we need to understand and accept that *pain is our construct.* We make our pain; we hold our pain; we wield the perspectives of our pain. Unless we let go of any thought or belief that says differently, that pain will stay there. We give it permission to stay there. It will feel justified staying there. When we believe the pain telling us there is something going on, there will be something going on.

And the second concept we are working with is understanding that with the increase in energy available to us, we are learning to bypass the long, drawn-out dramas we have needed for our evolution. We no longer need to go through lifetimes of hurt to find our way out of that hurt. We arrive at our resolutions more quickly…a lifetime versus lifetimes? Years versus decades? Minutes versus years? We figure out that hurting others hurts us, that *our* greed hurts *us.* And you can do this, too. You can realize that *your* anger is wasting *your* life. That *you* are worth loving. With the increase in energy, we are arriving at these Eureka moments faster.

The challenge is that the "clearest and easiest" way to release fear, shame, or rage is to go right into it. To get right in the middle of it. To sit down inside that discomfort, cozy up, and have a cuddle. It feels inconvenient. Counterintuitive. But that is how we integrate density into the greater field of consciousness. That is how we turn darkness into light. We sit in it with pure awareness. We sit in it with consciousness.

We are entering a time when we don't always need to go through the big drama to see the pain and bring in the wisdom. We can find our way into the wound, open it, lighten it, move it, and transform it, before it plays out in a generations-long nightmare. We see it is only our pain telling us, "Something terrible is happening." It is believing what pain tells us that continues to make it happen.

However, we cannot take advantage of this speedy evolutionary process if we continue to avoid, distract, deny, and feed our addictions, including (and especially) our addiction to blaming everyone else for our own discomfort. If we look away, we continue to drag ourselves through our own muck.

We have, all around us, growing opportunities to go right into the pain and bring the energy of pure awareness with us: without judgment, without expectations, without perspective. We bring in a new multidimensional story—a meta story—to replace the old story. We bring in new energy and send it to that story. And out pops the wisdom. Without the drama. At some masochistic level, we want the discomfort and pain. We want it to reveal itself, not hide in the dark, pulling the levers of our life, making us go through a dramatic dance like a puppet on a stage. We want it, but we also want to change our relationship with it.

Pain only has the meaning we give it. On this journey, it is the next frontier, the next opportunity to bring more awareness, more light, and more love into our reality. On this journey, pain is our potential, our path to expansion.

Ego as a Virus

Ego exists to protect and preserve its own existence. It wants to convince you it is there for you, that it is doing you a favor, keeping you alive with its perceptions and opinions, beliefs and fears, rage, and shame. Upon deeper reflection, we can see that ego has little interest in its host. It will allow the host—you—to die before it will allow you to see any other reality. How does the egoic infrastructure work? Consider these examples…

Fear of Failure

Fear of failure is common. If you have identified it as one of your fears, you will be familiar with the coping strategy of not bothering to try in order to prevent feeling that uncomfortable feeling of failing. It's the ego that tells us that we can eliminate the threat by not even making the effort. If we see fear of failure as shame based (i.e., I don't want to experience feeling not good enough), by not making an effort, we can guarantee we never feel good enough. Because we have nothing to measure accomplishment against. We lock in that experience by ensuring we don't achieve, don't experience our creativity, don't show up to the party. Ego ensures that we live in the very thing we are afraid of, and then it hides that truth from us.

Fear of Abandonment

If we are terrified of being abandoned, ego can tell us the best way to manage that fear or keep ourselves from feeling that fear is to hold on super tight. We want to control our partner's movements, monitor their behavior patterns, ask for reassurance, display jealous behavior, and make our partner responsible for our feelings by blaming them if we're anxious when they're around other people. We'll monitor their phone and other communications, manipulate them into isolating themselves, etc. Our ego/pain infrastructure tells us this is the only way to manage this uncomfortable threat of abandonment. In fact, what we all know (we know it when we aren't in it) is that jealous behavior is a sure-fire way to have your partner leave you, landing you in the exact thing you have been working hard to avoid. At the very least, it lands you in a relationship that lacks trust, safety, and loving communication. Even though a person might be there, the connection and intimacy aren't, which still perpetuates the feeling of being alone and abandoned. We may feel abandoned and not be aware of it, because ego has told us that as long as they are there, we're good. And we believe it.

An old abandonment classic, the one that keeps the world going 'round (or keeps this dimension going 'round), is navigating through parental abandonment. When I say abandonment, I mean all the ways we, as adults, are angry or disappointed in our parents, seek parental approval, depend on our parents, etc. At their core, these manifestations hold the fear of, and the need for resolution of, some abandonment wound we have felt from one or both parents or primary caregivers. These places where we hold painful stuff are not just worth exploring; they are the motherlode. This is where the deepest, densest stories can lie within our three-dimensional beings.

Our fear infrastructures can ask us to spend years of our lives seeking resolution with our parents, and most of us don't know we're doing it. We spend years trapped in our own anger or rage with our parents, and ego tells us we need to hold on to these feelings to protect ourselves from them. Many of us have ancient, subconscious alarm bells that tell us we must seek parental approval and validation or we're going to die. And while we don't really think we'll die; we still twist ourselves into torturous knots and do exhausting mental and emotional acrobatics as if death is chasing us. We stay stuck in our anxiety, guilt, rage, and shame. We often wrestle with an inner tension, jumping between wanting and loving them, then switch to judging and resenting them. Our ancient wiring tells us we need to keep looking at our parents to solve the problem—for them to see the light, to change, to apologize—when the resolution is so much nearer.

Our wiring, our ancient egoic infrastructure, does not want us to see that our parents take part in the 3D reality, too. Within us, ego has set up an expectation that our parents are here to keep us safe from fear of abandonment/rejection. We feel too vulnerable to see them with flaws, trauma, or with their own parental abandonment wounds. Well into adulthood, we hold them responsible for our discomfort. We are trapped in our childhood expectations of them. We are set up from day one to have a delusional relationship with our parents. Our egos engage us in this fruitless pursuit of needing our parents to see us, affirm us, validate us, or whatever other expression of *unabandoning* we need. And if they aren't equipped to do these things (because they are carrying their own boatload of ancient trauma in their bodies), we can ensure abandonment wounds are going to stick to us. We send them forward into the future onto our children, and on it goes. To date, that's just how human beings have worked. It has been explained in attachment theory and other models that work with childhood family trauma.[28/29] We human infants are vulnerable to a species— our own—that has been adept at treating each other badly.

The parent story is hard to see and to heal because that fear is a part of our deep, inherited, 3D survival wiring. But when we pay attention, it is accessible. We're entering an age of awareness wherein we'll get our sights on the ancient parental burdens we hold, because when we release parental 3D noise, it's the most liberating healing a human being can engage in. It moves us along our path to transcendence. Transforming the mommy wound and the daddy issues are the penultimate steps to letting go.

Workaholic/Busyness

Let's picture someone who works hard. Extremely hard. Twelve-hour days, no vacation, flimsy relationships, maybe a few other habits on the side to keep them going, like cocaine or coffee. Of course, they do this because they need to pay the bills or buy a lifestyle; whatever their egoic mind is telling them. Of course, their therapist tells them they work too much because they're trying to manage the shame of not being good enough, or they're looking for the approval they never got from their father. But this hard-working person's

---

[28] Diane Poole Heller and Peter A. Levine, *The Power of Attachment: How to Create Deep and Lasting Intimate Relationships* (Louisville: Sounds True, 2019).

[29] Amir Levine and Rachel S.F. Heller, *Attached: The New Science of Adult Attachment and How It Can Help You Find - and Keep - Love* (New York: Penguin Publishing Group, 2010).

answer to that is, "Whatever." They continue with the sleepless, amphetamine-driven productive existence.

Then the day arrives when their body screams, "I've had enough!" It has itself a multi-week panic attack. Or their heart shows signs of being overwrought. Or they develop neuralgia and parts of their face and body go numb. All of this is followed by complete exhaustion and unending tears. And through all these signs and symptoms, taking their body to hell and back, there is still that voice in their head telling them, "Feel guilty. You are doing something wrong. Your symptoms aren't real. This is weak. People are relying on you." But what most people don't see is that the guilty voice is the same voice that put them in this situation. The voice that tells them they must strive for success at any cost is the same voice that will ensure they never, ever succeed; that they'll be too miserable, or too alone, or too dead to feel their success. They will break themselves in their attempts to be good enough, ensuring they never get there.

Someone can tell us death is right in front of us and what we can do to keep ourselves alive, but if our primary egoic pain management tool is denial, ego will choose denial over survival. For example, I know of someone who is in the middle of cancer treatment. Instead of taking the rest she needs for her body to recover and heal to beat the cancer, Jane is staying extra busy hosting, shopping, and visiting. She doesn't want to see her body or her pain. As a result, Jane is returning to the hospital repeatedly as her body collapses in exhaustion, making recovery an unlikely outcome. No matter what the doctor says, no matter what her family says, her busyness/denial is the priority. Not feeling is the priority. Healing is not the priority. And I don't judge Jane's priorities. Alternatives may be too painful to consider. But Jane's situation sums up the human experience in a nutshell. This is a powerful example of how ego will drive us into the grave before it will allow us to feel the fear that's there in our own bodies. Which, under our old paradigm, might make sense. If we knew we were stuck with the fear, we could support a healthy dose of distraction. But now we're entering a reality where that fear is not what we thought it was and we are not trapped as we believed. To shift paradigms, we need to look, not look away.

Many of us make living with harmful violations in our own home acceptable in order to not feel alone, abandoned, or rejected. If we've been taught that to have a relationship, we must compromise ourselves—be invisible, deny our wants and needs, or not voice our opinions—we are living in a boundaryless existence. This means that a part of our immune system is not functioning—ego has shut it down. Ego shuts it down because it constructs a reality based on a core belief that might say, "If I express an opinion, I will be rejected. If I say 'No,' I will be abandoned. If they disagree with me, I'll be alone forever. I'm not valuable enough to be respected or spoken to with kindness or love." Ego believes it's protecting you from being alone by turning away from all the other parts of you that need to be seen, heard, and loved. It shuts all of that down. We allow bad behavior in our lives because the alternative—risking rejection—is not tolerable. We allow people into our lives who can't or won't see us, who mistreat us, disrespect us, or deny us. Not because they are malicious but because their pain doesn't allow them to see us. Ego tells us, "To hell with your immune system! If you say no, if you push that person out, you're going to die alone!" Then the body (which is aware of how much toxicity it is absorbing when it's not protected) will go into overdrive and activate its protection system. Flailing with the need to keep out the poison, it will attack itself. The body and the wound were never listened to, the poison kept coming in without end, and now the immune system attacks whatever it can.

It attacks its host, the source of the toxicity. And now we have an autoimmune disorder.

Ego says, "The stress is too much." So, we drink to manage the stress and we end up with even greater stress: health problems, failed relationships, failed jobs. The coping strategies land us right back to the place we're trying to avoid, and as I said, most of the time, it will kill us before revealing that truth. This is ego's M.O., and it's something to bring into awareness as we continue to reveal the ego's nature.

Feeling First

To oversimplify and to rehash a bit, our bodies are built to stash away emotional events that we can't understand or make peace with, as well as unresolved stories from our ancestors. The mind is wired to use that emotional debris to construct our perception of reality and to alert us to threats. The mind often determines if something is a threat based on what frightened us when we were infants or toddlers, such as a parent's anger or a snarling dog. Or it can have a deeper response or distrust of other human beings that was not taught but felt; felt from the deeper recesses of our human coding, the collective memories within our body.

For our healing, it helps us to understand that when our ego constructs our inner world, it is the *feeling* that comes first. For example, a feeling lands, and then the egoic mind tries to construct a protective reality around that feeling. We can also call that protective reality a core belief. For example, a protective reality for a teenage boy whose first girlfriend cheats on him might be, "All women are evil." He might use rage against women to construct a new belief that his ego says will protect him from ever experiencing a woman's rejection again. He'll allow his rage to keep women (and intimate relationships with women) at a distance.

Another common example of a protective reality is getting fired. We get fired and we use shame—the core belief could be, "I am bad; supremely flawed"—to help us navigate the uncomfortable experience. Or we use rage: "Everyone is an idiot, and I am a victim of all the idiots." Shame tells us to stop striving so that we never risk experiencing that kind of rejection again, and rage keeps us from feeling the shame and the rejection.

We can see that the big feeling (the hurt) around which ego constructs a core belief is our launching pad. Ego thinks interpreting the feeling and codifying it in a core belief is protecting us from future pain. What it does, in fact, is derail us from expressing ourselves authentically. We construct our life around old, stale pain and pain management. We can also see that the bigger the pain, the more derailing the core belief. The bigger the wound, the more you steer toward living in a world in which you are coping instead of living. Our egos construct a reality where we are just surviving, fending off the next wound rather than being in life.

Our adult minds are connected to hundreds, if not thousands, of unprocessed feelings that were imprinted on us when we were children and that come from our ancestral trauma pool.[30] The mind then uses those wounds as reference points for the present. We have countless experiences that create our unique frameworks for life and living. For you, dogs might be scary; for my neighbor, dogs are cuddly companions. Which is true? The brain and sympathetic nervous system, under the tutelage of the ego, don't care one iota about truth. Their priorities are safety and survival. They care about not being left alone to die (they want to be safe from rejection and abandonment).

A thousand years ago, our survival depended on gaining the approval and favor of, for example, the feudal lord. In our current privileged existence, safety and survival are often interpreted as having the biggest house, or being most liked at the gym, or being most feared at the office. They are dedicated to scoping out growling dogs and being sure to ignite a fight-or-flight response when exposed to even a picture of a dog. Add emotionally charged

---

[30] Richard Rudd discusses a collective emotional matrix that we are also all connected to and that connects us to each other. This is a shared record of human emotional pain.

childhood experiences such as, "My brother is always stealing my toys!" to "My friends laughed at my new pants," and our worldview begins to take shape. We live in perpetual risk management and assessment. Our reality is constructed upon many emotional warning signs trying to steer us away from experiences of rejection and abandonment.

Most of the time, we are not aware these alarm bells against rejection and abandonment exist. They float in the background of our psyches, believing they are doing a great job of steering us away from pain and disaster, telling us we're right and everybody else is a fool. They create nice, safe limitations within which we exist. Sometimes these are disguised as little alarm bells; like your heart beating just a little faster if you must talk to a stranger. Sometimes they are bigger alarm bells: "If I have to make a speech, I am going to die!" Or "How dare you think that way?" We can have thousands of micro-alarm bells going off all the time. The mind leaps on them, tries to make sense of the feeling by applying some "rational" thought that it believes is there to help us navigate through the dangerous world of humans. It tells us: "Don't share that about yourself." "Don't look them in the eye." "Don't say too much." "Be sure to smile." "Don't smile too much." "Make sure they like you." "Make sure you wear that shirt." "God, don't wear that shirt!" "Did I talk too loud?" "Will they think I'm an idiot because I haven't read that book?" "Apologize for yourself. A lot." "Never say you're sorry." And, more often than not, there's no thought attached to these coping strategies. These are automatic responses that trigger feelings and behaviors that show up uninvited but committed: anxiety, avoidance, irritation. We are stuck in our automatic responses with these emotional imprints talking to each other. So much so, we create perpetual *feedback loops* in our own mental and emotional inner landscape. We get stuck in this unconscious network of pain perceptions and responses.

A feedback loop might look like this: We have an experience that triggers an uncomfortable feeling. The uncomfortable feeling triggers an alarm response (i.e., fight-or-flight), which then triggers the mind to find a way of thinking about it, a way of perceiving, a way of organizing the world to make it safer again. Which then validates the repressed emotion: "Well, if I am running, it must be a threat." "Well, if I am angry, they're an idiot, and if they're an idiot, of course I should be angry." We create a thought that validates the uncomfortable feeling, telling us of course it is okay to be this uncomfortable because our thoughts tell us so, keeping that feeling locked in place in our reality framework. Out of this feedback loop, we construct a lovely, impenetrable fortress of core beliefs. Around and around we go, living within our fortress, wandering the halls of our fear, shame, and rage, telling ourselves our thoughts are justified. Our thoughts, in turn, tell us our feelings are justified. This fortress can last a lifetime, and we can pass it down to the next generation. Ego (individual ego and collective ego) also makes it uncomfortable to challenge these loops. When we try to step outside of this constructed reality, it tortures us. We get punished— with deeper anxiety, deeper anger, deeper pain.

My podcast, *Dismantling the 3rd Dimension,* is available to provide clarity and guidance into deepening our seeing into the 3rd dimension, bringing our pain stories into focus. The episode "Who Took the Zen Out of My Zen?" shares an experience I had at a silent retreat where for days I was confronted with ego's agonizing resistance to sitting in nothing; sitting with uncomfortable feelings. At this juncture, it may serve to deepen your sense of the level of resistance ego has to change, seeing our pain and letting go of our pain.

Podcast: *Dismantling the 3rd Dimension: The Journey out of the Tribe and into the Collective.*
Episode: "Who Took the Zen out of My Zen?"
https://podcasts.apple.com/ca/podcast/who-took-the-zen-out-of-my-zen/id1588908885?i=1000538224610

∞

The pain I experienced while sitting and doing nothing at a retreat is a microcosm of what ego will do to us for years and lifetimes. It keeps us trapped in our delusion by promising us enormous amounts of pain if we step away from or confront its framework. It's committed to feeding us threats, lies, and torment if we so much as entertain the idea of changing our way of thinking, or letting go of the drama, or stepping into our power. But this is also where we see the nature of ego as a virus. When we try to step out of the delusions, let go of the pain and the loops, it feels like ego—the virus—is trying to kill the host. It makes us sick—physically, emotionally, and mentally. At a certain stage in dismantling the densities in your body, things get a little messy. Well...a lot messy...uncomfortable, painful, and disgusting. When we step out of the feedback loop, we purge all the stories connected to that loop. The entire body (emotional, energetic, physical) excretes the virus, detoxing the pain infrastructure. We experience the toxicity of the density as it moves through: inflammation, nausea, sweats, fatigue, vomiting, etc. Once it starts, it can be a challenging time that can go on for quite a while. In the addendum, I share some tips on recognizing, facilitating, and surviving this giant detox. I believe many of us will experience this detox in the coming decades, and this is part of the time of intensity to which Richard Rudd refers.

I invite you to look at your thought processes, your thought reflexes, and your core beliefs about yourself that feed those thoughts. Use those thought loops, and those core beliefs, as a bread-crumb trail to the original story, the alarm bell, and the feeling underneath. Our entire identity and our mental and physical health are built on a foundation of repressed emotion. We will dive into this concept in the coming chapters.

Sometimes Ego Serves Us

Ego is part of our unique expression in this dimension. In the expression of our 3D vehicles, ego can serve us by protecting our beings from genuine physical harm. Ego can fool us into believing some things are harmful when they are not. But sometimes ego can get it right, at least in the short term. For much of our journey, we need to keep our bodies safe from harm. Put on your seatbelt. Don't eat rotten food. Wear your sunscreen. Don't make the big guy mad. All can be superb advice when we're trying to survive in the parameters of the 3rd dimension. Because so many of us have experienced significant trauma in our lives and have some pretty hefty alarm bells, that sense of safety is necessary to keep traveling our path.

What ego wants to do is take care of us, and sometimes it is good to let it. We can use the egoic sense of individuality to turn safety into a cherishing of oneself, a commitment to oneself, which we need in order to move through trauma. This body needs to feel safe in order to look at the scary places and feel the scary feelings. We are processing trauma. It doesn't feel very good, and it rarely feels safe. So, we're going to use identification with the individual—the idea that this unique being needs to be protected—to our advantage. We're going to take care of ourselves, get the care we need from others, treat this vessel as a gift, and be grateful for the work it's doing as it moves us through our dissolution. We're going to protect this body and set up boundaries and self-compassion, good nourishment, exercise, and sunshine. In this way, ego will become our ally. We will allow the ego to treat us as special, give ourselves a little extra compassion and TLC, and allow the nervous system to feel loved and soothed enough to keep going into the scary bits for as long as we need.

Exercise:
Journaling – Detecting Ego

Ego has been telling us for millennia that to survive we need to believe everything it's telling us. Ego wants us to hold tight to the repressed fear, shame, and rage, convincing us it's vital for our survival. We can recognize ego has been *trying* to take care of us, but maybe its method is now outdated. Our job is to see the subterfuge of the ego infrastructure. We want to bring ego into focus, which diminishes its power, dissolves it. When ego dissolves, the pain stories underneath dissolve with it. As our energies rise, we wake up and release the ego from the job of designing our reality. And we find out it's quite safe to hand that job over to higher vibrations of consciousness such as love and compassion.

○ Explore fear underneath anger (i.e., when you are irritated, annoyed, or angry at another person). Abandonment and rejection are the biggest threats to ego. Rage/anger are common tools to manage/hide feelings of abandonment and rejection. There are layers and layers of conscious or repressed/suppressed feelings of fear and rage. We're going on a quest, deep into those caverns within to find what's lurking in the dark.

○ What is your identity? Make a list of those elements you consider to be part of your identity. See the egoic stories we attach to when we hold on to identity—an egoic construct based largely on others' perceptions of us. There's a gold mine of stories of ego protection in human history. Human beings have hurt, abandoned, rejected, even killed people for challenging their identities. For example, we can risk danger when we challenge a church's identity of being merciful, safe, and an authority; when we challenge some men's heterosexual identities; when we challenge a police officer's identity as an unhindered authority; or we challenge someone's need to be right or the best. These are, of course, generalizations, but they're also common threads throughout history. Our ego needs us to see it in the image and idea it's created of itself, or it collapses, explodes, or implodes under the weight of threat or rejection. These deep challenges are rich opportunities for uprooting and breaking down the 3D infrastructure. Make your list and continue to reflect on and build on it. Consider this a working document.

○ Seek out your ego story of victimhood. When do you feel like a victim? When do you feel wronged or treated unfairly? Are there more subtle ways that you feel like a victim? Of the family? Of your partner? Of the world? They're there. I can almost guarantee it. Often, they're subtle and difficult to detect. There are no victims in consciousness. We're here to bring these into clarity since they can't go with us to the next realm. Remember, this is tough to crack. Until it's not. Keep looking at it with increasingly neutral eyes. If you're feeling like a victim, you're in one of your stories. You're in ego. You're in your delusion. You're in your dream. Make this another working document.

What Is Mind?

The mind is a multidirectional projector. It will project thoughts, perceptions, and judgments outward into the world and will reflect those back, into the body. And our projections will express what we have in our system; the inner emotional, physical, and energetic terrain of our bodies. The mind is a projector of that terrain out into the world. Ego hijacks the mind for its own purposes, which is to keep that drama/pain in place, projecting outward and reflecting inward to the body's felt reality.

If our body is holding old pain, tensions, anxiety, and depressions—from childhood or our ancestors—and/or disordered states such as poor digestion or breathing problems, then the mind uses that felt sense to interpret the broader reality. When we are anxious, the mind is going to follow with an anxious assessment of the world and will therefore make decisions based on that information. It will also decide to use the tools of an anxious being. Anxious decision-making will be rapid, erratic, ungrounded, and fear based. If we're angry, we'll decide to use the tools of the angry mind. In that state, fighting and aggression might seem like the best way to solve any problem. We construct a reality according to the egoic pain in our body, and we believe it. Ego asserts a reality based on pain, and its thought processes and decisions reinforce that experience. It validates the internal experience and from that experience, it facilitates that uncomfortable feedback loop. We feel at the mercy of every impulsive thought that comes across our radar and feel powerless to change it.

But there's a lot of potential to interrupt or recreate the mind/ego dynamic. If we feed something different into the projector, we're going to be creating a different image of the world. If our bodies are in states of rest—breathing deeply, laughing, experiencing quiet and spaciousness, our physiology moving with ease and order—our minds are going to project that outward in their perceptions and decision-making. Our minds will also project those expectations inward, back into our physical, emotional, and energetic bodies. They will continue to reinforce the inner and outer reality based on the data they receive. Much of this is pretty basic. When we are drunk on love, everything seems magical; we have more energy and vitality; our grocer is the best guy in the world. We write the best poetry, and our boss gives us a raise. When we are depressed or angry, everyone looks like a threat. We are fatigued, and our digestion and sleep suffer. But in our busy, urban impatience, we have lost touch with this basic principle, which is why we're on so many mood-altering medications and managing stress through substances or harmful distractions, such as damaging amounts of alcohol, narcotics, and the internet. We either don't want to spend the time or don't believe we have that much influence over our own thoughts, feelings, or physiological responses.

We can see that the mind is connected to whatever we consciously or unconsciously connect it to. The thoughts (if they are thoughts, for often people describe not even thinking) of people who describe being in a state of flow—that space where we create effortlessly, as in a channeled state—are a product of that inspirational space. A place outside of 3D ego. If you experience a state of joy, your thoughts are going to emerge from that and give meaning to events based on that state. The mind will sketch a thought-based world on the palette we give it.

The egoic mind, therefore, is the mind connected to, and given orders by, ego. And since most of the world exists in a left-brain, fear-based, hypervigilant, achievement-driven state of being, if we're not paying attention, the mind will create and organize itself according to that data set. And we've not been paying attention for a long, long time. In Western societies, we rarely look at our minds. They operate without scrutiny. The growing practice of mindfulness is challenging that history, but we still tend toward mind*less*ness (which is different from a "no mind" state, wherein you are "thinking" with pure awareness). And many people live in an egoic reality anchored in a belief or feeling that there's no longer an option to believe or feel anything different.

Learning to discipline the mind becomes essential on this journey. Dismantling this dimension requires us to detach ourselves from the 3D artifacts of egoic fear and pain. We intend to feed the mind an alternate reality so it becomes a product of the journey toward consciousness versus a product of egoic pain-looping. To accomplish that, we bring into focus what our minds are doing. We pay attention. Most of our waking life, the mind is a tool of ego. And, as we have seen, since ego's MO is fear, the mind is a tool of fear. Many of my clients share with me that when they pay attention, they're shocked or disappointed when they realize their minds are consumed with negative thinking throughout their day. Bringing that into awareness is a big step out of the 3rd dimension. So, I look forward to that disappointment.

The mind, therefore, is the front-line, semi-conscious tool of ego infrastructure. Our thoughts emerge from fear and emotional pain that we've stored away in the body and programmed never to forget. Most of us would agree there are some things that are not worth remembering. There are things we just don't need to keep recalling repeatedly, especially if recall is not leading to resolution. But the mind rolls around in the negative thought cycles like a pig in mud. Constant recall and rumination are tools the mind uses to support the ego.

So, what do we do with our minds? Stop believing them! Don't take it on blind faith that your mind knows what it's talking about, because I can almost guarantee it does not. Every day is an exercise in not believing anything my mind tells me. The mind is too limited for an expanded reality. It is a tool of the 3rd dimension. *We are expanding beyond that space and time, and the mind cannot follow.* We are in a place in history where we are being allowed access to the whole magnificence of ourselves, and the mind has great difficulty in believing this magnificence exists because ego tells the mind it is dangerous to believe anything outside of the pain infrastructure that it has set up within this five-senses physical dimension. Our work in expanding is to get familiar with what ego looks and feels like so we can stop following its limited perceptions.

When we loosen our grip on this physical reality, we also detach ourselves from the objectives and processes of the mind. Once we comprehend that the mind is an unreliable source, we lead ourselves into the healing process. This happens in layers. We take ourselves deeper and deeper into our new reality, creating distance between ourselves and our mental projections. This new place is less connected to thought and more connected to feeling.

When we have detached ourselves from our minds and created space, there is room to direct the mind to where we want it to go. We can change a narrative, bring in affirming thoughts, use creative visualization, and slow the mind down, training it to be more discerning, or to respond instead of reacting. But the mind shifts as we heal the emotional body, the energetic body, and the physical body. I have found that by working on those three, all I need to do with mind is not believe it too much and allow the dissolution of mental stories to happen.

Use the mind as another clue to lead you to the egoic structure, to the core belief and to the repressed emotion. To study your thought patterns is to reveal the stories you are stuck in.

Exercise:
Finding Ego in Our Thoughts

1. Write in your journal every time you become aware of some of these common 3D thought patterns and themes:
   - I am not good enough.
   - I don't belong.
   - How dare you!
   - I can't inconvenience anyone.
   - Everyone always inconveniences me!
   - I always give but I never get.
   - It's not fair! I can't do that. What would they think?

○ Good things never happen to me.

○ Everyone hates me.

○ I hate him/her/them/everyone.

We often need help in seeing our 3D mental manifestations because when we look at our pain within our own egoic infrastructure, it's camouflaged. Learn to recognize when your mind has hijacked your reality. Develop your ability to identify when your thoughts are not reflecting your truth.

2. Identify and write out when you become aware of your thoughts as manifestations of a 3D story. When we see and identify a story, we work at interrupting those stories every day. When we interrupt them, we have space to do something, like replacing the thought with a higher vibrational thought. Maybe you find a feeling hidden underneath the thought (which we will explore in Chapter V). Maybe they'll lead to you introducing a new behavior.

This is in line with, and can benefit from, the therapeutic processes of Mindfulness and Cognitive Behavioral Therapy. We can use these tools to bring awareness and choice with our thought process for the project of waking up and metabolizing this dimension.

It's vital that you build in a healthy skepticism of anything your mind is telling you. The more you examine your thoughts, the more you discover the mind is not a source of wisdom but instead is connected to a delusional system that can terrorize you. Finding your way out of the labyrinth of your mental trickery can feel like you're feeling your way through a dark room. You might grasp a rope to guide you, but it turns out it's the tail of a tiger. Is what you believed to be a benign thought connected to some deep, fearful agenda? With a commitment to being an observer and creating the space to detach, we can feel our way out of this dark, sticky 3D system and find our way into the wisdom of consciousness. The more we let go of mind and ego and our connection to the pain infrastructure, the more consciousness will direct our reality. When we are immersed in love, that is what will appear in our reality. Our mind cannot compete with consciousness.

So, plug your ears. Stop listening. Start being.

Expanding Beyond the 3rd Dimension

When we move beyond the 3rd dimension, we heal ourselves from the 3D, loosen the contraction of its limiting reality, move into other states of potential and flow, and expand into the next reality. Our potential for expansion is accessed in our deep dive into our pain and into our collective healing.

People are turning to alternative forms of medicine and healing, not just to seek root causes of illness but to empower themselves in their own healing processes. They're learning how to become their own healers. As our medical systems are stuck in low-frequency states of crisis management, we find the need to rise to higher states of caring for and healing ourselves—we begin to live lives of health, not just pain/symptom management. We are undergoing a similar process, on a larger scale, on the journey out of the 3D. We heal not just our bodies but our entire beings—our present beings, our past beings, our ancestors' beings. In doing so, we become not just healers but creators. We are learning how to transform a contracted state into one of wisdom. We are transforming pain into light. We are creating consciousness and love.

To access our inner process of transcendence, we need to see our pain as a legacy, not as reality. We see it as our inheritance. It's here not as a failure or as punishment but as our potential. We can launch a new reality out of the cycles of agony. When we hold pain with compassion, respect, acceptance, and a deep seeing, we access and transform the trauma held in our emotional collective memory bank.

Summary: Bringing the 3D into Focus

This is an experiential process. My intention is to direct your attention toward expressions of consciousness so you can dive in and find your way into yourself, in your own way. My intention is to deepen our dive into the concept—and to understand that none of this is real. But first we need to see all the parts of us that are trying to tell us it is. We need to see what we are holding in our own bodies that is enforcing and retelling this story of contracted existence. Our reality is steeped in suffering, and suffering is nothing but a projection—and an expression of our contracted dream state. However, there are lots of ancient, childlike parts within our bodies that don't yet believe that. The journey is to bring seeing into those contracted, pain-filled parts by finding creative ways to deliver the message to whatever part of us doesn't yet know... *nothing is happening.*

Life here is a play, a drama with many players. All the actors are within our mind/body. We want to know who's there so we can get an eye on them, bring them into focus, and see their agendas. We want our pain stories to come into view so that the players in them are no longer in the background pulling the levers and turning dials without our awareness. We want to ensure they're no longer contributing to the giant manufacturing of a pain reality.

We bring how our mind functions into focus so we can see how undisciplined and attached the mind is to states of contracted pain. Our pain wants attachment, and our mind is ready to serve it up. To discipline the mind is a project on our journey, so we're not an unwitting slave to our pain. We are bringing the feminine principle into view so we can wield energies for growth, balance, and transformation in our expansion. This is the foundation of our process of letting go, dissolving, and dismantling our densities.

We are seeing what makes up the 3rd dimension and what we need to do to deepen our awareness. We are being with our pain differently; in a way that aims to open and transform instead of suppressing or denying. These are just foundations, tiny building blocks of awareness on our journey. They are little pieces we continue to assemble. As you proceed, these concepts will develop, open you up to seeing more, and deepen in meaning for you. They all have a unique life of their own within you, and your relationship with each of them will change and shift as you do. Don't attach too much, but don't let go.

Many of us are changing and evolving. Along with that comes a rapid change in how we are healing trauma, pain imprints, and key aspects of the 3rd dimension. We are learning we don't just have to live with our pain, work around it, avoid it, or numb it out. An important part of this journey is discovering we can turn trauma into love. Working at an energetic and feeling level and accessing the energy of consciousness that is floating around, we discover we can turn 3D pain into higher vibrations of compassion. We can transform suffering into awareness. The flow of consciousness is working on our tribal realities. All that trauma is here to teach us how to create and expand into connectedness. I believe that is where therapy is going. That is where healing is going. That is where trauma work is going.

Historically, we have transformed the trauma stories because we spent our lives trying to figure something out: Why am I not happy? Why can't I find a good partner? Why am I angry/sad/depressed all the time? Why does greed keep us from connecting? Why does fear keep me from living my life? Why do I live with so much guilt? All these are just us figuring out how to love. But now, with the increase in energy and growing number and availability of energy delivery mechanisms (see Glossary and Chapter VI – Consciousness Delivery Systems), we are finding our abilities within ourselves and sharing with each other the capacity to bring in enough he aling and transformative energy that we don't need to spend an entire life figuring it out. We are learning how to direct that energy of love into our trauma imprints and bypass years of "problem solving."

Chapter IV

Building the New Narrative

Introduction

In the first two chapters, we explored the nature of this multi-dimensional dance we're in and how the 3rd dimension plays itself out in the tribal dramas. We then explored some of the major characters in the 3D drama in order to get familiar with what exactly we're trying to dismantle. We see trauma and its role both in constructing the 3rd dimension and in leading us to our expansion. We looked at the mind and ego and how the two are connected. We looked at what it means to be asleep and how we get stuck there. We explored a common language of consciousness and how we're bringing its metabolic potential into focus, meaning consciousness' power to transform pain into another reality. We now understand that we are in charge of our process of moving out of the us-versus-them reality, the state of separation and aloneness, and that we do that by inviting the energies of connection, of consciousness, into the states of aloneness we hold in our bodies.

We'll move forward by building the foundations for inner transformation and transcendence. We are seeking to transcend the 3D reality; this dense, sticky, slow reality that exists in our bodies. Now we can develop and encourage consciousness and bring in frequencies that shift us to our higher Selves and that resonate with our metaphysical Selves. These frequencies heal us of 3D trauma. We have set up the infrastructure to welcome in new awareness, to absorb a new narrative, and to *receive* the energy necessary for change. We will now introduce the building blocks of raising our frequency, of bringing in the energy of the next level of our evolution. Because there are a few key ingredients necessary to encourage metabolizing densities, we will discuss this metabolic process in the following sections. But first we need to set the stage to allow this dissolution to take place. We want to ensure we move through the tough stuff safely, with support, with understanding, with a good dose of faith and a lot of love.

Framing Your Process

I will start by reiterating some basic concepts and introducing some new ones to feed the foundations of your understanding and reflection. Every concept or practice I introduce will evolve in meaning and depth as you move through your journey. As you shift your inner landscape, the tools and subjects of your perception change. I can say the same thing ten times, and each time it may mean something different to you. And as your inner world shifts, your outer world will follow.

This section will include discussions of practices and concepts such as Safety, Boundaries, and Self-Compassion, and some exercises to assist you in deepening your connection to these concepts. I advise you not to attach yourself to the meaning of any one thing. We're here to witness any attachment we have or any clinging we do as 3D agendas. We attach out of fear. Fear needs to hold on. Love, on the other hand, is fluid. If you're holding on to anything, you're activating a fear story within. The same goes for rejection. If you're repulsed or angry, you're in a story.

Use your response to anything you read here as an opportunity to witness your inner 3D landscape. Our minds are involved in our interpretations and meaning making because they're still attached to the 3rd dimension. They determine what we consider desirable or undesirable because most of us are operating with a hearty pain infrastructure that selects and judges from a stack of survival-based inner narratives. A good place to start is to practice not believing anything your mind is telling you.

The most potent source of *tribal looping* in the angry dialogue of North America is reflected in everyone believing what they're saying. Making it safe to detach from and disbelieve all the stories to which our fragile egoic minds cling is fundamental on this journey out of an existence of suffering. We want to make it safe for ourselves to detach from our judgments and conclusions and we want to foster a safe and supportive community around us, where others can more easily detach from their thoughts and beliefs without judgment.

Exercise:
Reflection

Others may not want or need to be in the same place you are, but that's not a sign that you should step in to prove yourself right and them wrong. That is an egoic trap. The moment we need to be right is the moment we fall fast asleep. This journey is about opening up and developing our capacity to see our attachments and neutralize them with a compassionate witness. Explore some of the following patterns and signs you are lost in the 3rd dimension:

○ Are you harsh toward your inner realizations; toward the things you discover about yourself?
○ Can you be mindful of how you judge your attachments or your judgments?
○ How do you judge another person's attachments or their judgments?
○ Can you see your judgments for the 3D illusion that they are? What does that feel like?

The New Frontier Is Within

Historically, our focus has been an outward one. We have been engaged in the activities of survival and accumulation for thousands of years. Much of that survival has been hinged upon cooperation/obedience from our tribal members, and the group's welfare has largely been dependent on a shared self-interest. We have needed each other to be or to feel safe. We have lived in shared states of vigilance to protect ourselves from attackers from the outside (e.g., we created a national military) or from internal members who go rogue and attack from the inside (e.g., we created the penal system).

There is a massive, complex pain infrastructure connected to this ancient, externally focused reality. Human beings have accumulated a lot of traumas, but we've needed each other to survive. A mutual self-interest led us to help each other out so that we could hunt better, graze more, grow more, and protect ourselves from the elements better. But by and large, our external focus has been on the need to protect ourselves from other humans. Our 3D bodies are invested in staying safe from the threat of each other.

We are still obsessively focused on people and things in the external environment. The internet seems to have captured and capitalized on that obsession. To not focus on the other, throughout much of the world, ignites the fear-of-missing-out (FOMO) response. To turn away from approval of others is considered unproductive, unaccomplished, even unsafe. Safety has been about finding a secure place in a hierarchy. It involves proving "how worthy I am." Or it's about developing a hearty rage to scare away a threat. And it's this persistent, age-old trauma that keeps most of us focusing outward—fear of the dire things that'll happen if we don't get that validation. This fear is ever present but also well hidden. It keeps us negotiating with the tribe so we can be told we are okay, that we're valued, that we're worthy, that we're good enough, and what to do to avoid rejection and receive approval.

What our ego has not wanted us to see (and it has been dangerous to see), is that all reality is *within*. Our reality, in this dimension, is held in each individual's pain, and this pain creates our perceptions of the world and of self. So, if my reality is within me, then the reality of connection or separation is within me as well. Within my mind, my body, my ancient programming, I hold the idea (stemming from trauma) that I'm not safe unless you, outside of my being, deem it so. This pain idea gives birth to the belief that I'm not safe unless my parents, my boss, my partner, or my neighbor tell me I am. The pain within my body tells me I'm a victim, at the mercy of every other fool or baddy in my vicinity.

So, during moments of clarity, when we see that maybe we *are* all connected through a field of consciousness, we also see that the old programming within our own bodies keeps us from knowing and feeling that. We see that there is no threat and yet we feel a familiar anxiety. We understand no one has done anything wrong, but we feel an old irritation. The frontier for change is *within*. We all hold the layers of darkness within us. And sometimes those stories clash or reinforce each other. That's the condition of being in this physical dimension. Within our global group, we hold the vibration of fear stuck in this density. Everyone's stories and darkness bounce off everyone else's stories and darkness. So, the darkness we experience without reflects our darkness within.

Your attempts to "change" another person, to tell them they are wrong, or to shame them so you can find safety in being right, is your density. Believing there's no place for another person's pain, or there's something wrong with their pain and how it's showing up in the world, keeps your pain in place, keeps the victim story locked in. Looking at "the other" as the source of your discomfort is part of the distracting agenda of ego because fear drives that agenda. It's looking to another so I can feel comfortable/safe. The egoic mind tries to convince me the source of pain and discomfort comes from outside of me. That is part of the oppressive framework we live in. It is part of ego's need to keep us from tending to the fear, trauma, and drama we're holding within our own bodies. It needs to make the problem about everything and everyone else. And all of that is a condition of, a result of, and a product of this dimension.

You're here to expand beyond the density that clouds your awareness. We're uncomfortable and because we feel stuck and powerless, we try to manipulate the outside world to numb out or push away the discomfort and pretend it doesn't exist within us.

We hold the stories of trauma and victim within our beings and therefore, to change our reality, we need only look inward. What we experience when we look outward is *perception*, and as we know, perception is a manifestation of the mind carved out of repressed emotions. We are shifting from believing we're in an outwardly directed experience to knowing that it's all an inward experience. We know this at an intuitive level, which is why meditation and yoga retreats have exploded in popularity within the last fifteen years. We know this when we go to plant medicine retreats and we not only release the pain from within, but we feel the deep connection to everything, to the Whole. As we increase these practices of healing the body, we're exiting this manifestation of the outward experience. We are graduating from it. We understand that our whole reality is a manifestation of inward experience. It's the manifestation of the fear, shame, and rage that has stuck to us like glue. Until now.

What Does Integration Mean?

On this journey, when we wake up or see the bigger reality, we're metabolizing pain and burning off trauma. That means we convert the stored energy of pain into the fluid energy of consciousness. We bring pure awareness to the dense, pain-oriented stories within, and in doing so, we expand our consciousness. We burn off our belief in our own suffering and separation, and in the parts that keep telling us to continue to repeat and relive the suffering.

We are carrying a gazillion little stories of pain in our body, and each one is a version of the story of aloneness. Each pain we hold, each program of fear, rage, and shame, is a little or big story of isolation, separateness, and aloneness. Each one is here to be metabolized. Each one is here to be told it is not alone. And we heal those stories of separation/aloneness with the connecting energies of consciousness.

Becoming Nothing and Everything

Integration is bringing the high energy of connection into the low energy of fear, raising that vibration, and burning off the debris of separation that has stood between you and the Collective. It is transforming isolation into connection. Connection is integrating pain into the Whole, the unity of all.

As we know, it takes energy to activate metabolic processes. And when we peel our way out of this density, we apply energy to the 3D delusions in the physical, emotional, and energetic bodies.

Where do we get this energy? Led by the egoic mind, we spend an enormous amount of energy maintaining our state of suffering, instead of spending energy in the present moment. Most of our energy is spent thinking, feeling, and doing our way out of pain. We want to put all that energy into the present moment. Most of the time, there is no particular drama toward which we must direct a lot of survival energy. So, we have a bunch of untapped energy available to us. When we get quiet, we free up that energy, energy that goes right to the nearest density of aloneness. The energy works on the density, the pain, until it raises the low vibration, burns off 3D toxicity. It raises the vibration and allows it to connect—to the Self, to the Whole. But this is just one source of energy within. There are a growing number of sources without.

The framework we use for redirecting energy is the feminine principle. When we bring in elements of the feminine, we redirect energy from the masculine egoic infrastructure and dream state and release the pain from the contracted dream, which moves us into expansion and healing. There is a tremendous amount of energy available to us as humans within our own beings. We've been directing that energy into the activities of the masculine: doing, running, judging, fighting, fleeing, and oppressing ourselves and others. The qualities of the feminine free up that energy, moving us into states of being, accepting, meditating, sensing, and loving. The feminine leads us toward inward-focused *being* versus outward-focused *doing*.

When we come into contact with pure awareness, nothingness, we are activating a process by which we teach all the parts and pieces within—all the pain of the unsolved problems, the undeterred threats, the unresolved terrors—that there are no problems. One by one, or a thousand by a thousand, we let all those bits know there is nowhere to go, nothing to fix, and nothing to do. We bring all that pain and discomfort into knowing *there is nothing happening*. Not anymore. Not in this place. In other places, there may be lots of problems to solve. But not here. Everyone who is reading this is doing the work, is part of the shared project of dissolving all that running and fighting and freezing and pleasing because they all come to be part of the whole that knows there's nothing else to figure out.

The process of integration, therefore, is turning the energy within us into the energy of consciousness, the energy of awareness. We're becoming *aware* of all the painful tribal expressions of aloneness, and through the energy of consciousness, the aloneness becomes the energy of the Collective and the connectivity of everything. They are seen. Everything is seen. Everything is seen and accepted by the whole. Everything becomes the whole. Everything becomes consciousness.

Layers and Layers

We are on the path of removing trauma, ancestral karma, and other potent stuff, and most of us move through this process in layers. I believe each layer is timed. Each layer is a triumph and has its rewards, and with each layer we get closer; to ourselves, to our truth, and to the expanded Self. We dismantle dense pain, create more space for consciousness, and increase the potential for the creative universe to enter us with order and love. We take the next step in our liberation. But these steps have a process, one that our minds often resist.

Imagine you were told that instead of being male (which you have known yourself to be since the day you were born), you are female, that you have two days to live, and that you were born in a laboratory on Jupiter two hundred years in the future. To permit that new information to become part of your reality, your mind may need a little time to adjust. Often, when I'm on the edge of letting go of an old fear story, I can feel another fear story come up, and the story seems to ask me, "Are you sure? You don't know what is going to be there if this fear is not here. Could be scary!" If I had asked myself to let go of more, there wouldn't have even been a question, it would have just shut down the process. My egoic mind wouldn't have been able to accept and integrate this new reality...too much, too soon, too fast (the very definition of trauma itself). I know there are people who have let go of the 3D in an instant, but I haven't yet found the magic door into that wonderland.

My body has also needed time to adjust. As we release the 3D from the body, it has to filter out toxicity as it brings in extra energy and a new order. Depending on how much energy is coming through and for how long, it can be uncomfortable, even painful. I have included an addendum to speak to the physical manifestations and challenges and to share some things that have helped me through the transition.

We Heal in Safety

Human beings find it hard to heal when they don't feel safe. When the body is busy running or fighting, it doesn't prioritize healing trauma. It prioritizes survival.[31] To allow the trauma to come to the surface, we may need to do a few things, and two of the most important things are:

1. We have to love the bejesus out of ourselves; and
2. We have to keep the low-frequency stuff out. The two tools for accomplishing that are to practice self-compassion and set boundaries. To do that, we need to step out of the stories of threat that we impose upon each other.

Most of us don't feel safe. We don't even recognize we don't feel safe. Over the last hundred years, a large part of our global community has created intricate systems of cooperation to assist

---

[31] Peter Levine, *In an Unspoken Voice: How the Body Releases Trauma and Restores Goodness* (Berkeley, California: North Atlantic Books, 2012).

in our mutual survival and peaceful co-existence (of course, that system was built upon colonialism and the exploitation of continents). Humanity has created systems of government and economy, resource allocation and waste management, punishment and safety, food production and distribution, education and health. These extraordinary systems and technologies (albeit flawed and insufficient) support not just survival but our capacity to thrive, find our creative potential, and show up in authentic ways. And we are screwing it up. Why are we screwing it up? Because we don't feel safe.

In North America, we are coming full circle. We are less than two hundred years from an existence mired in deep threats to our survival, where we needed boatloads of adrenaline to fight for land, and food, and to survive the elements and enemy attacks. Here in North America, we need only a little adrenaline to survive. Yet our bodies are flooded with it. We're not in danger, but we're signaling our own bodies that we are. We create predators and prey—out of each other. We construct danger. We have manufactured a world to match our anger and our fear. This doesn't support our survival. It threatens it. We don't feel safe, so we make our world unsafe. We make everyone the enemy. We vibrate in fight-or-flight all the time and accept that as our normal, baseline existence. Our ego convinces us that to survive, we have to keep running or fighting, or freezing, or pleasing others. But this level of fight-or-flight is coming to the surface at the perfect time. Many of us will see it right when we have enough energy and awareness to know what to do with it. And unless we connect to fundamental levels of safety, we can't do anything with it.

To raise our frequency, to heal, it's important to deepen our sense of safety. The body is less likely to let go of anything while it's in survival mode. It clenches in fear, contracts, resists release, and asks the mind to problem-solve. It can't shift, change, or reflect in a state of fear. It braces and looks for distraction to escape the uncomfortable state as quickly as possible.

Held in states of contraction for millennia, our bodies have been waiting for a time when we feel resourced enough to go into fear, shame, and rage to transform it with light, with consciousness, and to release it from the body. Now is the time for many of us, and we need to get our nervous systems on board.

But the speed at which we're living these days blocks any effort to signal the body that we can relax now. It's safe. We are coursing with adrenaline and cortisol, stiff with muscle tension, delirious with sleep deprivation, and hopped up on toxic stimulants like sugar, coffee, and other common drugs. When and where are the cells of the body ever going to get the chance to feel safe? The "masculine" part of ourselves has taken over the show, telling us that perpetual states of busyness, anger, productivity, and oppression are the only way to be: the safe way to be. It says that there is something to be fixed or improved upon all the time. The masculine tells us there is a problem, something is wrong, and must problem-solve continuously. Our masculine-driven egos say that to be any other way is lazy, unproductive, inefficient, and inadequate, and that we're not contributing to society, not keeping up, not successful, not worthy, and not lovable.

To shift inner gears, we need to shift the outer ones, creating safety for the mind/body. Bringing a sense of safety into the mind/body is delivering the frequencies of love and compassion and is a first step toward our journey of merging into love. As we get closer and closer to the vibrations of consciousness, we need to cultivate that sense of care for ourselves. We need to be the first (and the last) frontier to build that love. By doing so, we allow ourselves to delve more into the ancient traumas within, because we've built a safety zone, a buffer, around us. We cocoon ourselves within this zone of care. We need to create this physical and emotional container of compassion and kindness before we can let go into the boundarylessness of our metaphysical selves. We help raise the vibration within by raising it without.

A lot of our work is about taking care of ourselves so we can create opportunities for letting go. We want to increase our feelings of safety as we enter story after story of pain and discomfort within. We need to take care of ourselves so we can move into the density and then return to the light. We have so many parts within us that believe that to let go, to let light in, is too risky and change is too dangerous.

Our job is to tell every frightened, contracted part within us that, "It's okay now. We are safe. I know you are scared, but I got this. I will never leave you and I am going to get us to the other side." Sometimes those parts don't want to—or know how to— listen to messages of safety because it has been just too scary, so we may need to get some help to get that message in there. That help can come in the form of your friendly neighborhood therapist or from other allies. But every time you get that message, you're healing and expanding your inner world to another reality.

If you were hurt by a parent or caregiver in childhood— through violence, rejection, by a self-absorbed parent, or in another traumatic way—then, of course, it was their job to keep you safe. But if they couldn't accomplish that (and many are/ were unable to do that because they themselves never felt safe), then it's now your job. Challenging though it may be, it's your task to go into the pain you inherited and teach yourself how to feel safe; teach yourself how to love; teach yourself that you're worth it. This is not easy, but we have so much energy and wisdom and love available, it is more possible than ever. You have more support now than your ancestors ever did.

Here I'm attempting to construct a reality in which it's safe to be in pain. That means making it safe to screw up or not know, without expecting that everyone else will dump their rage and disappointment all over. Therefore, you can make it safe to own it when you screw up or violate another person's boundary. We are not likely to change our behavior, to reflect on our beliefs, if we are in a defensive state in our relationships. If I'm protecting myself from attack (hostile criticism, judgment), then I can't be vulnerable with the people close to me, and I am less likely to reflect on my behavior and be open to changing. The converse is also true. In my life, I am making a conscious choice to construct a reality in which it's safe to communicate when I feel unseen or unheard. And conversely, I make it safe for others to communicate with me when they do not feel safe or heard. Clear communication of my experience and my needs not only nourishes safe relationships but encourages a reality wherein it is safe, acceptable, to access the egoic stories that always show up in relationships. I encourage you to construct your own social reality where you bring in others who encourage you to do safe inner exploration. These are conscious relationships, wherein the shared goal is not to win but to encourage each other's path to freedom. There are some excellent resources available on conscious relationships.[32] I recommend making one part of your reflections.

On our path toward deepening love and consciousness, we want to build additional infrastructures and processes that nourish our awareness. We have hinted at the important role of boundaries in building our sense of safety. Let's explore the role of boundaries on our route to a boundaryless existence.

We Are Worth Boundaries

We are on a transcendental journey, waking up to our inner Self and letting go of all that is not us. Walking this path is about knowing we have created our own pain, seeing our opportunities to heal it, and comprehending that while we may live in a great deal of discomfort, discomfort is no longer our reality. We can see pain is a reality that our egoic minds construct or hold on to from our ancestral trauma pool.

---

[32] John Wellwood, *Conscious Relationships: Where Is Your Relationship Going?* (Louisville: Sounds True. Audio Book, 2015).

Our 3D body is built from wounded parts. Sometimes these are deep, unimaginable wounds, but it's these wounds that keep us from seeing a bigger reality. They are threatened if we do anything other than run from, avoid, or deny pain. My wounds resist any suggestion that I'm responsible for my suffering. The wounds are afraid of that reality; they don't believe they're powerful enough to undertake it, and they're looking for validation, to be rescued and made safe. "See me. Protect me. Save me."

A human, 3D wound has a process of healing, and we need to respect and honor that process to move it forward into the higher realms. Our job is to get these wounds ready for expanded existence. We do that by working with what we know about how humans change. We know the nervous system and mind allow healing and change to happen when they feel safe. Safety is all we have been looking for. We feel safest when we feel seen and protected. That signal of protection is sent to our 3D pain through the message of boundaries.

Boundaries tell our wounds, "I see you. I am keeping you safe now. You no longer need to be afraid. You don't need another person to keep you safe. That is now my job." We see the pain and we're with the pain as if it is our child. Which is, in fact, what many of these wounds are—parts of us that got stuck when we were wounded or felt vulnerable as kids (or when our ancestors were wounded or vulnerable). Those parts got stuck in the state of childhood. They feel volatile, and they vibrate with the fear of being alone and abandoned. They want to be rescued and they get frustrated, angry, and feel rejected when they're not. They have a limited perspective on life and their role in it. To allow these parts to feel seen and heard, to facilitate a connection to the whole, our job is first to keep out the bad stuff so healing can occur.

Grown-Up Boundaries

As adults, it's our job to discern what feels like a threat, what feels unsafe, and to put up protections. Instead of asking what many of us ask, which is, "What do they want me to do?", it is our job to ask ourselves, "What do I need to feel safe right now?" So many of us were not taught how to say "No," how to walk away, how to understand our worth, or that we're not obligated to experience another's rage, shame, or hostility. And even though we can understand at a soul level that nothing bad is happening at any given moment, that everything is as it should be, there are still parts of us that are not yet ready to believe it. We feel afraid. It's our job to protect ourselves until most or all parts of us are convinced everything is taken care of and safe.

For example, if I was raised in a household where I felt unheard by my father, in my adulthood I may get upset, or feel frustrated, agitated, emotional, or triggered when I'm with my father. To step out of that loop (that story with my father), I may need to take some time, and make some space, so the part of me that feels unheard gets a break from that feeling, and from not being heard. It will feel protected. In that space and sense of safety, I'll create a long, quiet, healing conversation with the part of me that is looking for my father to see me. I'll let that part know: "I hear you; you deserve to be heard, and you are worth hearing." In this way, I'll recognize that it's my job to hear myself and to hear what I need to feel connected. It's no longer my father's job. In fact, I need to give my father permission to not hear me so I can be realistic about who he is and what my expectations are. It's my job to bring in people who hear me, want to hear me, and can hear me. And it's my job to keep out people who don't or can't. It's my role to create a reality in which I feel heard. I don't leave that job in anyone else's hands. Once I release my father from that job, it may feel "safer" to be around my father because I have reset my expectations and no longer look to him to be seen or heard. Or I may decide that I no longer live in a reality where I have anyone in my life, father or not, that does not hear me.

Boundaries are often challenging and confronting because so many of us have been told that to set a boundary, to say "No," is going to be met with disapproval, disappointment, or rejection.

All our trauma is telling us that "No" will lead to our demise. We may face many generations of programming that tell us it's dangerous to set a boundary. But with boundaries, we create a path of safety, allowing us to take a deeper journey inward to explore and examine our inner pain. With boundaries, we calm the external noise. We can see, for example, that our fear of rejection allows people to take from us without limits. Or we see that our inability to say "No" is because we are terrified people will abandon us. These are all challenging things to see, but boundaries are a necessary part of creating a safe environment so we're more able to draw that uncomfortable reality into our awareness.

I have a client who experiences repeated anger and frustration when her mother cancels plans they make. Her mother has never kept plans or fulfilled her commitments. Now, in her thirties, we can see and explore her abandonment wound that was ignited in childhood; a wound that still stings today. We see it's a wounded little girl within that felt she could never count on the most important person in her life—she carries a wound caused by her sense of feeling her protector didn't see her. The wound is still making plans and still has expectations of her mother. My client needs to explore new boundaries with her mother. These boundaries tell the abandonment imprint that it's her job, not her mother's, to keep her safe, to protect her from not being seen or abandoned. When my client learns to put up boundaries (e.g., not making plans with her mother, or if they do make plans, then knowing and being okay with the reality that she might have to go on her own), she will send the message to the abandonment wound that she has "got this." She is there for her own feelings, taking responsibility for her own needs, and keeping herself safe. She's seeing her mother's current capacities rather than who she needed her to be as a little girl. She protects herself from her mother's behavior. With boundaries, she'll create the safety within herself that she'd been looking for from her mother for years and could never find. By owning it, she'll release the expectations of her mother that feed her anger. She'll find her own power to take care of herself and her life rather than feeling victim to her mother's choices.

If we've set a boundary and we still feel resentment, we need to rejig the boundary. Resentment is a clue that something has got past the gates that doesn't feel safe or doesn't resonate with the reality you are trying to create. Own all your resentment. Explore what you need from yourself to feel seen, heard, and taken care of.

This is not an overnight healing. The process can go on for years (especially with mother stuff). But the profound healing that comes from setting boundaries feeds the energy of safety and care that all our young and old wounds are seeking. We activate a power within our own bodies. We create a new, high-frequency reality that says, "I am in charge of my healing. I oversee my safety. I create my freedom."

Late-Blooming Boundaries

I was thirty-three years old before I set a boundary in my relationships and thirty-five before I set one at work. At thirty-three, two years into my marriage, I realized I had married a narcissist. After we separated, upon reflection, I realized I had married my mother—a mother facsimile. The end of the marriage was the beginning of an enormous expansion where I saw the parts of me that were taught that my needs are less important than others', which was my mother's lifelong lesson. She taught me that if I wanted to be in a relationship, I couldn't say "No," not in any way that mattered. She taught me I shouldn't expect to be seen in my most intimate relationships; that my job was to see the other person. The end of my marriage was a multi-year journey into healing layers of ancient wounds of invisibility, unworthiness, and feeling obligated to own everyone else's discomfort to feel safe.

In addition to our intimate relationships, our careers are vast landscapes where we feel unseen, unheard, and unsafe. Leaving my previous job was the single biggest energetic explosion I had felt to date. I decided one day that I'd no longer work in a toxic environment with oppressive superiors who couldn't communicate with integrity. I quit in a flurry of confidence. Along with that big "NO!" there was a release of big energies. For the first time, I saw *myself* instead of seeing my life through fear. My life trajectory changed on a dime, and I found myself racing toward a new career and a new purpose. I was holding on for dear life, not knowing where I was going or how I was getting there. I synced up with a magical reality that would unfold and expand for the next many years.

Declaring "No, that pain is no longer my reality" is a tangible shift. It raises your vibration, sending you off in unexpected directions. I've seen it countless times. I cannot understate the power of a loving boundary. It's an energetic and emotional maturing. When we declare the unapologetic "NO," the wounds within get the message, loud and clear, that someone here is taking care of us, and the healing begins.

Some objectives of boundaries on the journey to our expanded selves are:

○ to provide "protection." People are not entitled to dump their pain on us. We do not need to ingest everyone's pain to feel loved.
○ to see and feel that we are worth protecting. To love ourselves, 3D bits and all, and to recognize we are valuable and worth the effort.

Exercise:
What Might Boundaries Look Like?

○ Take out a pen and paper and write down key people in your life with whom you need to draw boundaries.
○ What would those boundaries look like?

○ Why and in what way would they provide healing? Safety?

○ In what way would it feel unsafe?

○ If you feel anxious with the idea of putting up a boundary, with saying no, is that feeling of it not being safe a real threat? Or an old habit and familiar response?

○ If there is pushback or resistance from another person in response to your new boundary, does that mean you are doing something wrong?

I'd like to encourage you to set boundaries mindfully. We're all on the journey of healing our pain, whether we're aware of it or not. If we can look upon another's painful projections and expectations of us and know that their behaviors also came from thousands of years of PTSD, we can set boundaries with the higher vibrations of compassion and love versus judgment, shaming, and rage. We don't determine or judge another person's path, but we protect ourselves from recycling pain stories with another. If someone close to us tells us (in words or deeds) they'll only accept us if we never object to anything, we know their trauma is dictating the terms. We can put up a boundary by stepping away, without judgment, and acknowledge that the reality their pain is asking us to take part in is one in which we no longer want to exist. *They* may exist in that reality for as long as they need to, but it's our choice to break from it. Part of that break is walking away with acceptance, love, and forgiveness. We put up boundaries around the *behaviors* of others. In those boundaries, we are not rejecting another person or judging the journey they are on. We're determining that the behavioral manifestation of their story is one we no longer accept as something we can have in our reality. But they may still need that behavior, that energy, in their own life for a while. If it's not for you, it's great that you recognize it. Try to honor the other person's journey and respect the path they need to walk to figure out their own stories. If you decide, for example, that the low-frequency behavior of gossip is something you no longer want to create or have around you, great realization. If others are still working through that story, give them permission to do so. Watch and see if your ego wants to judge. Judgment may be your next story to work on.

At the other end of the spectrum is where we find those of us who set up exaggerated boundaries. We kick people out at the earliest sign of conflict or don't let people come close to begin with because we've already assumed that bad things will happen. There's a big "Flee!" response. A pre-emotive strike. Here, your fear and rage have most likely told you that when people get close, the only thing you can expect is to be hurt and disappointed. So why bother!? I suggest you do some work with a professional who can assist you in figuring out how to make the discomfort in intimate relationships something to be explored and used for your expansion rather than something to avoid. In relationships, our old 3D wounds are revealed and reflected to us. We find out how to love ourselves through the exploration of loving others. There are always going to be sticky points in a relationship. We are not seeking a perfect relationship, but we do want to find people with whom we can negotiate. We may not want or believe the same things, but how do we see each other so that we can co-create a reality?

There are many resources on boundaries.[33/34] I would suggest exploring a few to see what speaks to you. If you have a history of not setting boundaries well, if it feels challenging or unsafe to set boundaries, or you have set up big giant walls around yourself to feel safe in the world, do some reading. Maybe find a therapist to guide you through your journey toward expansion. Boundaries are about

---

[33] Anné Linden, *Boundaries in Human Relationships: How to Be Separate and Connected* (Bancyfelin, Wales: Crown House Publishing, 2008).

[34] Henry Cloud and John Townsend, *Boundaries Updated and Expanded Edition: When to Say Yes, How to Say No to Take Control of Your Life* (Grand Rapids: Zondervan, 2017).

learning that you're the creator of your reality. Setting boundaries is a fundamental process for acknowledging your compassionate Self. However, crafting boundaries can be challenging work, and it's one of the many reasons we need to develop the practice of Self-Compassion—which we will explore soon.

Boundaries, Anger, and Rage

Anger has its functions. Healthy anger tells you that something got past the gate; something violated your boundaries. You determine what it is (because sometimes it's not clear), and then follow up with some form of boundary. Once you listen to what the anger is asking of you, and get the message, it's up to you to follow through with the resolution. There is no need for more anger. Knowing that you're in charge of your reality, if you bring in someone's unwanted behavior, it's up to you to negotiate something new. If that doesn't work, push it out of your life. Out of your reality. This could take two minutes or two decades. Once you own your anger and your decision-making, you see that beyond the moment of understanding what you need, anger is not useful. If anger hangs around after its usefulness, you are floundering in the ego infrastructure. A minor wound is having a big tantrum. But you're here to realize, and to remind the anger, that the construction of your reality is up to you.

Anger lingers because underneath there's a fear or grief that doesn't feel safe to emerge or be seen. Anger stepped in to manage that discomfort, promising protection through oppression and ferociousness. This is why anger at parents or spouses from whom we have felt betrayed can go on for years. When we're unseen in significant relationships, we feel vulnerable—until we're ready to own and step into the fear, grief, shame, etc., and heal it. Acknowledging there's something underneath the anger allows us to be tender with it, giving it room to feel the stuck feelings.

This brings us to rage. As discussed earlier, rage is an epidemic, especially here in North American large urban centers. We are pulsating with it. It reflects the deep sense of powerlessness we feel when we don't feel seen. But how can we be seen when there are millions of other people around us, all trying to be seen, busy navigating their own pain stories minute to minute, day to day? How could we have power over the behavior of all those hurting people?

It's our job to see our rage for what it is. Rage is our pain infrastructure chiming, desperate to make its own discomfort someone else's responsibility. We're trying to vomit up intolerable feelings. And where do we vomit our feelings the most? In our intimate relationships and our families. When we own our big pain, we make setting up boundaries around our rage possible. Just as we protect ourselves from other people's stories, we need to protect others from our stories. When we hurl our rage onto another person, we deepen, build, and rebuild the 3D infrastructure. And the first place we reinforce it is in our own bodies. We're the ones emitting the low-frequency density. That's our creation. And it's ours to own and transform.

When anger and rage show up, we want to be mindful of the futility of hurling more shame or rage at our rage. Our rage is there to protect us because we have felt unprotected in our lives. For example, we may have been told since childhood our voice doesn't matter and our "No's" are unwelcome. This suppression can cause sticky states of depression. At some point, our rage might want to step up with a powerful voice after not feeling heard for so long. Or the rage wants to assert its power and take up space after we have experienced physical violence. So, we need to honor, love, and be grateful for our rage, as it may be a necessary part of our finding safety, asserting boundaries, and providing care to a deeper wound. But we also need to see rage and its role on the bigger journey. For rage is a dense energy. What is it trying to accomplish? What does it need? How can we meet that need without the density of rage? It's an opportunity for us to shift from creating protection and safety through rage into creating it through love and higher vibrations of consciousness. Our job is to come forward into power without pain. So, we don't shame rage into the corner or spew it up on someone. We allow it to relax, soften, and be heard; to transform and merge with the voice of love itself. To be transformed into higher wisdom, a higher vibration of the next reality, our rage needs to be seen, and then accepted and honored. Which means our safety needs to come first.

There are lots of resources to help us work with our anger and rage. If those stories come up, find a good book or two, and a good therapist (or other ally), to assist you in bringing light to that story. There are generations of rage and anger deep within our beings. Try not to get discouraged when it doesn't dissipate right away. The anger has been trying to protect us from the emotional and physical brutality of other human beings for thousands of years. It will take time to transform all of it and get the message into those deep, old crevices that "We are safe now." There are many messages and behaviors circling the globe trying to tell us the world is still not safe. Keep your focus inward.

Boundaries and Guilt

When I first launched onto this wild, terrifying path, I met with an intuitive in my efforts to find help interpreting my upended life. He provided me with a profound but confusing reflection. He said, "You need to figure out what's your stuff and what's other people's stuff." I didn't know what he was talking about at the time—and I didn't realize that was my first conscious foray into understanding boundaries. Now, I see a whole new generation of human beings that navigate this terrain better than I was able to, so I believe we're heading in a beautiful direction. Still, I see daily in my practice how trauma and family dynamics train people to take responsibility for other people's pain. An exploration of guilt is a good place to ask that question, "Is this my stuff or is it theirs?" Good guilt will say, "Yep, this is my stuff. I don't feel good about this choice or this behavior. There is something here I need to change. Sorry if I spilled some of that on you. Let me clean that up." Once we implement the change or lesson, the guilt fades.

If we were raised in a family home where parents or caregivers blamed us, their children, for their discomfort, we can get confused, especially when we face disapproval. Often these are homes where kids had to walk on eggshells around their parents to keep some sense of safety and peace in the home. If a parent responds with anger, grief, or shaming at a child's poor grade, or getting injured in the playground, or at the child having an uncomfortable emotional reaction, a child can get a deep message that they are at fault and that it's their responsibility to make the people closest to them happy. Which is translated as, "Other people's happiness is my responsibility."

This type of guilt is an inherited pain story—and a false signal. It tries to tell us, "It's your job to fix their pain and discomfort." It says, "You are bad and not safe unless they are content or they approve of you and your choices." We can carry an old childhood message that says, "If I feel bad, it's because I am bad. If they feel bad, it's because I am bad." So, when we face someone else's disapproval, we can have a strong emotional response that says, "It's my responsibility to resolve the problem," even if we know we have done nothing wrong. We scramble for approval and compromise ourselves. We give up our needs and wants and we lose focus on what we need to feel safe and heard. The guilt we can feel when we're told by another that our choices or behaviors caused their discomfort can feel overwhelming—and convincing, especially when we make choices other than what the guilt wants us to do.

Exercise:
Dismantling Guilt

We understand that people are allowed to disagree. They may have their own pain and perceptions, and they may not behave the way we want. In fact, they came here to this dimension to misbehave and to find their own path to resolution, to healing, and to transcendence. Our job is not to take on their inappropriate behavior, own it, or fix it. Our path is to put up either emotional or physical boundaries to protect ourselves from their pain stories, and then to bring our guilt story into focus. When putting up an emotional boundary, here's a possible internal dialogue to help you make sense of your new boundaries: "They may not like me or like what I'm doing. They're entitled to be displeased or think differently."

○   Is that my business? My concern?
○   Does that have anything to do with my value as a human being?
○   Does it mean I'm not safe?
○   Is there something I could learn about myself from this?
○   Is there something I want to do differently?

If you can answer "No" to all these questions, you are on track for setting and practicing good internal boundaries. Give yourself permission to not have to resolve someone else's discomfort. Get out of people's emotional spaces. Your focus is to heal your guilt, not save people from themselves.

Self-Compassion

Throughout history, many groups have seen the physical self as the source of evil or badness. The body is seen as a profane thing, keeping us from union with God and deserving of our disdain and contempt. Both early and medieval Christian ascetic practices have used forms of inflicting pain (such as self-flagellation) as tools to exorcize or purify evil from the body. Purification and punishment are centuries-old traditions seen in almost all parts of the world. (And I believe those traditions still echo in our collective memory banks.)

Our bodies are breaking with the burden of the self-inflicted pain we have carried. The idea of caring for oneself, even for those who understand its benefits in principle, still carries a sense of shame for many people. It confronts the parts within us that feel weak or unworthy—and often, it feels more appropriate or natural to punish ourselves than to treat ourselves with compassion.

When we try kindness, compassionate self-talk, or self-forgiveness, we can feel like we are being indulgent. There are many reasons human beings resist self-compassion. Women are often told their value is in how they sacrifice themselves for the tribe; that love is meant to be extended outwards. It's one-directional. Women are recognized and rewarded when they are the sources of compassion for others. Often, we see women who take time for themselves or say "No" as selfish. Self-compassion is rarely supported or even recognized as an option.

Self-compassion has historically felt unnecessary for men. They may take what they want and need from the world around them already. Love and compassion are expected to come to them from outside sources, but men do not see love and compassion as things they give themselves. We expect the feminine to direct compassion toward the masculine. For men, compassion for self is perceived as a weakness. We expect both men and women to suck it up, and "take it like a man," which we have defined as a strength and a desirable quality in a mate or leader. Compassion and self-compassion are feminine, childlike. The practice of being kind to oneself, gentle with oneself, forgiving of oneself are rejected, consciously or otherwise, by most men and many women.

In the last few years, the field of psychotherapy has recognized self-compassion as a valid and impactful therapeutic intervention.[35] Self-compassion regulates the nervous system and soothes and heals such emotional states as shame and guilt. Mainstream psychotherapy is confirming that no matter where it's directed, love heals. To have any credibility, self-compassion had to move into mainstream psychotherapy. The concept felt foreign, even laughable, especially to our North American sensibilities. Almost without exception, every client new to psychotherapy flinches when I introduce the concept of self-compassion. Their discomfort and resistance are palpable, and typically, they dismiss self-compassion as being a vacuous therapeutic ploy.

Such visceral resistance to self-compassion indicates how separate we are, both from ourselves and from our own source of consciousness. We're born into families and bodies crushed under the wounds of survival and self-loathing. We see ourselves (and others see us) as broken, dangerous, threatening, insufficient, and not worth loving. Driven by egoic pain stories, we've been choking on the expectations of others. But we realize that what people want from us are projections of their own fear, shame, and rage. It is their fear, shame, and rage determining what they want and need from us. And these projections are what we are here to liberate ourselves from; they are part of our toxic connection to the tribe.

At the most basic level, at a physiological level, self-compassion heals the body. In directing compassion toward ourselves, the body has the same (or a similar) physical response as receiving compassion from another person. Our body releases oxytocin, serotonin, and dopamine, for example, then the nervous system regulates, and we shift into parasympathetic activation, a state where healing occurs. At an energetic level, compassion is a high (and maybe the highest) vibration.[36] To deliver compassion,

---

[35] Kristin Neff, *Self-Compassion: The Proven Power of Being Kind to Yourself* (New York: William Morrow Publishing, 2015).

[36] David R. Hawkins, *Power vs. Force: The Hidden Determinants of Human Behavior* (Carlsbad, California: Hay House, 2012).

no matter the source or the target, is to receive the energies of expansion and awareness. Self-compassion not only contributes to our healing, but it also furthers our evolution and our experience of connection. When we practice compassion, it delivers the energies of consciousness, which, in turn, deliver intelligence and order into all levels of the beings. We are all connected, so when we direct compassion toward another, it lands as compassion toward self. It acts as an internal scrub brush, cleaning out low-vibrational stories within our own beings. When we deliver compassion, we activate that high vibration in our heart space and generate energy in our own bodies, which releases contractions, creates openings, and feeds our expansion and healing.

Exercise:
Seeing What's in Between You and Self-Love

When you first launch your journey of compassion, it may feel weird to be tender with yourself, to speak gently. My clients describe feeling "inauthentic, hokey, mushy," etc. Take that as a clue. Explore:

o What is standing between you and you? Between you and love?

o If you sit in the weirdness, what comes up underneath?

o What feelings or thoughts emerge?

o Can you witness them?

o What in your body is resisting feeling love toward your own being? If it could speak, what would the resistance say?

o What within you is telling you that loving yourself is wrong, inappropriate, unattainable, weird, etc.?

That uncomfortable feeling is you hitting on some density, pain, suffering, contraction, or ego; a story you are holding in your being, blocking your access to the flow of love. See it. Witness it. Practice being with it without judgment, because it is asking you to bring in the energies, the creative force within, that will turn that blockage into love.

We Need Credibility

Our energy body and our emotional body are connected. To heal the energy body, we need to feel love. Our cells need to receive the emotional and energetic message, the instruction of love and compassion activated in our heart space. That doesn't come through as thought; it comes through as feeling. So, we need to explore what it feels like to love ourselves.

When you speak compassionately toward yourself after you've been hostile for most, if not all, of your life, it's going to feel strange. It won't feel real. You may need to give it a couple of *years* before it does. It will take that long to develop credibility in your own being. Our nervous systems expect and have been bracing against our self-directed hostility, likely for decades. It's the norm. You need to give it time to adapt. It's like having your dad yell at you for a dozen years and then one day, out of the blue, he walks in the door and says, "Hey kiddo! Come here and give your dad a hug!" You don't trust it. You may even feel creeped out. You get your back up. You're suspicious. You have difficulty feeling the kindness of those words because it's never happened before. It's unfamiliar. It's not what the relationship has been about, and it's not what you expect, not what you trained yourself to cope with to survive. You don't know what to do with it. So, when you change the temperature of your inner dialogue, give it time and practice. Just because it feels foreign and fake doesn't mean that the love you are giving yourself isn't healing. It doesn't mean that love isn't a reflection of consciousness. It doesn't mean that it isn't penetrating the density of ego and your wounds with a higher vibration. It may take time before we notice a shift. Then we notice that our self-soothing has an impact, and we believe and respond positively when we provide kind, supportive self-talk.

When you deliver the higher frequencies of compassion to yourself, you invite and direct the energies of consciousness to penetrate the densities (the wounds) within your body. You bring in the energies of healing. So, accept the possibility that the healing energy will come into contact with a pain story. They will connect. If something surfaces, observe it. Allow. If it's uncomfortable, observe the mind's need to think about something else or the body's desire to escape by doing something different. Allow the feelings to surface. Let your body release the tension— maybe through tears. Then, be grateful. Unconditional positive attention brings in the mother's energy, the one who accepts all and heals all. If something arises and is released, afterward, practice appreciation for yourself for being able to let go of the lower vibration, the pain story, and integrate a higher vibration of love and acceptance. And appreciate your capabilities.

Bring it in through your heart, not just your mind. Keep your eye on the egoic stories of disappointment, anger, fear, shame, guilt, and judgment. Instead of seeing them as failures or flaws, see them as opportunities to direct consciousness. We have been seeing our pain as something to avoid and deny, which has kept it in the dark. Now we are learning to see our pain as a *signpost*. As an opportunity for expansion. As a place to see our internal drama, not abandon it.

Self-loathing is another common internal drama in humans. We can host the thoughts, feelings, and behaviors of self-loathing and not be aware it's happening. But if you see it, no matter how convincing it is, your journey, your Self, asks you to see your self-loathing, and see your self-judgment as an ego trap that is there to be dissolved. To be loved, not rejected. To be seen, not believed. It's your doorway into awareness and expansion.

Self-Compassion: Tribe to Collective

When we are taking care of ourselves, when we see our own worth and honor our obligations to bring ourselves into states of love and compassion, we're also disconnecting from the tribe. We release ourselves from the need to look to another person to tell us we're loved and we're OK. When we feel afraid, we make alliances with an oppressive "other" in order to "make us" feel safe. We hand our safety and power over to another and stay in the pain story of oppressor/oppressed. The journey is to work our way out of an interpersonal dynamic that says, "I am not connected, complete, seen, or safe." We open ourselves to knowing that no family member, friend, or boss is there to tell us we are loved, loveable, or worth loving. That is all within us. Therefore, the journey toward self-love is the journey toward the multidimensional, complete, whole, collective, high-vibrational Self.

When we experience what it means to not compromise ourselves for the approval of others, when we stop fearing rejection or isolation, love shows up. Genuine love. We bring the vibration of unconditional love into our bodies. When it shows up within us, it shows up in spades outside of us. The world feeds it back to us. We step into the flow of consciousness. It won't look like the mind thinks it should look. It will be how the intelligence of consciousness constructs it.

Explore self-compassion. Reflect on self-compassion. Make it part of your growing conscious dialogue toward yourself. It's a necessary element in your expanding Self. It's not only part of the construction of safety for healing your body; it is also a consciousness-delivery system. Allow how you express compassion toward yourself to shift, change, and take on new meaning. There are lots of books on self-compassion these days, so I don't have to reinvent the wheel here.[37]/[38]

---

[37] Neff, *Self-Compassion*.

[38] Tara Brach, *Radical Self-Acceptance: Embracing Your Life with the Heart of a Buddha* (Louisville: Sounds True: Audio, 2008).

Exercise:
Bringing Self-Compassion into Focus

When you launch your practice of self-compassion, here are some things you can ask yourself:

○ Can you spot your resistance when you say something kind or supportive to yourself?

○ Does your mind tell you, "This is stupid," or "It feels too weird," or "It doesn't feel authentic"?

○ Is there sadness or grief? Maybe because you haven't been able to deliver much compassion to yourself in your life? Maybe because you haven't received much compassion from others in your life?

○ Is it a game changer?

○ Is it just a lovely addition to your growing toolbox of love?

○ Can you notice your body/mind shift and change its response to your attempts at self-compassion over a week? Over a year? A few years?

Through our painful walk toward our suffering, we can see, feel, and experience that compassion is consciousness expressed in all directions, to all things, that leads us to God, Goddess, Source, the Universe, and to Self. We have an opportunity to be the creator of our next reality, and self-compassion is a fundamental part of our creation.

Self-Care

Most of us suck at taking care of ourselves. We ignore our own needs. We don't recognize our needs. And yet, how are we to know how to give or receive care unless we have felt it in our own bones? We know our needs best. Other people who come into our lives can't know our needs until we tell them what they are, so we must figure it out for ourselves first. Denying oneself comfort, care, and safety expresses pain and the 3D. It's not, as so many of us were taught, martyrdom or selflessness. It is a rejection of self. So, the pain of rejection is within us, and we hold it in place when we martyr ourselves and reject ourselves.

Exercise:
The Egoic Story of Self-Rejection

Not taking care of yourself?

○ Do you feel you are worth it, or good enough, to receive care from yourself? How so? How not?

○ Do you put others' care before yourself? What is your motive?

○ Is there something you don't want to see or feel that arises when you do take care of yourself? For example, do you feel guilty? Is it uncomfortable to be alone with yourself?

○ Do you allow others to care for you? Do you do this instead of caring for yourself?

○ Does care only feel real when it comes from someone else?

○ What does it feel like when you put yourself first?

○ Do you prioritize busyness over care?

○ Explore ways that you would wish others to care for you. Can you provide them for yourself?

○ If you're aware your self-care has been lacking, make a list/project of adding some daily, weekly, and monthly self-care practices to your routine. Journal about how they felt. Was there resistance? From yourself? From others? Has it created greater ease?

To not take care of yourself is to feed the 3D, keep it alive, remain in your delusional reality of pain. You may not know it's there, but your stories (and your nervous system) ensure that you circle around the pain and never get near it. To continue moving forward, you must see the pain for what it is, beyond the stories of your egoic mind. You deepen your knowing, understanding at a profound level that if it's pain, it's not real. It needs to be soothed, loved, integrated, and released. Taking care of yourself is an act of dismantling. It dismantles and dissolves the pain stories that have defined your value and your reality as anything other than magnificent.

On this journey, we are witnessing the suffering we hold in our bodies, and we do it with vigilance and discipline. To carry yourself through this challenging, extended journey, you want to create times and spaces that acknowledge the incredible being you are. When we're living under the strain of our tribal pain stories, our ego wants us to forget our magnificence. So, create those reminders. Construct moments in which you acknowledge yourself. Create a favorite room, book, music, chair, altar, or blanket. Find a place to visit, or a favorite person to call. Create delicious, nutritious food, and find places where you love to move and breathe. Keep a list of favorite caretakers: massage therapist, naturopath, acupuncturist, Reiki practitioner, coach, or therapist. Go where you feel nourished, seen, and reminded, where you see yourself and hold yourself in high regard. Find ways of celebrating yourself frequently.

I invite you to reflect differently on self-care. We need to open up a new way of loving ourselves. Self-care is part of the energy needed to see and dissolve egoic infrastructures. Self-care reveals that to hurt yourself, criticize yourself, not forgive yourself, put yourself last, or compromise yourself is to be under the hypnotic spell of ego and pain infrastructure of this dimension. It's the same stuff. To shift out of this trap, we need to see how we live, behave, think, and feel the painful emotions of a construct we've built since we were infants, and see how we host our ancestors' similar experiences. In doing so, we can see this construct is not real. How we ignore, insult, and reject ourselves are all manifestations of ancient pain stories. They're not real. Not anymore. If you're not loving your being, or you call yourself stupid or doubt you deserve forgiveness, you are fast asleep in the ego trap. Never doubt you should take care of yourself. Hostilities will show up because many of us have treated ourselves dismally for...ever. *See* the hostilities close and personal. Stop believing them through practices of self-compassion and self-care. Construct a new reality that confronts old pain stories.

We may believe that what we do now is self-compassion, but in the future, we'll look back and see it wasn't. It was avoidance. Self-loathing. Fear in disguise. Be kind to yourself. Allow this process to unfold. Don't attach to any concept or behavior. Don't hold on too tight to what you feel *now* is the "right" way of loving. Continue to reflect. Ask yourself, "Is how I talk to myself, how I behave with myself, and how I feel about myself a reflection of love or pain?"

Chapter V

5 Pillars of Dismantling

Introduction

Since 2006, five practices have consistently shown up in my journey. They have been fundamental to the continued deepening of awareness, moving things along in a consistent and reliable fashion. They anchor me and keep me focused, mindful, and connected to the next reality. They feed me the higher frequencies of consciousness and encourage and strengthen my ability to see the 3D, at all levels, within my own being. These practices are *Meditation, Vigilance, Reflection, Owning Everything,* and *Feeling.* Each one shows up for me daily, even hourly, guiding and revealing the path forward.

1. Meditation

There are many beautiful books and online and community resources on meditation, so I do not need to explain what meditation is or why it's the best thing ever. A large percentage of the world is already sold on the idea that meditation is a powerful practice. What I will share with you is how I see meditation applying to—and being essential to—the path out of the 3rd dimension.

For many people, meditation is an opportunity to check out, to take a break from a busy mind and daily activities. That may be what our nervous system needs…to take a break and to regulate our adrenaline- and cortisol-flooded body. However, for the project of dismantling, in meditation, we check into our internal landscape, into the stories ready to be revealed. The conscious energy available around us can be used to heal us. We check in and give permission; we make space for those energies to come into view and come into our bodies/minds.

In Chapter III, we explored how the mind is a tool of ego. Or, more accurately, how ego enslaves the mind to serve its goals. Meditation challenges those bonds of enslavement. It allows us to witness ourselves and develop our ability to see our mental antics versus believing them and following them blindly. In meditation, we develop distance and space to observe and discern what the mind is projecting.

With minimal observation, we can see that we are noisy. There is noise inside and out. We all vibrate with mental activity and pain management, humming all the time. Meditation leads us into the space where we get some distance from the noise of ego to release the energy underneath. Our stories are everything that connects us to this physical existence. They're all of our past—childhood past, ancestral past, past-life past—and they show up like a movie reel in our minds. The thoughts create conjectures about the future and narratives about what the future should look like. In meditation, we develop silence and space within that creates a portal to our metaphysical Self, where none of the stories exist.

This is the present, a reality and energy not connected to the 3D but connected to the Self beyond the 3D reality, the density, the pain.

We use silence to get into our feelings, to see and bring connection to the 3rd dimension and how it shows up in our bodies. Feelings are difficult, if not impossible, to shut off. They come in overwhelming waves, and we feel compelled to ride them or push them down with disgust, annoyance, or fear. But there they are and there they remain. Our entry point becomes the mind, or rather the discipline of the mind. Not connecting to our thoughts as they move through, finding the space between the thoughts, and finding extended periods of silence slow down and cut the feedback loop. We stop sending signals and energy that keeps the feedback loop alive. We stop feeding the imprint's rationalizations; ego's arguments for staying alive and taking up so much space. Without that energy, the imprints unwind, unravel, and dissolve. This is not an overnight process, but with persistence, change happens. We access the layers and we let them go.

When we allow ourselves to bring in silence, we introduce the energy of pure metabolic potential instead of feedback loops. Below mind, below body, below time, is the organizing force of everything. Our world, the universe, and everything work within the principles of that energy—it is a force of creativity and order. When we enter states of real silence, meditation, or creative flow, we invite the energy of pure potential—the energy of order—into our beings. Stepping into the flow every day, through meditation, through generating compassion, and through feeling gratitude, are all ways to contribute to your metabolic process, igniting the state of order within and around you. Each moment in presence is a drop of consciousness, a drop of potential, bringing you out of the chaos and closer to Self.

In silence, we can create a sense of safety in the nervous system, in the mind, in the body. If there is big-T trauma, it may take some time for that silence and the unclenching to feel soothing versus threatening, and therefore your journey into silence may be gradual and strategic and you may need a little extra help to get to that quieter place. Whether or not you have big-T trauma, we all need to feel safe to let go, so the more work you do on feeling safe and regulating your nervous system, the safer your meditation will feel.

In the space and safety of extended silence, we get glimpses or insights into what is blocking us, what we are resisting, what is keeping us from moving into our higher Selves, and where we need to let go. To surround and infuse our body with the energy of pure presence is a deep practice of unabandoning. We learn to be present with ourselves, without judgment, without egoic interpretations, without story-making. We are practicing being with ourselves, in completeness.

In meditation, we are also creating and remembering the journey inward. In the dramas of everyday life, the ego takes over and tries to tell us all that noise out there is important and real and needs all our attention. When we meditate, we connect to the other reality, which is that everything that is happening is happening within us. We connect to all perceptions, thoughts, pain, and inspiration. In meditation, we remind ourselves to keep looking inward. Instead of focusing on the drama without that keeps us trapped in the delusions, we dismantle the programs within.

Exercise:
Meditation – Connecting to You Under the 3D

In your meditation, find that part within you that's not connected to the stories, the trauma, the discomfort. Connect to your Self, which is connected to the universe, the everything, and the nothing. I connect to my heartspace in meditation. I sit in the most powerful part of my subtle being, the center of everything, allowing the energies of order to flow freely while I connect to the place underneath all the 3D agendas.

Explore the Subtleties of Your Self:

○ Where does Self/Universe sit within you?
○ Can you sense it? How does it feel? How does it move?
○ Is it familiar? Does it feel strange? Unusual? Separate?
○ Can you connect to the varying nature of your inner landscape?
○ Can you tune into where your body might hold more density, contraction, tension?
○ Can you feel where it might flow more easily? Can you deepen presence?
○ Can you find your way into the physical densities/discomfort? Allow yourself to sit in them, around them. Can you see/feel judgment or expectations arise?
○ Can you connect to the repressed emotion beneath?

Group meditation and silent retreats are my favorite ways of inviting in big energies. When we meditate together, we magnify the potency of silence and consciousness. I make giant leaps forward after a week at a meditation retreat. I find it to be as powerful as plant medicine for cracking the 3D open. Finding a group to meditate with is a gift: to yourself and to the Collective. An annual or bi-annual retreat is a potent commitment to Self and keeps you grounded in the journey.

We are connecting to the part of us that lives in total connection. We see a reality where we no longer need those ancient protective mechanisms for survival, because we are eternal. Eternally connected. In meditation, in silence, we continue to nourish safety in the body and loosen the grip of our 3D agendas. We allow the energies of presence to permeate our dense reality to transform and release it from our beings.

2. Vigilance

Vigilance means that we are consistent, turning into and bringing awareness to the 3D as it appears in our day-to-day living. Vigilance helps develop our capacity to be the witness, so it's always watching, observing, and detaching from the egoic drama. We look under every internal rock to see if there is density hiding underneath. We are persistent in exploring and examining our thoughts, behaviors, and feelings to determine whether we are perpetuating the 3D in our bodies or nourishing a higher vibration. We commit to detaching from our fear narratives and bringing light into those stories as they appear. We hold our egoic stories accountable to our higher Selves, and we bring in individuals and communities that support creating safe spaces for honest, difficult inner work. We examine the energy we're putting out into the world and what we're allowing in. We become a moving meditation—existing in mindful states, bringing awareness into every moment. When anger shows up, we don't stop there. We use it to turn inward. The anger is a signpost. It's not a place to take a break, believe the story, or allow it to take root. We take the time to see it, maybe explore it, over minutes, hours, or days. Every time anger shows up, we change the direction of our gaze from outward to inward. Every time guilt shows up, we go into the feeling—we don't believe the story. Every time shame shows up, we sit with it—we don't react to it.

When we live a vigilant existence, we may not be able to shift and heal everything, but we keep our eyes open to see where ego is hiding. Where is it trying to convince us that our jealousy, anger, or fear is truth? We don't accept our big feelings as truth. We use each uncomfortable moment as an opportunity to dissolve the layers.

Exercise:
Practicing Vigilance

Here are some examples of practicing vigilance throughout the day.

○ When on the freeway, bus, or subway, observe the irritation, judgment, or other ways you contract and feel separate from others. Observe, breathe, allow.

○ When in an argument or disagreement with someone, even though a part of your egoic mind believes you're right, consistently activate another, more zoomed-out part of you that knows you're in a story and are not accessing the truth. Once there's distance from the argument, examine and (kindly) challenge the part that needs to be right. Explore what the lesson/pattern might be. What is it you're attached to? What do you fear?

○ When you're about to do something that makes you anxious—e.g., a job interview, going into a crowd, a first date—observe your anxiety. Be curious. Keep breathing. Even though it might not change in that moment, activate that part of you that knows nothing is happening.

○ When you become aware that your mind is going in circles trying to resolve a problem, move your awareness to your heart. Sit in your heartspace. Breathe pure consciousness into your tensions and contractions. Do this many times a day.

○ Observe your mind wanting or needing someone— anyone—to act, think, or feel differently than they currently do. Bring that thought into awareness. Don't feed it. Just let it sit there. Where does that thought show up as a feeling in your body? Observe that. Bring lightness into that. Breathe.

3. Reflection

It is vital that we direct our mind into the energies of consciousness. Feeding the mind with high-vibrational thoughts and concepts contributes to shifting out of lower frequencies at all levels. Potent reflections open gates, release limitations, and unleash the energy of your truth and the power of higher frequencies held within the wisdom. I suggest you read (and reread) high-vibe texts. On retreat, when we allow ourselves to ponder concepts that whiz by our minds on a normal day, we experience a depth of understanding and often a shift in perception. When I'm on silent retreat, my favorite texts to read are books by authors Richard Rudd and Eckhart Tolle and the Seth books. Each time I read them from a place of quiet and contemplation, I go deeper into myself. You will find these and other authors and titles in the Suggested Readings at the back of the book.

Reading high-frequency words, contemplating their meanings, and feeling the energy they activate or transmit feeds your expansion. They shift your state from victim to creator. The truth of something has a profound effect on all levels of our being. Our field of awareness embraces and feeds on truth, so nourish your journey consistently with high-vibrational wisdom.

Exercise:
The Practice of Reflection

Find an inspirational book and pick a passage or page in that book that strikes you as meaningful or relevant to what you are experiencing in your life at this time. Read this passage before you:

○ Go on a walk.
○ Cook a meal.

○   Begin your meditation.
○   Finish your meditation.
○   Have a bath.
○   Go for a drive.

Allow some of these times of quiet and introspection to be filled up with higher frequency thoughts and feelings.

4. Own Everything

After a few forays into plant medicine, I was at a retreat where I was encouraged to try one of the highest sacraments: Bufo Alvarius, a powerful toad medicine. It was the last offering at this retreat, and I was pretty shaken up already. I had experienced a deep resistance, a terror, of doing any more medicines after having already done three, six hours each, involving extreme discomfort. And I was not feeling at home with this group. I felt a bit like an outsider, invisible, not connecting. It was not a comfortable week for me.

I knew it was about me. Always is. But I was not shaking it. I had rationalized myself out of doing any more medicine. "Why does it have to hurt? Why must it be so painful? I don't have to do this to myself anymore!" The morning of the offering, I paced and ruminated, and my mind spun. I could see the path of terror my ego had taken me on. So, after a few hours in this clenched state, I stopped trying to decide, sat still, and allowed the truth to come through. And in that silence a persuasive push that led me toward the facilitators emerged, and without thinking, I expressed a firm, "I'm in." My decision was met with a big, knowing smile, and it was decided among them that I would go first. (I assumed this was so I'd start before I changed my mind.) I was led to a grassy patch in the garden next to the dining room.

I was told to lie down on a mat and was instructed as to how to inhale the medicine. All the while, my heart thumped, and my hands shook. When the time came, I took a big inhale, strained to hold it in, and slumped to the ground. Just before I slipped into the hold of the medicine, I could see all the facilitators—shamans, powerful healers—all standing around me, eyes on me as I slipped into nothingness. And that's all it was: nothing. I remember nothing. I did nothing. The moment arrived when I came to after an indeterminate period. I opened my eyes, and there were the facilitators, standing around me in the same places they had been when I'd left. Except they all looked different. The world looked just a little different. Brighter, truer. A strong thought rushed into my mind. JOKE'S ON YOU! it said. I felt a sense of amusement and celebration accompany that thought. A full, joyous, almost hysterical laugh erupted. I couldn't stop laughing. Which launched everyone around me into laughter. It became so clear to me...there was nothing going on! All of my anxiety, anger, frustration, disappointment, all of it, all of my life, was nothing. I had created it all! I had made it all. The joke really was on me. Now it was my job, my journey, to unmake it. Because there was nothing happening! After I finished my long laugh, I rolled over to my right, facing Cesar, one of the facilitators, a powerful Mexican shaman who was sitting in the chair a foot from my head. He looked down at me, shrugged, and said, "No hay nada." (There is nothing.) And I responded, "Yes, I see." I rolled over and threw up on the grass, my body purging my pain and the toxic density of belief in this reality.

Ownership Is Access

Letting go of this reality requires you to acknowledge that it is *your* reality. You live it, you create it, you have always created it. You just haven't come to that realization yet. In order to get access to my manifestations, I have to recognize that they're all mine. I need to see and practice full ownership over my experiences, especially the uncomfortable ones. Owning everything—meaning looking at all our embedded fear and shame and rage in all of our programs—is difficult. In fact, it goes against everything that global ego has been trying to establish for the last few thousand years. We see it in the stories of victimhood that have dominated our politics, economy, and relationships. To some people, the idea of ownership can look obvious at first blush, but it turns out to be rather confusing, and just about everyone meets it with resistance—at least in the beginning.

Owning everything means acknowledging that everything is within you and *everything in your body is your responsibility*. This includes all thoughts, all feelings, all perceptions, and all pain. You either signed up for it coming in, or it landed on you along the way. Either way, since it's in your body, it's yours to own, yours to transform. It's there to serve your journey and your expansion. It's not here for someone else to transform; it's all yours. The transformation and expansion won't happen unless you own it. Every experience, every feeling, every painful event that happens in your life, no matter how shitty or unfair it might seem, own it. If you are the center of your universe, and your own creator, and all pain is a story you carry around in your body, and your expansion depends on you seeing and transforming everything within your body, then looking outside of yourself to feel better, different, or safe is a trap of ego and the 3D infrastructure. Your discomfort is in you, not out there. Blaming and victim stories are a delusion; more density keeping you in pain. Projecting your pain, displacing your pain, and deflecting your pain are all sure-fire ways to cement you in the 3D.

During this great shift, I am going to speculate that many high-vibrational beings signed up to burn off, heal, and transform hundreds of generations of pain. We're bringing big energy into dense, tribal programs to facilitate the collective transition from pain into freedom. Many of us have been hanging around for a couple hundred thousand years so we can deliver this energy in this critical time of change. If you're one of those beings, you will serve your journey well when you catch your victim stories; see them for the ancient trauma they are expressing. In order to liberate our bodies from hundreds of lifetimes of pain, we can't shirk our responsibility—and until now, we have been experts in shirking.

We have inherited an ancient bad habit: looking outward. We all do it. Our aversion to seeing our pain leads us into a global culture steeped in blaming. Blatant forms of blaming, such as raging and shaming, seem to be in vogue. There are more subtle forms of blaming, such as patronizing righteousness. We are all uncomfortable and to cope, we point fingers at everyone else.

On this journey, we are trying to rejig our perspective. If you're uncomfortable, it's your responsibility. Anything within you that blames someone else or declares you a victim is part of the 3D egoic infrastructure, and that too is your responsibility. If you understand this, you step out of the victim's story and transcend it. There is no victim in consciousness or in the present moment. I know this is contrary to much of the Western psychotherapeutic model, which can often frame ownership as victim blaming. Ownership goes against all the politically correct discourse we are so invested in, and it goes against much of what I believed and fought for in the first thirty years of my life and career.

All this protection of "victims," I believe, has been necessary. It may even have been part of a larger, historic boundary-making apparatus. Until now. There are no victims in the next reality.

Only in full ownership do we unleash the power to create a new reality and let go of our identification with the old one. We are zooming out of our limited 3D existence and the drama we have engaged in from a distance. We zoom out in deep silence or in higher vibrations (such as in meditation or at a plant medicine retreat), where it is common to sense deep connection and to know our pain is teaching us something. That there's a bigger picture, a bigger story going on. When we're uncomfortable, we zoom in. When our bodies are in pain or a wound is triggered, ego keeps us focused on the discomfort, telling us it's the only thing that matters, the only thing there is. When we're obsessed, enraged, or frightened, we zoom right into a limited aspect of ourselves. And that's all we see; all pain wants us to see.

We are here to experience ourselves, to experience pain, and through the pain, to find our way to a greater awareness that tells us, "I create my world." That knowledge leads to expansion, to greater love and ease. We let go of this reality and all the things that ego wants to hold on to in this reality—including victim and perpetrator dramas.

Integrating this as truth—that this is all yours and that you are creating all of it—is enough to launch you on the path. It is a colossal leap in frequency. It begins by dislodging you from the dream, distancing you from delusion. It loosens the hold of the 3D within your body. I feel it all the time in my clients, that energetic loosening. As soon as they *see* the story, I feel the sticky density dislodge, become mobile, fluid, accessible…and BINGO! We have lift-off! The pain separates from the being. They heal mentally, emotionally, and physically. Merely seeing it as something they can change versus something they are trapped in shifts their reality. They create space between the Self and the pain.

This doesn't mean that you haven't experienced terrible things in your life. It doesn't mean uncomfortable things won't happen to you. But our potential lies in our approach, our attitude, and our attachment/detachment to the discomfort. We need to own our residual feelings about any event in our life. We decide if we hold this in the dark or bring it to the light. And we may need to go through a long process of forgiveness to get to that light. Forgiving ourselves and forgiving others.

Forgiveness

The journey of forgiveness is a transformative and liberating experience of integration and release. It permeates the stickiness and lightens the pain. Question a mind/ego that tells you forgiveness is about losing or being weak or unsafe. That's an egoic distraction. Sometimes it's a necessary one, but eventually we regain our focus.

Resistance to forgiveness, to letting go, is a classic 3D infrastructure. Forgiveness with boundaries is a superpower.

We open up when we own the oppressive beliefs that have emerged from our DNA and repressed emotions. If we look to another person to feel freedom, we imprison ourselves. Our liberation is in the journey inward, in looking at our belief systems in a new, empowering way that says, "My feelings of joy, love, belonging, and connection are all within me. Therefore, anything that stands in the way of those expressions of consciousness is also within me. I am responsible for those, too." In the most subtle, non-egoic way, we're creating a critical mass of empowerment that's not about force but about the power that comes from shining from the inside out and from knowing that you are the creator of that light and therefore your reality. Owning everything brings power and capacity into your hands. It's the opposite of the victim state. Victim states keep us in a feedback loop, believing nothing will change. Victim states imprison us in the idea that in order for me to be okay, the other person needs to be different; think differently, behave differently, or understand differently. See your tendency to want others to be different. Let it all go.

Many of us need to revisit how we see others' pain. Many of us are compassionate, but our compassion is wielded by fear. We want to heal the world, rescue, fix, and save it. But maybe we are ready to see others' pain as their journey, their responsibility, and their potential. Try honoring the path another person took and thank them for revealing something to you about you. Their pain is no longer your business. It asks only for your presence.

Your path is to turn your gaze within and bring greater awareness to where you are holding pain and 3D contractions. Your process will get stuck or slow down if you look to another person for your resolution. It starts to flow again when you sink back into the realization that "I am only a victim of my core beliefs." Reflecting on that at every challenging turn will propel you forward and assist you in letting go.

Another powerful tool of letting go is forgiving self. But it's typically a dance between our own inner wounds. One wound/ego story feels another story has betrayed us, shamed us, or weakened us. Often, what we're so angry or ashamed of is something we did as a child, so how can there really be anything to forgive? But we need the forgiveness to work its way into and between our wounds in order to engage the process of letting go. In order to arrive at the place where we can see that nothing was happening, nothing was wrong. You were doing exactly what you needed to do to survive then and what you need to love in order to heal now.

Forgiveness is not a linear journey. Your commitment to owning everything will be challenged more or less depending on the depth of your pain story. As we ground ourselves in our truth, we use each challenging time to deepen our practice of ownership and letting go. And we will need to go really deep to own the biggest 3D stories, such as shame and rage.

The Delusion of Rage

Rage is a part of our 3D selves that does not want to own anything. And rage cannot pass the threshold into higher dimensions. It's too dense. The challenge is that rage tells us we need it to survive. It asserts how right we are and how bad the other guy is. We are addicted to this 3D density. We need to bring awareness to our rage addiction to get access to this seductive narrative.

As I mentioned in Chapter III, at the beginning of the section entitled "What is Ego?", most of us construct our reality based on pain versus what is happening in the moment. Rage is a perfect (and extreme) example of how far we can exit from the present moment. It's easy to recall when our anger/rage led us to say or do things that, upon reflection—an hour, day, or week later— we think, *Oops! Maybe not the best response. Maybe that didn't get the results I wanted.* When we're in rage, we enter survival mode and ignite fight-or-flight systems in our mind/body. We release lots of adrenaline and cortisol, and the brain's executive functioning (which allows us to be flexible in our thinking and exercise self-control) shuts down. When you're being chased by a tiger or are fighting a battle, executive functioning doesn't keep you alive; you need speed and strength to escape your enemy. Many of us live in a privileged part of the world where most people experience a high level of safety. However, the egoic mind still wants to ignite a fight response, wants to tell us there is something enraging happening, at a frequency that doesn't seem to reflect reality. Everybody's rage is poised to spring into action, dukes up. You can feel it when you drive down a freeway in any major city or when you do an online search for "anger management" (where you will find groups, books, and therapists in abundance).

In states of hypervigilance and anger, the mind/body will take physiological cues and add a story. Ego sets up the story so that you are the good guy, they are the bad guy, and you are conquering or winning. In order to reclaim what it feels is a vulnerable place, a place where it feels powerless, it brings a story of being victorious over an enemy. We may feel powerless in the face of an offense or in the face of another person's unpleasant decisions. Ego will construct a story that helps your mind/body feel it is reclaiming your power. Blame is your number one tool. They're stupid, arrogant, evil. They're no good at their job, at relationships, at driving, at breathing! Our rage feels justified amping it up a notch because, of course, it covets the victim's seat, thinking it's protecting us by making sure we're not at fault. And this maintains our victim story. The world is on fire, and ego is addicted to telling you it's everyone else's fault. Around and around we go in circles with each other and our ego stories.

The moment you're in rage, you're buried in your pain infrastructure. Ego has taken over your reality. For a moment, you may need that anger. Anger or rage may give you a compelling signal that someone or something has crossed a boundary. So, you pay attention. You get the information you need to make the next decision, to make a correction, or put up a boundary. After you come down from the anger, you can reflect and reframe. Reflection assists us in reasserting ownership over whatever victim story arose during an event. Your anger reveals you have trauma that feels so powerless, it needs rage to feel safe.

When rage takes over our perceptions and we believe the victim story behind the rage, we are locked in delusion and the density of that pain. We're living in the tribal reality. This reality says we need the other and their approval to feel okay, to feel safe, to feel seen. This reality says, "If they don't give me their approval, then I'm betrayed/rejected." But that rage is too dense and too heavy to go with us into higher states of being. In order to transform that rage, we need to own it. When you're aware of the inner drama and see it for the pain it is, you transform it and free yourself. Here is an example of my own transformation process.

Betrayal. A really popular ego story. By chance, I was told about a colleague who had behaved in a not-so-respectful way, taking advantage of my openness and willingness to share ideas, plans, and projects. The moment I understood what had happened, I felt this old surge of white rage come through my body: heat, a pulse increase, and overpowering low-vibe thoughts. It was a reflex. Something old and buried deep within me rose up—a hot surge that ran through many generations of women in my family. I could witness this age-old rage response. It hadn't appeared in many years, so it was easy to spot. I could see all the energy it was consuming and the story it wanted to tell me. That I was wronged. That they were bad. That I was a victim. It was uncomfortable, yet seductive. My higher goal was to not allow the story of the betrayal to take over my understanding of the event but to use it to metabolize the deep, ancestral rage in my body that had made itself known.

To dive deeper into my process, I went for a long walk. As I circled the park, I did some of the most challenging work of my life as I directed my attention and my energies into my body, to be with this powerful rage and all of its sensations. My mind wanted to hijack the experience with rationalizations of why this other person was so bad, why I was so wronged. Those rationalizations then tried to shift to something a bit more righteous—maybe I needed to have a conversation and share how I felt so they would at least know what they'd done, so they could learn from the event. My mind was searching for a plan, something I could do to fix this. But I could see this was a distraction and an attempt to manage, control, and escape the discomfort. I kept going deeper, bringing in more energy, diving into the feeling, into the pain. I breathed and sometimes gagged and coughed as old, stale, stuck energies surfaced.

After walking for an hour, bringing in energy and breathing out pain, directing love into this story of rage, I could feel it loosen. Waves of tears came. I allowed suppressed wails and deeper agonies to emerge. My mind was desperate to find a place to land, to organize this experience into something I could feel comfortable with—to make myself right and them wrong. Or make me not care. I wanted to tell myself I was taking the higher road and that "They will get their lesson by experiencing some reckoning in their career." I could still see the ways I was gracefully going to teach them the error of their ways by sharing what I felt and articulating my needs. Supposedly all good things, right? But with each thought, each attempt to navigate and negotiate with this story, I emptied my mind and directed more energy, more space, more consciousness into the pain. I could see that this was not about them. After an hour and a half, I could see/feel the thoughts show up as frequencies, a fresh experience for me, a new capacity. I was able to actually feel the difference between the rage and then the freedom of this not being my reality, my drama. I could feel the heaviness of the rage and lightness of the acceptance. I could feel that each thought that wanted to wrestle with them and get them to change, to see, to be sorry, was a low-frequency part of me. I could feel the hum of their behaviors as lower frequencies, low vibrations of pain manifestations. And every time my mind wanted to change their minds, contrive conversations where I would get them to see the error of their ways—which means believing their reality—I was lowering my vibration to that level by negotiating with that reality. I had to talk to my mind and ego that wanted to fix it, to make it right, to protect me. I had to tell my pain story: "Everything is okay; it's safe not to go there; I am safe not to be in that reality." I could bring in more space, more love. Believe less, let go more. Think less, breathe more. The pain continued to loosen and let go, loosen and release. And then that blessed moment arrived. I felt it all let go. I could feel myself letting go of the reality that I'd been a part of just moments before.

I found myself in the park, radiating light energy, bubbling like champagne, feeling grateful to this person for this most profound lesson. I found my mind loose, my body light, and I felt connected in a way I had never experienced. I was connected to the world by vibration. I felt my thoughts, feelings, and body in terms of vibration (instead of right and wrong, good and bad). Everything became clearer, less messy.

I went home to cook dinner. Fifteen minutes after walking through the door, my liver started spasming. It felt like it was throwing up, again and again. I bent over, clutching my right side as it surged and purged. I fell to the kitchen floor and the old, stale rage and fear emotions came out in tears, sobs, and vomit. Now the body was letting it all go. By that evening, my thoughts were light. I rarely thought of the other person or the event again. And in the rare moments it did appear in my mind, it had no emotional charge, no weight, and there was no reason to linger on the thought. It moved through effortlessly.

Turning your rage into an opportunity to heal may take time, and it could reveal layers of stories before you get to the center. For years, I have been dismantling generations of anger and rage that I inherited from the women in my family. It's a gradual detoxing of generations of vulnerability. So, allow the process. Try not to judge. It will be uncomfortable. And that's right where you need to be.

Exercise:
Bringing Your Victim into Focus

1. Every time you want to blame someone for anything, write it down.
2. Every time you want to shame someone, write it down.
3. Every time you want to blame yourself for something, write it down.
4. Every time you become really angry, have an explosive argument, or get lost in your rage, write it down.
5. Every time you feel sorry for yourself, write it down.
6. And then wait and watch.

A day or a week after each of these events, revisit your writings and attempt to have a different conversation with each one of them. Use the questions below to start that conversation:

○ Can you ask yourself where your power lies within each event? Power that your anger has kept hidden from you?
○ Is there a fear under your anger that you have not yet seen/connected to/understood?
○ Can you recognize where a boundary was violated? Where you need to set a new boundary?
○ Is there something that needs to change, and you have not felt safe enough to change it?
○ Can you recognize where you made a choice about your life—the people, the job, the home—that anger does not want you to see as your choice?
○ Is there a fear of/resistance to forgiving getting in the way of letting an old wound go? (Which is OK. Forgiveness can take time.)

5. Working with the Feelings: Disassembly Required

Human beings dislike feelings. At least the uncomfortable ones. We're all over the good ones, but the second it gets uncomfortable, we flee for the hills. The reality is that by choosing to be in this dimension, we're uncomfortable most of the time. This is a heavy, dense place to be, with lots of low-frequency experiences. Many of us in North America (if not all over the world), have not found a reliable or consistent way to deal with many of those feelings. We reject them and often cannot see the opportunity in them. In fact, we spend trillions and trillions every year on cocaine, alcohol, sex, pornography, and various internet diversions, and years of our lives on violence, shaming, and rage, all in order not to feel. And without the distractions we still usually don't feel them. Or aren't aware we're feeling them. Many times, I've been with people telling me about their happy lives, but I can feel the pain stories they're holding within, often not far from the surface.

The pursuit of not feeling our feelings builds the foundation of our economic, political, and social existence. The magazines we buy, the cars we collect, the money we stash away, the technologies we accumulate, the things we watch, the internet we troll, the drugs we take, the sex we have (or don't have), the jobs we get, the politicians we elect, the garbage we dump, the rage we inflict (on ourselves and others) all lead us away from our uncomfortable feelings. We're in a persistent state of pain management.

Pain Management

Pain looooooves, wants, and needs pain management. And pain management needs pain. Historically, the two have gone hand in hand.[39] We feel pain, and we spend a lot of time and energy trying

---

[39] I want to emphasize that I am referring primarily to emotional and mental pain. Physical pain needs more direct attention, more energy, as it is a deeper manifestation of trauma. Healing interventions need to reflect that intensity.

to manage, ignore, and deny it. There is a lot of activity, busyness, and attention in the pain/pain management partnership. But we are entering a new reality that says maybe all that pain doesn't exist. Maybe that pain is done.

Exercise:
Reflection on Our Relationship to Pain

○ What if that pain were part of a project that is coming to completion or reaching a climax? What if it served no purpose?

○ What if there is nothing going on? What if all of it was just your perception bouncing off another's perception?

○ What do we do with that pain if there is nothing going on?

○ Can you ask the pain what it wants or needs? Does it have an answer for you?

○ What does it mean to accept fear? Guilt? Jealousy?

○ What does it feel like to hold acceptance and fear in the same space?

Let's look at how to use our various forms of discomfort—little feelings; big, giant feelings—to learn many ways that we can direct that energy of awareness, acceptance, compassion, consciousness, and love into all those hidden, dense wounds in our bodies. And with all of that energy that we're bringing in and all the energy in those stored wounds now being released, we're going to expand, expand, expand. That pain is going to allow us to spread our wings like big multidimensional butterflies.

To Feel Is to See

Your mind, at some level—at a growing level—may understand that none of this 3D drama is real and that it's becoming more and more antiquated in your reality. But there may be many places within you that haven't yet been informed of the new reality. Our job is to deliver the message to all those places that have yet to receive it, and in doing so, to bring consciousness to those places that have not held consciousness before. Or, more accurately, we are allowing consciousness to move freely where it was kept at bay or squished into silence. We are bringing awareness into the darkest, deepest, heaviest, most contracted places. We're bringing consciousness into fear. Fear we've stored in the shape of shame, rage, guilt, grief, or disgust. And where do we host these little gems?

In our bodies. These bodies are vessels of torment. We are hosting these lower frequencies like a boat hosts barnacles. They shape how we experience this reality. Now we can bring big energy into big wounds, big traumas, big imprints, big programs. That's why we're here…to scrape off the barnacles so we can experience freedom, expansion, and the next level of being. And with, let's say, a quarter or a half of the planet engaged in fear-busting, can you imagine where we can take each other?

Of course, I am trying to seduce you into this journey because it is uncomfortable. Awareness at the feeling level means *feeling the feeling.*

We have spent so much time not paying attention to our feelings or running from our feelings that many of us don't know how to make our way into one. Or we don't know what it looks like when a feeling arrives. What I want to introduce (and re-introduce) and encourage is that when we create the conditions of presence, when we bring in the energy of consciousness, having uncomfortable feelings is going to be part of the detoxing of this dimension. We're bringing in the energies of the universe to dislodge and dissolve the toxins that no longer sit in that higher vibration. Emotions/feelings that aren't connected to what is happening in the present moment are toxins. And that toxicity may have served us in the past but it's no longer necessary. We may need to feel them when they're on the way out. It's a bit like having too much to drink. Most of us feel the effects of the alcohol on the body as the body tries to purge the poison. We sweat it out. We pee it out. We feel our bodies go out of balance—mood, appetite, digestion, energy—as it resets itself. This happens when we release 3D density from our bodies, too. We release the energetic disorder. We release the physical toxins or the physical parts of self that correspond with the energetic imprint. We also detox the lower-vibrational emotions that correspond with that story and that are connected to that pattern. We feel them when they bounce off our nervous system as they leave the body. So, while there is an emotional release, we need to remind ourselves that there's nothing happening, even when our nervous system is sounding off all the alarms. To move into an understanding of the nothingness, that the drama does not exist, is to transcend the imprint and its pattern, to rise above the lower vibrations. Richard Rudd described transcendence as a process "that can only be triggered by such a deep submersion into our human wounding that it becomes the catalyst of our transcendence."[40] Our wounds, our feelings, our emotions—the things we've been avoiding, denying, repressing—are the key to our transformation. Let's discuss how we can often experience resistance when we're in our metabolic process and what you can do with that resistance to minimize its effect on your expansion.

---

[40] Rudd, 438.

Sitting in the Feelings Is a Metabolic Process

We want to allow the energies available to us, both within and without, to get access to our wounds. There's more energy available than ever before on this planet, so we want to direct that energy into those low-vibrational imprints, those dense places within, and raise them to a higher frequency. We need to allow the light energies of awareness to penetrate the dense energies of pain by being in pure presence. Pure presence allows feelings to move, to flow, and to be seen and felt so we can allow the intelligence of the universe to move through us unhindered.

Beautiful things can happen when we create opportunities for intelligence to flow. But what usually arises first is resistance. For example, in a therapeutic session, or in meditation, a yoga class, or a plant medicine journey—all places and experiences in which we activate presence—uncomfortable feelings can come to the surface. Often, what we do in the face of that discomfort is forget what we're trying to accomplish. We leave the present moment. Our nervous system takes us back to the time the event first occurred, and the presence heads for the nearest exit. We enter flight mode before we know anything has even happened. The egoic mind hijacks the mind/body, rallies around the pain, and tries to keep the status quo.

In sessions with clients in which uncomfortable feelings arise, people get struck with amnesia. Their minds clamp down and hijack their reality. They forget they are safe. It is okay to feel something uncomfortable—it's normal and to be expected. For example, many of my clients have read *The Untethered Soul* by Michael Singer. They adore it and connect to its wisdom. But when the time comes to get uncomfortable, they don't know what to do. What do you mean *feel it?* Where is the feeling? What do I do with it? What am I actually doing? Rather than sit in the uncomfortable feelings, their mind gives them a thousand other places to be. There's no space within the mind and an uncomfortable nervous system to conceive of remaining in that discomfort. Conceiving of doing anything other than escaping from pain feels impossible. You might as well suggest jumping out of a speeding train.

As soon as we're uncomfortable, our mind shifts into problem-solving/pain management. I see clients benefit when they allow me to hold them in the present moment when discomfort arises in a session. I assist them in releasing pain—and that can lead to big shifts in their life. They may see positive movement, opportunities open, or perceptions change. They may let go of old behaviors, allow new ones to come in, and discover things that bothered them before no longer do. But the next time we're in an uncomfortable feeling with an opportunity to let go of a 3D imprint, their minds take over the narrative again. I see ego get busy, trying to distract them, directing them anywhere but into the feeling (again). They chat, analyze, remember, or change the topic. Exit stage left. Return victim state. They fall into a reflex that says, "Sitting in this uncomfortable feeling is impossible, even dangerous." Their bodies go on alert. At any sense of threat, they grab onto old pain-management reflexes. They clench, distract, deflect, displace, or try to escape at any cost, by any means. Sometimes it doesn't matter how much evidence there is that sitting in feeling and sensation heals and transforms. We're going to find many reasons and rationales and escape methods to keep us from that feeling.

Our process becomes even more challenging when we're trying to direct consciousness into uncomfortable stories that arise during daily life and living. Maybe we got fired, our partner dumped us, or we got cut off in traffic. We want to practice bringing enough presence, enough awareness into those contracting, hijacking moments to create opportunities to dismantle the 3D...to see it while it's happening and allow presence into the uncomfortable feeling that wants to run, hide, fight, blame, please, or freeze.

I have been burning off old stories since 2006. In the early years, when I was working through some big fear, I spent a lot of time avoiding discomfort only to find myself face to face with it at a later time. This was a gradual process. There was no way I would've been able to sit in some of the pain back then that is coming through now. I had to become accustomed to experiencing bigger traumas coming through with more frequency. I had to develop a sense of safety and trust in the process, which allowed me to dig deeper and uncover more buried discomfort. If ten years ago I'd had to experience the density of traumas I move through now, it would have been too much for my body/mind to manage. Even today, I get caught in the stories and mental problem-solving. Our ancient egoic infrastructure is a robust system that has perfected the art of distraction and the delusion of victimhood. I believe it's essential to know what we are up against and to know that your mind will want to distract you when something uncomfortable comes to the surface in your day-to-day life. It will become useful to recognize the urge to exit the building when you are in a healing session/class/meditation/retreat/plant medicine ceremony/integration right when there's the biggest potential for transformation. You're going to flounder and wonder what the hell you're doing and why it's not working. Which is why we're going to continue to discuss the many creative ways our being, our ego, is going to distract us from our discomfort and keep us stuck in 3D density.

Incorporating Eckhart Tolle's teachings as a guide for you and your practice of being in the present, developing the witness, and trusting what is happening in the now will help you get resourced for dropping into the potential healing that awaits in pure awareness.[41]/[42] But I suggest we keep remembering that we're here for each other. There's big pain, and with big pain comes big belief and big attachment. Bringing someone in to assist us who

---

[41] Eckhart Tolle, *The Power of Now: A Guide to Spiritual Enlightenment* (Novato, California: New World Library, 2004).

[42] Tolle, *A New Earth*.

is *not attached* to our pain stories can bring in a bigger energy to help us through a stuck wound.

We're stepping out of an outdated 3D framework and we're here to build a new one. In doing so, we create a new belief that we don't have to believe everything we're feeling. Not unless you're being chased by a bear. If you're not being chased or about to be hit by something, then it's time to (kindly and maybe with some help) challenge your beliefs, your responses, and your relationship with your uncomfortable feelings.

Everything out of balance has a repressed feeling/emotion contained within it. Ayurveda has told us that for thousands of years. A repressed emotion that stays repressed is a bit of our 3D being that continues to believe in the pain state, believes we are that small and powerless, and then constructs a reality around that belief; behavioral reality, thought reality, emotional reality, and physical reality. In my personal journey, I've released thousands of deep, repressed emotions and have seen my mind/body change and heal, lighten, and loosen. My perceptions shift. In fact, most perceptions to which I was attached have disintegrated. They continue to shift. I continue to zoom out of this reality as I go through rapid stages of integration and release. It's all facilitated by turning in and not turning away.

The Big Kahuna—Fear of Rejection/Abandonment

We love to avoid hard feelings, so it serves us to bring the really big ones into focus, to see how they land and play out in our lives, to see how, when, and where we *feel* them in our beings. The terror of rejection and abandonment ripples through our tribal existence. I speculate these two fears are the primary substances from which we construct our egoic infrastructure. They are the building blocks of our giant 3D fortress. Throughout history, to be rejected has been life threatening. This vulnerability we feel in abandonment plays out in our adult relationships, and we see it across cultures, time zones, languages, eras, and genders. Our constant states of lamenting, running from, avoiding, avenging, and healing from the broken heart are a giant trail of evidence of our struggle with rejection. We see it reflected in our myths, our love songs, the eons of literary ambassadors exploring the inner workings of the broken heart.

Since our eternal Self exists in connectedness, when we come here to dive deep into the experience of separation, it's a shock to the system. Which is why we crave intimate relationships, why we resist detaching, and why, when we break up an intimate relationship, it can feel so devastating, at all levels.

Sometimes our resistance to rejection can override all other impulses, facilitating many creative ways we compromise ourselves. Relationships are a balm to soothe the burn of this isolating existence and the persistent threat of rejection. That's also why a breakup can launch enormous drives for healing and change. We're confronted with such a big "Ouch!" that we're propelled deep into the wound, trying to figure out why it hurts so much, how to make it stop and ensure it never happens again. When we dive deep into our wounds, to reveal, to heal, to bring in our own sense of connection, often we find what's there all along: our profound connection to Self and to everything else.

To be rejected as a human infant, until this last century, in almost all parts of the globe, meant imminent death. For a girl or a woman to experience the rejection of her husband or father meant facing homelessness, hunger, violence, even death (and in many places, including here in North America, it still does). Any form of dependency has carried with it that low-grade hum of threat of rejection and abandonment.

If we're born into a home that does not provide a strong attachment—a deep sense of safety and acceptance—entering the larger tribe of playdates and elementary schoolyards can activate the ancient story of rejection. A safe, loving home can mitigate the persistent fear of rejection. However, if that secure foundation isn't available, fear of rejection goes into overdrive and appropriates all thought, feeling, and behavioral patterns. We rarely see how it operates within us or others, since it is the dominant mode of operations in social, political, and economic interaction. It's not seen as what we do because it's who we are. It operates in the background of awareness like the air we breathe. When air becomes too poisonous to breathe, we notice it; it comes into our awareness. But with ego, we don't seem to have that crisis detection system. We just keep on living in and creating our own poison.

As a global community, we're now more aware of the impact of the childhood experience of rejection on human development and quality of life, which is why we monitor and regulate bullying in schools. Psychological frameworks, such as attachment theory, have moved into mainstream self-help literature in recent years. In our school years, once we face the large schoolyard tribe, most children manage and negotiate their position in the tribal order to find a secure spot of acceptance and approval. We replicate the tools of survival we inherited from our ancestors and learn from other children to do whatever it takes to keep from experiencing rejection. The compassion of children is adored by all, but the meanness of children sets families on fire. The stress parents feel as they witness their child being excluded from a group, picked last for team sport, or threatened or harmed by their classmates can put them into states of high alert, anxiety, and rage. The school years are decade-long-plus re-enactments of the *Lord of the Flies* for many children, and parents are along to watch their own childhood fears being replayed through their offspring.

A client of mine, Sara, told me she went to a spa to enjoy a group sauna and do a class on breathwork, a new spa therapy entering the healing zeitgeist. She went alone, and when she got there, she saw a lot of attractive women, which confronted her insecurities. What made it more uncomfortable was that they all knew each other. While Sara sat alone and silent, they all chatted around her. She was uncomfortable but was able to witness her discomfort with curiosity rather than with a victim's mind. She recognized the emotional trigger, a memory of being eight years old and rejected by her friend, who accepted an invitation to hang out with the popular girls instead of with Sara. She recalled in vivid detail how she felt excluded from everyone for the whole school year. She described coping by making herself invisible, being alone at recess with a book, hiding. Over thirty years later, the painful imprint activated in the sauna. She recalled how her family responded to her experience of rejection as a child by not talking about it. More invisibility. Their rejection coping strategy? Avoid, deny, and suppress.

The trauma of not being accepted by other eight year olds can feel so threatening, so terrorizing, that it can set the trajectory of adult life. It becomes the foundation on which we build our self-perception. It becomes how we judge our own value or worth, how we navigate relationships, and how we develop strategies and goals to move through challenges. In order to survive, ego rejects the feeling of rejection, because to an eight year old, rejection feels like life and death. It needs to be buried. When the memory surfaces later in life, the eight year old's pain overwhelms the adult's nervous system, throwing them right back into that eight-year-old reality with all the fear and vulnerability. Our fear of rejection penetrates at the most personal level as well as systemic levels. Corruption in governments is constructed upon the fear of rejection. Political leaders can leverage the fear of people in order to ensure fealty. For example, the disapproval of a dictator invokes deep terror. The more trauma a nation has experienced in their history, the more likely people will protect themselves from the threat of rejection by appeasing the tyrant. The more abusive power a leader has, the more likely they will have others orbiting them, vying for positions to assure their approval/safety. While deep ancestral rejection trauma exists within our bodies, the desire for approval often will outweigh the desire for truth. The desire for tribal acceptance will outmaneuver the desire for justice. Until a person or group discovers that their need to heal is bigger than their need to just survive. That their drive to find their power within is bigger than their fear of relinquishing their power to oppressors without. Until their desire to live in a connected existence is a stronger force than their fear of tyranny/separation.

People say corruption is about greed, but I would say that greed is about staving off the fear of rejection. Having more money and more power over our external world provides a 3D sense of safety. It's an egoic story that tells me if I get more money, more resources, and build more walls to keep out the bad guys, I will have control over my environment and can protect myself from the threats of the dangerous world.

The fear of rejection will be there as long as the ancient programming in the body is left intact and continues to dance with others who share the same program. We won't change anything by trying to make the bully understand us, or the sociopathic president see us, or the narcissistic parent hear us. We are going to release ourselves from the tribal story of the terror of rejection by seeing it in our own bodies, bringing the feelings of rejection into awareness, and owning our part in this traumatic human drama.

Fame is another unconscious tribal antidote to terror of rejection. I have many clients who work in the entertainment industry. When we analyze wounds and motivations, it's soon revealed that people are seeking the big applause, the big signs of approval and acceptance. "See me! Love me!" What we almost always see (and, of course, what I see in my practice) is that no matter how much applause, political power, or money a person has, it will never be enough because the wound is rarely, if ever, healed by someone or something outside of us. We may feel good for ten minutes after the curtain falls, or feel safe for a day after we've achieved that salary bracket, or satisfied the week we were elected. But the fear of rejection is not healed by external events; it'll find another story to latch onto. It'll look for another source to explain its feelings of rejection and seek another solution. But such solutions rarely work. In fact, they often highlight or elevate the issue. For example, once we become famous, we realize that we've made ourselves even more invisible (meaning more rejectable) because people can't see *us*; they see only the aura of fame. We may find political power, but having control over people will ensure less intimacy, as our relationships are constructed on a foundation of fear/greed/shame. Once again, you're not seen; only your power and how you wield or ease fear is in focus. Ego leaves no room for you to be seen. I also want to suggest everything is as it is meant to be. Those who want to continue to suppress or to oppress may be here to do just that. Maybe because they're working up the energy to burn off the story the next time. Maybe they're here to reflect our own terror, our stories of victimhood, our feelings of powerlessness back at us. *How much love must we gather, create, find within in order to be bigger than the oppression?* It may be here to ignite within us the desire to step out of the paradigm, to access our processes of healing, change, and expansion. I'm not here to judge a single act of avoidance, oppression, or even violence. I'm here to ignite awakening, healing, and awareness within those who are ready to walk that path. I'm here to bring awareness to the hidden pain we're ready to liberate ourselves from. You're not a victim of another's story of oppression. You're not a victim of your own oppression, or greed, or fear, or rage. You're a part of a historic drama. You can leave now. The exit is within you.

My gentle suggestion is that you become familiar with the feeling of rejection/abandonment so when it shows up, you can see the story, and your mind is less likely to hijack you and your response to the feeling. A couple of years ago, I led a silent yoga meditation retreat with a group of people who connected right from the start. They chatted and laughed the first evening over dinner. After dinner we talked as a group and then initiated our practice of silence. The following day, during our group reflection, a participant, Sue, shared how she experienced our collective transition into silence. She said, quite humorously, it felt like a family fight. The silence triggered the echoes of family members arguing and then freezing each other out with the silent treatment. For Sue, silence held a big story of abandonment. I think we all had a good giggle, and then connected to where that feeling resonated within our own bodies.

Witness the stories of abandonment and rejection that show up in your life and in your body. *Feel* the story in your body. Feel where it might be sitting. Get familiar with it, as well as with any other repeating stories. Write it out, take notes, do your research. You may need some assistance, a loving eye, a trusted therapist, or other ally to help you identify your rejection and abandonment stories for the first little while. The ego camouflages our stories quickly. When a story comes into awareness, your job is to notice the sensation, and notice any physical pain, tightness, or contraction. Then, if it feels safe, feel the emotional pain below. If that feels safe, let go of all resistance. If it still feels safe, bring in the energy of love and acceptance. We'll dive into this process more in just a moment.

Feel It, Don't Believe It: Doubling Down

We have been discussing how to not believe the pain infrastructure, the drama, and the turmoil we exist in—how to see it but not follow it down the garden path. Where we open ourselves up (and where the challenge lies) is in holding on to our disbelief while we're right in the middle of it. When we're vibrating with our shame or rage and we get quiet *with it,* when we merge our detachment *with* those uncomfortable feelings as they are happening, that is the miracle. That is the alchemy. We change everything when we connect to that presence. We change our past, present, and future.

With all the energy moving and surging in our planet at this time, we can advance a giant collective detox. We can allow the suffering of the last many hundreds of years that's recorded in our bodies to burn off. But if we continue to believe the ancient traumas that have started surfacing, and that will surface as the energy rises around the globe, our egos will sabotage or stall the process.

Our bodies feel discomfort, and our mind jumps all over it at lightning speed. It constructs a story about that discomfort and convinces us it's true, at least at some level. We do this, for example, when we've had a bad day at work, then come home and take our anger out on our partner. They didn't have time to pick up the apples we wanted at the grocery store, and it's because they don't love us anymore or they're too thoughtless to care. We do it when we go on a date once and they don't call us again, and that experience launches a giant, uncomfortable shame story about how "There must be something wrong with me," because, of course, someone we've met once is the authority on our dateability. My clients who feel stuck in a depressive episode have a mind telling them to just stay home, sit on the couch, don't exercise, don't talk to anyone, eat more ice cream. These are clear examples of a mind giving some bad advice, coming from an unreal, delusional, pain-filled framework. Can you imagine how creative your mind might get when it's releasing your ancestors' hundreds of battle wounds or slavery traumas?

Your mind, most if not all the time, is looping in one or many childhood, ancestral, and/or past-life stories. Our lives comprise feedback loops that hijack our reality and convince us that whatever our mind is telling us is the truth. Then we replay this drama repeatedly in our thoughts, behaviors, and relationship dynamics. But most of us don't see this happening. We don't see our minds at work, and we don't scrutinize our minds. We resist assessing our minds for consistency, humility, or validity—especially when doing so might reveal that we're wrong. We ask other people to be paragons of unflinching principle, but we rarely ask it of ourselves. If we take an honest moment to observe ourselves, we'll see our own hypocrisy at play. How many times have you been annoyed at someone who is speeding while driving, and then a day or an hour later, you are heavy on the pedal? Conversely, maybe your ego weaponizes shame to keep your inner victim alive and well; "Everyone else can speed, but if I do it, then I'm bad." The stories we tell ourselves are all fear. Fear directed in or fear directed out. Directed in or out, it is the same thing—we are all part of, and therefore reflections of, each other.

The egoic mind keeps us from seeing ourselves. It camouflages us from us. I know it camouflages me from me all the time. I can still struggle to see myself through most of what the egoic mind is telling me about me. It terrorizes us into believing our pain stories. This terror is the 3D density hard at work.

But we need to go into these tough places and those hard feelings and take high vibrations with us. To do so, we need to develop our inner witness, through multiple means, that will accompany us while we are in the discomfort of lifetimes of pain in our healing process. We need to nourish a witness that will always remind us: "Feel it, but don't believe it." Develop your inner witness to help erode the power of the egoic mind, that tells you what you're feeling is actually happening. Be vigilant. Remember, we produce our own plays, our own dramas, products of the stories imprinted in our bodies. We create them or inherit them in order to transform them.

The process asks us to let go of the egoic mind's interpretation of an event so we can step out of the tribal suffering we host in our bodies. It asks us to let consciousness flow and penetrate the infrastructure that keeps pain in place and tells us, "This suffering is still real." Ego is here to tell us how small and threatened we are. Consciousness/awareness reveals to us all the treasures of safety and love, the learning and potential, that have been sealed within our pain.

Feel, Observe, Breathe

You would think feeling our feelings would be easy, since it seems we're feeling all the time. When feelings show up, we have a way of shaming them, rationalizing them away, running from them, or throwing them up on others. I have witnessed a lovely new dialogue opening up in families where parents teach their young children that feelings are our friends, that feelings are to be listened to as a source of information, maybe even wisdom. They're taught to honor their feelings as a source of self-love. But most people in my culture, who have centuries of training on how *not* to relate to their feelings, are now reversing that trend. More and more we're connecting to our feelings, creating opportunities to experience the potential, the wisdom stored within the repressed emotion. I believe there's a shift where parents and children are finding the potential consciousness and healing embedded within centuries of trapped feelings.

Our new relationship with feelings is to give feelings the space to be. Without thinking. Without judgment. When a feeling comes into view, we sit with it. We observe it. We don't attach a desire—"I want it here. I don't want it here." We don't attach analysis, assessment—"Why am I feeling this? Where is it coming from?" That can all be done later, if at all. We sit in presence and allow whatever the body needs at that moment. We let go of egoic control over the event and give ourselves permission to just *be* in a profoundly attentive way. As a parent would with a child who's fallen down and scraped their knee for the first time, we sit with the feeling. We hold them. We stay regulated. We stay quiet. There is space for the wounded little one. We let their bodies release the tension through tears and snot and shaking and hiccups. As it subsides, we tell them we love them, that they are good, that the body will heal. We tell them all is well and say, "Good job."

If the density doesn't move when we go into the feeling, we keep feeling it. Maybe we get some help. Maybe it's a sign to head off to a silent retreat for a deep dive into consciousness. When the feeling is stuck, we need to bring in more detachment, because something in us is still attached. A part of us still believes the pain. So, we witness our attachment, bring space into our attachment, until we're ready to bring more space directly into the pain. Pain is only a new area in which to direct energy, attention, and nothingness.

The mind's job the moment an uncomfortable feeling arises is to do nothing. It's to watch. No calculations or judgments or assessments or analyses. We're the audience, so we observe the wonders of nature and consciousness doing their magic. We step aside and allow forces that are much bigger than our mind to take over for a moment and lead the way. We humble ourselves to the powers within and without, powers that the mind cannot comprehend. We take a back seat. Asking the egoic mind to take this back seat requires practice and discipline, since it will resist because it's uncomfortable. As noted earlier, it will want to take over and tell you, "This is what's happening. This is why it's there. The problem is real! This is bad! This is urgent! We need to do something!" Our job is to not believe that voice. We need to deepen our witness and practice silence and presence.

Then, while the storm is moving through, if there's space and awareness, we want to breathe mindfully. We can take deep breaths in through the nose and release out through the mouth, helping our energy system clean out the old, repressed emotions and bring in is energies to help reorganize the body. We bring more energy, more life force, more intelligence while we surrender into a state of being and healing.

Don't Expect It to Be Easy

The only reason I write this discouraging-sounding heading is because I want to bring attention to the reflex we have to flee when things don't happen right away, or they get uncomfortable. This journey is about coming up against our resistance. We may need to make the extra effort, focus more, and keep trying and not look away. I have worked with people who can't feel something separate from their minds. Because the mind appropriates so much of their experience, they can't understand how their thoughts and feelings are, in fact, different. I was one of those people. My body existed in my conscious mind. Or rather, consciousness did not roam in my body. This is why feelings can feel so inaccessible, especially to mind-centered people such as academics; people who have been living and even thriving by using and listening only to their minds.

Ego has trained humans to do everything in their power to avoid doing what I'm asking you to do. It asks people to work eighteen-hour days and stay busy until their bodies collapse. It asks you to mutilate your body in search of perfection; cut yourself to avoid; starve yourself; consume lethal narcotics; drink yourself out of a family, out of a job, or into a coma; and kill yourself, all so you don't have to feel. I'm asking you to ignore and disbelieve your egoic thoughts and allow all the feelings. We want all of the feelings to come out of hiding when the time is right. I suggest you turn off the mind and feel, but with no story attached. Feel from a place of awareness. Feel from a place of surrender. If it hurts too much to surrender, then we get our helpers, our coaches, our therapists, or our teachers to guide us deeper into surrender. Again, Michael Singer's *The Untethered Soul* is an excellent coaching and inspirational resource for observing your thoughts and allowing feelings.[43]

When we feel the resistance to "just feel," when we struggle to let go of what the mind is telling us about our discomfort, remember, the mind cannot compete with consciousness. Any belief to the contrary is, I suggest, the arrogance of the egoic mind and its attempt to appropriate everything. We let go of the "brainwashing" of mind, telling us it knows what to do with pain. Let go. Fall inward to the place below the mind where consciousness comes in to do what it does: heal and bring order and love.

We see it in nature. I see it in my clients. I see it in myself. Trust that your body is part of the intelligence of nature and connected to an even bigger intelligence. It knows how to heal itself. The egoic mind, repressed emotions, and ego loops interfere with the

---

[43] Michael Singer, *The Untethered Soul: The Journey Beyond Yourself* (Oakland: New Harbinger Productions, 2007).

ordering energies of our bodies. There has been enough research to know that practices such as meditation heal. Meditation is a potent consciousness delivery technology. When we get the mind's fear agenda—the energies of disorder—out of the way through the practice of meditation, the body's ecosystem allows the higher vibrations to come in and to move within, creating order out of egoic chaos and suffering. With the expanding energy, we'll expose healing opportunities and shifts in energy. The energy, the expansion, will expose us to more opportunities for feelings to surface and move through without letting our resistance impede our healing.

So, I say again and again, "This is difficult," not to discourage you but to set up your expectations. This is a lifestyle change, not a one-week-long retreat. If we're anxious, we set up our checks and balances in our life to bring tranquility into the anxiety. We build a life of meditation, nature, no caffeine, a slower-paced job, gentle yoga, etc. If we do not shift our life toward less anxious stimuli, we won't have a less anxious life. The work of dismantling a dimension is an ongoing creative process. It's a lifelong project of transformation. It's the infusion of awareness into every level of our being until we cross the threshold into the next realm. This is a tough concept to grasp for a culture that wants everything and wants it yesterday.

Not being easy is evidence of the potential in this transformative process, not evidence that it can't be done. We're here to transcend a reality! We're here to stretch our limits. It's important we take care of ourselves. We need to practice. I ask you to be aware of the pain you're examining at any moment. Because all pain is going to resist being examined, explored, or brought into the risky light of day. Is this pain resistant? Does it have a little tantrum when you ask it to sit still, or get on the yoga mat, or dive into a feeling? Or is the resistance going to hijack your month with anxiety? Will it ask you to get a divorce, dissociate, or go for the nearest addictive behavior? Will it want you to do anything instead of getting into that feeling? If it's a little tantrum, take the feeling by the hand and invite it into the uncomfortable (but held) space. If the feeling is having a meltdown, stop. Get a cup of tea, crawl under a cozy blanket, and put on your favorite movie until next time, or until you bring in some reinforcements to help you get in there. Read the room. Don't force an unwilling inner participant to do something they do not want to do, but do guide a child that doesn't yet know how good it is to eat your broccoli and practice your piano.

Bring Awareness to Your Judgment

I suggest you look at your repressed feelings as sensitive little clams. It doesn't take much to trigger them to shut down, close up, and go back into their shell. A guaranteed way to send a feeling back into the deep, beyond the grasp of awareness, is to ignite the egoic loop of judgment and self-criticism.

Our project is to bring the kind, gentle energy of awareness into those difficult feeling places. When we bring in self-criticism, we bring in opposing energy. We hurl another dark, dense pain story into the feeling we're trying to heal. We attack ourselves with the 3rd dimension. What's the feeling going to do? It's going to disappear and hide. It would be the same if a parent approached their distressed child and told them, "I'll give you something to cry about!" The child is going to get quiet and shove that pain into a deep hole out of sight. Our egoic wounds follow suit.

The practice of dismantling asks us to bring the judgment itself into awareness, to see it so that it too can be burned off, creating access to the other layers of repressed emotion. We can see the judgment as just another trap, another program, and another repressed emotion tied to another story, ready to be liberated. But our liberation also requires us to bring awareness to judgment of others.

To judge others is to slip into the 3rd dimension. For example, to call someone an "idiot" when you witness or are subjected to someone's raging, shaming, or dismissive behavior is to keep the infrastructure alive. To recognize that the other's non-loving behavior comes from their pain infrastructure, and that your job is to recognize the feelings it activates in you, is stepping into the next reality. To see such behavior as separate from the person and know that it's up to you to put boundaries around it is lifting yourself above the 3rd dimension. To say to yourself, "Yes, I see the pain and I release that from my reality" is dissolving the density in your own reality. To judge others reveals where we judge ourselves. To free yourself from the pain, use your inner judge as a signpost to your own opportunities.

Find a Feeling and Its Route Inward

I suggest you explore a little shift in the language of your self-inquiry. Begin by moving your inquiry inward from the question of "How am I feeling?" to "What Am I Feeling?" While asking "How?" is a great way to engage the feeling body, when we ask "What?", we increase the capacity of the witness, we increase our ability to just see it, versus trying to understand it. We need to know less about its nature and instead want to just bring it into awareness. To do the work, any uncomfortable moment will do. Anything that's uncomfortable is a place to bring awareness versus feeding the feedback loop. Here's an example of a recent uncomfortable event I believe is shared by thousands of people. I was forced to travel during the pandemic. Being around a lot of people swirling in their fear and frustration in an international airport afforded me lots of opportunities to see and work with some of my own trapped stories.

I made a last-minute flight to British Columbia, Canada to be with my father as he was passing. It was in the second year of the pandemic, and, of course, anything to do with travel was still at its peak of chaos and stress. At Pearson International Airport security and screening, I faced many irritated, exasperated airport staff. One staff member in particular, who was guarding the gate, my passport in hand, made it his personal goal to demonstrate how rude a human could be. With angry relish, he admonished me for not scanning my boarding pass before putting my luggage up for inspection. He tried to shame me by telling me that others could not scan because of my ineptitude, and that I was doing the unconscionable thing of holding everyone else up. So, I scanned my boarding pass, then checked in with him to make sure I'd done it correctly and was clear to proceed. It was easy to see he was making a conscious effort not to look at me as he gave me an irreverent wave, dismissing me.

The next attendants at the metal detectors were abrupt. Non-communicative, they offered no signal to tell me whether I should walk through or not—just a frozen, dead stare, intent, it seemed, on communicating how little they cared.

As I found my way through the craziness of gate security, I noticed I was stuck in the feeling of being a victim of rudeness. This feeling didn't want to move through. It was lodged in my chest, pressing down on my lungs. This story is deep for me. Rudeness signals an unfathomable intent to not cooperate. Rudeness has always triggered anxiety and anger for me. It is a big affront to my Canadian sensibilities. I know it makes sense that they were rude, short, and irritated. Who wouldn't be, working at a country's biggest airport in the middle of a pandemic? It's logical to expect that the place would pulse with hostility—hostility that had nothing to do with me.

With my blood boiling a little, I collected my belongings off the security conveyor belt and got myself organized. I could see the part of me that wanted to hold on to the righteous indignation. My mind flashed through a few thoughts, trying to convince me to: Go back and tell him off! Where do I send a letter?! I could feel that anger poking at me, trying to get some traction. I noticed that this stirring anger was a fraction of what it would have been a few years before and I found a pleasant spot for gratitude to co-

exist with my anger. But there was still something uncomfortable trying to give meaning to this event. So, here was the opportunity. Here, with awareness and focus, I saw the tribal connection. I could see/feel/sense the fearful part of me that wants everyone to be nice to me. I could connect to the old anger that wants to protect me from feelings of shame and rejection by getting mad at someone else when I am uncomfortable. It thinks it protects me from fear and feeling powerless when people choose not to cooperate, choose not to see the needs of others, or choose not to care how their behavior affects others. I could see the fear that arose...fear I can't see and don't have access to when others are polite. But I had it in my sights now, this flavor of fear. I had some awareness; I had an opportunity, thanks to the trauma-induced rudeness of the employees at Pearson International Airport.

And so...I felt it. I stood still in a crowded airport, hundreds of people hustling and milling about. I felt it. Then I walked and I felt it. I swelled up with it. I allowed the feelings to move, to be, without judgment, without wanting them to go anywhere, expecting them to go anywhere. I watched them kindly. I got out of their way. I invited space. Acceptance. I watched the stories of retribution, imagined arguments, letters I could write to the management flow by. I just felt it. And I breathed. I looked into every single crevice in my being and tried not to let any bit of that discomfort in my body rise unnoticed. I wanted to see it all; I wanted to feel it all. Until I didn't feel it anymore. Which is what happened. After about twenty-five minutes, I felt it trickle out of me. I felt it shift and move. Then I felt a new energy move in. I saw the part of me that was frightened that this release would not happen, that this pattern, this pain, would never change. That I was fooling myself into thinking this was real. But that heaviness cleared, and a lightness took over. I felt the desire to thank Pearson airport and the pandemic for the opportunity to transform this little pocket of 3D suffering in my body.

∝

You can also bring the 3D into focus when you try to change a behavior or an egoic pattern, and resistance arises. For example, you may want to change how you set your boundaries by practicing saying "No." But when you do, you feel anxiety, guilt, or shame. As you bring old stories into awareness, allow yourself to feel all of those things your ego has been keeping you from feeling. Get familiar with the ego loops. Go deep into the uncomfortable feelings, deep into the stories, deep into awareness. Surrender. Your body will heal itself. Just peel back the pain programs and unleash the energy of consciousness.

In this way, feelings become opportunities, versus something to be dreaded or avoided. When it becomes safe enough to pay attention, we tune into even more subtle ways that pain drives our thoughts, behaviors, and beliefs, and we can see the quiet judgments, subtle disappointments, and contractions in our bodies. We become detectives. We examine the motives for everything, committing to our practice of vigilance. What you thought you understood comes in even clearer or is turned on its head. You access a greater awareness of your pain and what it was trying to accomplish, and how it held you in a pattern for years without you even knowing it. For example, you could be an accommodating person and tell yourself, "That's a virtue. It's what makes me a good person, a nice person, a desirable person, a loveable person." But when you activate awareness, you can see that your accommodation of others can be motivated by the fear of rejection and abandonment. This awareness doesn't arrive all at once. It arrives at the right time for you—when you bring in enough consciousness and can see the story fully.

Some pain stories are obvious because they're obviously painful. For those, we should get some help. Childhood abuse, substance use challenges, partner abuse, severe or sudden accidents, chronic illness, acute grief because of the death of a loved one—these are big pain stories in overdrive. They take up a lot of space in the nervous system. They need enormous support and need to feel seen in big ways. Big pain, big help, big allies, big love.

But for many people, pain stories hide in the recesses of our being, below awareness. They're early childhood experiences stacked with reinforcing events. They're past life/ancestral experiences that we don't see as pain stories. We don't experience the encoded ancestral traumas and tribal stories as pain on the surface, but these small-t traumas and subtle pain imprints inform our worldviews, behaviors, and relationships, with ourselves and others. Many of us know that we hold the imprints of racism, sexism, homophobia, etc., within our psyches and our bodies. How can we not?

Painful thoughts/beliefs/energies have made their way into our collective reality, and while we may cloud them with our good intentions, they'll always be there—until and unless we accept they're there. To deny they exist ensures they remain. By bringing *awareness* into those nodules of pain, we release them from our bodies, our lives, and our tribes. We bring seeing, acceptance, and compassion into our hates, and our hates become our wisdoms. They dissolve into knowing, connection, and love.

It can be difficult to go straight into the feeling. There are so many mental and egoic guard dogs up, we can get diverted. The mind will want to deflect by blaming or shaming someone else for our discomfort, or it will distract us with busyness. But we can use the mind to our advantage. We can employ our intellect (or someone else's) to assist us in rooting through the history of our pain stories.

Exercise:
Seeing the Infrastructure of a Pattern

Is that pattern in your life taking you around in circles and producing the same uncomfortable results repeatedly? For example, you may look back and notice how many times, over the last fifteen years, you quit your job within a year of getting hired. It may not feel like it serves your highest self to do this again, so you explore the feelings you had when quitting, or you feel into the uncomfortable feeling that prompted you to quit. What are the thought patterns about quitting?

○ Is it the same each time you quit?
○ When you have those thoughts, what feelings show up?
○ What sensations arise in your body?
○ Are there feelings you notice now that you could not see before?
○ Are you able to explore a core belief about you and employment...or money...or commitment?
○ Are there feelings connected to that core belief?
○ Where are those feelings in your body?

There comes a moment when we realize we don't need to do the detective work—we just need to get out of the way. As each uncomfortable feeling comes along, we sit in it. We don't question it, wonder why, or ask, "Where did this come from?" We know that if it's not love, it's bullshit. We remain secure in not knowing what the pain is about and what we need to do with it. We tell ourselves:

I just need to love it. To not play this game anymore, to hand it over to something that knows what to do with this. To give my highest Self access so it can heal the wound. And, if there's a time when I can't get in there and move it, then I'll call in my team to assist me in bringing in a bigger energy to help transform this story. It's no longer my job to wrestle with the understanding or the stories or the problems. I don't need to know.

Exercise:
Gentle Seeing When We Are in Deep

Sometimes sitting in a story requires a gradual approach. If we move too fast, we can shut down our healing process. If, for example, I have a client who is in a contracted state—let's say they have been hit by a big break up—we won't eliminate all the pain they're experiencing at that moment. These are deep, acute stories of loss and separation. It's not just about that one breakup. It could be about earlier breakups, abandonment as a child, or ancestral stories of abandonment. We won't plow through all of that at once. But we can witness and therefore increase our awareness and insert consciousness into the experience.

○ Where is the body clenched and holding 3D pain?
○ Where is it contracted?
○ Is it in the heartspace? Is it in the belly? Is it in the back?
○ Can we breathe a little deeper?
○ To feel safe, what does the person need?
○ Does this feeling need anything else from me while we gradually move toward safety?
○ Is there something that it would like to tell me?

We feel moments of pain and allow the pain through. We breathe, we move, we soothe as much as possible to help regulate our nervous system. We bring in a little space, maybe some movement, until there's enough safety to transform and process the experience. Maybe we call in an ally, a therapist, to help us be with the big feelings, regulate the big feelings, when we feel overwhelmed and not quite ready to go right into it, to feel it all. But the more awareness we bring into that contracted state, the more ease unfolds afterward, when the heart of the drama is over. The event reveals itself because we created the potential for expansion. There is room to examine thoughts and to recognize potential patterns. Here's an example of how this works. During the pandemic, a sudden responsibility fell on me. My biological father, who lived across the country, descended into dementia. Too many stories flooded in too fast. I couldn't integrate them. All I could do was hold on tight.

A few years earlier, my father had shown the first signs of dementia. Years before, while he was still living with his partner, I had agreed to be his health representative and his power of attorney. Shortly after the dementia began, his partner kicked him out of the house and the relationship, and I was the adult left to manage a man in bad health, who just happened to have a slew of legal problems in tow. My days were taken over by lawyers, accountants, banks, financial advisors, and medical professionals—and a boatload of resentment, because he was my biological father, and not the man who had raised me. The kids he'd raised were nowhere to be seen. The pain stories came through at lightning speed. My mind/body was in fight/flight for a few months while trying to get him moved to a facility while navigating a legal battle. These stories were trying to convince me that all of this drama was real, that I was in trouble. Trouble for what, I couldn't quite figure out, but the feeling of threat oozed through my body. There was pressure on my chest; my mind was spinning. I even dissociated a few times. I had quite a few sleepless nights. I knew there was nothing happening. I could see I was safe, loved, fed, housed. But there were too many stories for it to feel safe enough to feel them all. There were so many ancient fears—not being good enough, being alone, being betrayed, being abandoned, being used, losing control of my life. The only thing I could do was continue to not believe the drama, not believe the stories, remind myself to hold on tight until this wave passed, and I could find the opportunity to dive in, feel them all, take care of them all, and pick these stories off one by one. At a plant medicine retreat just a couple of months later, I puked and cried and puked and cried and it all came out.

Keep Remembering

The 5 Pillars deliver the remembering. We're here to burn off all that keeps us in this suffering. Underneath the suffering is the Self that sees all, loves all, and forgives all. The intention here is to build an infrastructure of remembering that connects you to Self repeatedly and transports you below the stories, where *You* are waiting.

Bringing in a more feminine space is to live in the reminders, in the remembering, of who we are and why we're here. It's to bring in the silence, the peace, the allowing, and the presence. We create and imbibe these elements every day, moment to moment, to remember who we are, that we're not our pain, that we're not trapped in pain; and to remember to feel, breathe, and observe.

For those connected to this journey, it may serve you to create a schedule. The goal is to find your way to your center every day. Every day, we find that place within, where we feel the "Ahhh, right. None of this is real. Even *that* problem, still not real. Got it. Thank you!" We want to connect to where we can see the role the mind is playing in creating drama. We've been living in a "masculine" space and at "masculine" pace for so long that we've brainwashed ourselves into believing the busyness, the doing, the problem solving, and the raging are all immutable forces. We're surrounded by technological artifacts designed and built within the masculine, ego-steeped paradigm. It's hard to see how far we've swung into individual, defensive, busy realities, because we've been in it so long and our tribes have told us it's the most desirable place to be.

In order to swing the pendulum back, we create the time for nothing. We step away from our personality and dive into pure awareness. We create more space for being, observing, instead of doing. When we get lost in the doing, the egoic mind continues to justify the dominance of its existence by telling us that the meaning of life is defined by the next thing we do. It justifies its own existence. To step out of the paradigm, we practice presence...even though it is uncomfortable...especially when it's uncomfortable.

There's Nothing Going On

Remember this section. Bookmark it. Return here when you are in the thick of a story telling you, "No, there *is* something going on! This wound is real! They're all wrong! My rage is right! Don't listen to her!" Or the converse, "But I *am* that bad! How could I not be bad?!"

Your job (because if you are here, reading this book, this is what you have signed up to do) is to deliver the message repeatedly that *nothing is happening*. Your job is to find every bit of trauma and drama and fear and shame and rage that you have in every dark corner of your being and bring in the message, the vibration, the energy, the feeling, that *there is nothing going on*. If something within you is telling you there is a problem, there is a tragedy, you have been betrayed, forgotten, or mistreated, now you know: You're in one (or more) ancient pain story. You're in a disconnected state, in delusion, fast asleep. The delusion has taken over your power of thought.

You're here to remember that almost all perceptions in this dimension, in this pain infrastructure, are driven by wounds in the mind/body complex. These are wounds that landed when you were a child or through the traumatic experiences of your ancestry. A 3D wound is invested in staying put. This is the technology of ego. This is the pain infrastructure. This is the tribal reality: "Don't mess with the fear of rejection, and we'll be okay. Protect yourself with rage and fear. Keep doing what you have been doing, and you'll survive."

We're going to have big feelings, of course. We're going to experience pain. Life can hurt. A lot. We're all involved in our human dramas, and they're still playing themselves out. We're going to feel anger, fear, and shame. Our bodies will move out of order, out of ease. But to know they're no longer real means to not believe them. To not believe them is to allow them to fizzle out, detach, and not recreate the 3D density.

We may have an intellectual understanding that nothing is going on, but when the shit hits the fan, there may be some or many stories that show up, asking you to forget this knowing. I'm here to remind you that just because your discomfort is telling you something terrible is happening, it doesn't mean it is. It means there are wounds within you that have yet to get the memo. Your job is not to believe the drama is real but instead to deliver the message to all parts of you that they're safe, that this pain no longer serves them, and no longer exists, even if you feel it.

Your new story, your new reality, and your journey is to see all the density, all the discomfort, all the pain within you that holds those stories of rejection and abandonment and bring them into awareness, into consciousness, and into the Nothing. Or more accurately, bring the Nothing into them. The first step is to see them. The second is to not believe them.

You will come to understand that each density is something within you trying to tell you "There is something to figure out," "There is a problem to solve," or "There is something scary to fix." Each will try to say you are unsafe, that you need to run, hide, fight, shame, or freeze. It wants to say you're in danger all the time—and that it's dangerous to believe you're not in danger all the time. We blame everyone else for our discomfort. The guy in the parking lot or the cellphone company is the reason the world sucks. Or it wants to say *you* are an asshole and don't deserve to have good things happen to you. But one by one, or dozen by dozen, you see the stories, and you deliver safety to each one, releasing yourself from the suffering of this existence, stretching the boundaries of consciousness and creating a whole new reality.

We continue to look inward and find the ways of seeing the stories within because we're walking toward, expanding toward the knowing and the wisdom that there is nothing going on. This is an empty stage. We are emptying it of pain, thought, stories, ego, and all the 3D perceptions and problems. All the history of torment and torture our ancestors believed in and we thought we had to resolve? We are letting it all go and letting in the next reality.

Sensitivity

The people I work with who are on some version of this journey share a common element. They're almost all sensitive. Ask them to feel the feelings, and they are likely to respond, "Haven't I done enough of that already?" or "I seem to do that for everyone!" It seems sadistic to ask someone who is already aware of just how uncomfortable the world is to jump on in and take another big bite of that torment.

I ask you to reframe your sensitivity, if you haven't already, as the superpower that it is. Being sensitive is to have access to the heart of the delusion—the feeling, the sensations. The stories are at the surface, because you have cleared or transitioned enough to be in your connected, metaphysical self. You have access to the feeling, so you direct the healing energies of consciousness into it. You train yourself to be in it and not believe it. You disconnect from the stories even though the feelings may come on like gangbusters. You practice going into the feeling instead of judging it, being afraid of it, or denying it. You practice going right into it and taking consciousness with you. It is time to alter your approach to your sensitive self and see it as an asset on your journey out of the 3rd dimension.

The World Is Your Mirror

Everything we do, and every uncomfortable exchange and perception we have, reveals inner egoic stories. How you react to a friend's pain is not about their pain but about your perception of pain. We're perfect manifestors. That's a hard concept to manage when we're in a great deal of pain and we witness the never-ending pain that encircles the world. But looking at the world and revealing the stories within also reveals your power within.

For example, when someone does not return your call when they said they would, this can provoke feelings of anger, disappointment, sadness, or fear. You wonder, *Does it have something to do with a personal failing of mine?* Your mind jumps on board, and to protect you, it plans a course of action. Ego wants you to tell them, "You screwed up and disappointed me." Indignation or fear tells you, "Never call them again." These are all three-dimensional manifestations. When we're dismantling our manifestations of the 3rd dimension, the function of every experience with the outer world reveals our inner world to us.

Exercise:
What Does This Tell Me About Me?

When someone doesn't return my call, what's my discomfort telling me about my expectations, or about what I'm afraid of?

○ Is it telling me I haven't accepted something?
○ Have I accepted too much and need to create a boundary?
○ Can it tell me where in my body I'm not at peace, where a contraction lies?
○ Can it reveal a belief I have about my value, my worth? A belief about what I expect from others?

Every interaction and every urge I have, with anyone or anything, reveals the 3D within me. Other people's stories are their own business. I don't need to know about them. I want to look at the tempest in my own teacup. When we hurt another person, the world reflects how we're hurting ourselves. For example, if my neighbor is noisy late into the night and I want to shame him, tell him how he's acting like an asshole, the focus of my attention is not his behavior and seeking change. It's on my desire to shame someone to feel better. My anger reveals a part of me that wants to feed and recycle my pain stories. I have a wound that still believes I'm a victim. Once I burn off the victim, I can release the anger and heal the fear (or at least bring it into focus), and then I can negotiate something new with my neighbor—that is, if I want to and if they're capable. Allow the world to reflect at you your densities, your delusions, any part of you that feels it's still a victim, limitless, choiceless, powerless, stuck, or unseen.

The Perfect Landscape for Our Work – The Relationship

Intimate relationships are perfect mirrors for the deepest, most vulnerable, and most defended parts of ourselves. The two big stories we examined earlier—The Family and The Masculine and Feminine—demonstrate the profundity of egoic wounds in human relationship dynamics. These wounds are hidden well below our awareness (which is why they're the ones we keep repeating). Where else do we feel as abandoned or rejected as we do in our marriages and partnerships? Where else do we desire to be seen so deeply? Where else can we feel so invisible? This is the perfect place to dive into our egoic closets and find the skeletons. The big bells will ring when we're in intimate spaces. This is the heart of our tribe. This is where we believe we have the most to lose. This is where we also protect ourselves the most from losing anything at all.

I suggest, with rare exceptions, that intimate relationships in this heavy reality are in survival mode. We couch our relationships in love language and romantic gestures, but we want our partners to bring in what our ego tells us we need. We rarely see them for who they are. We don't see each other because we're too busy trying to survive each other. We don't see each other because we don't see ourselves. We live only according to the terms dictated by ego, and that is to survive. When we're googly-eyed in love, that painful gap of separation closes momentarily. Romantic love is a balm for the deep, ancient wound of aloneness. Ego wants us to keep our eye on that feeling of connection, no matter how minute. In that desperate need for connection, we'll ignore or deny the many ways we allow/create rejection and abandonment in that relationship.

Most opportunities for expansion lie in the exploration of intimate relationships. It's where we can create a deep honesty and authenticity about our pain stories and a safe space to burn away some of the foundational patterns of abandonment and rejection. Being in a relationship where it's safe enough to activate a deep seeing of the 3D brings in enormous potential for healing and evolving. If everyone in the relationship is there with the intention of seeing and healing stories that arise, then we see the stories not as deal breakers or failings but as densities to be transformed.

In a conscious relationship, we own our own stories. We see conflict as an opportunity to see the looping, the abandonment and rejection programs, and the trauma in the body. The goal is to grow and expand. In safe, intimate relationships, each partner can own their unacceptable behavior. Each is motivated by the evolutionary work and how that contributes to a healthier, peaceful, and more enriching relationship, and therefore a healthier, more enriching life. This is in contrast to an egoic 3D-driven relationship, which often subsists on the need to win the fight. The need to be right.

Many of us try for a perfect relationship, and we shop around until our romance bells ring, and we find all the characteristics in a person we think we want. Many people hold themselves to a standard. They don't compromise and will only accept the ideal fit. We want to make our relationship picture perfect, conflict free, but we'll contort, deny, and compromise ourselves to make it look that way (if only on the surface). We try to be the way we think our partners want us to be, or how we want others to see us—i.e., problem-free. However, the idea of perfection keeps us from changing. Perfection is an egoically defined goal and identity. It's a construct of the 3rd dimension. It keeps us from looking at what a relationship reveals about our most tender stories, our most vulnerable places. The stuff stays put because we're afraid of seeing ourselves.

On the journey, we want our partners there for our sacred growth, and we for theirs, to reflect to us all the abandoned places within that don't feel they're loved, or feel they need something, or feel they're not perfect or not safe. Our partners are not there to be perfect; they are there to reveal us to us. You may have had a lot of terrible partnerships because there was something big you needed to bring into focus through your discomfort, something you needed to see in yourself. If you feel your partner doesn't see you, I can almost guarantee you walked into that relationship with parts of you believing you're not worth seeing. The relationship is a painful little gift that reveals that wound to you. He/she/they reflect that truth back to you. Whatever discord you experience in your relationship is an opportunity to bring imprints into awareness. You bring your ego into focus and see its desire to stay in victimhood and blame others for your reality.

Exercise:
To See Yourself in Relationship

Explore what you're experiencing in your relationships and allow it to reveal your own as-yet-unseen stories and expectations.

○ Do you stay in conversations with others who talk only about themselves? Why? What would it look like if you were to remove yourself from this conversation? What emotions and feelings arise when you consider walking away? What are the consequences of walking away, and how does that make you feel?

○ Do you stay in relationships in which the other does not see you? Why? Do you, or parts of you, feel invisible in the relationship? What would it look like if you were to remove yourself from that relationship? What emotions and feelings arise when you consider walking away?

○ Are you in a relationship where you fear sharing what you're feeling? Do you never speak up when something is bothering you? Why? What would it feel like to communicate your feelings—in a non-blaming, non-shaming way—to your partner(s)?

We stay in a relationship in which we feel invisible because there is a part of us, below awareness, that does not feel seen. That part picks our relationships for us, and that part needs healing, not the partner who can't see us. If there is a wound within that you can't see—the wound will find someone who will reveal it to you.

We are going to make messes in our relationships. Maybe we'll vomit up a pain story on our intimate partners. Our work is to see the mess and hold ourselves accountable for cleaning it up. We want to create relationships where it's safe to flounder and safe to repair. We create space for one another in which it's safe enough to keep looking, keep seeing, keep feeling the 3D pain when it shows up. It will always show up in the vulnerable, intimate spaces of romantic and family relationships. Ongoing practices of vigilance, ownership, reflection, and silence will help reveal the 3D in our most guarded spaces.

There are a growing number of books and websites discussing conscious relationships. I recommend you dive in and bring their visions—how they see the evolution of relationship—into your energy field. Bringing high-vibrational texts in on a regular basis will not only assist you in creating a conscious journey but will also help bring your ego stories that have been constructing fear-based relationships into focus.

Summary: Unabandoning Ourselves

Our 5 Pillars are about engendering a process of being present, sticking around. We commit to being with ourselves consistently, unwaveringly. We agree to look and not look away. We're healing separation, which is rooted in the deep 3D feelings of being alone, rejected, abandoned.

We heal the abandonment by finally being there for the hidden parts within, not leaving them alone, scared, and in the dark. That's how we heal the aloneness. We bring deep seeing, feeling, and connection to our stories of separation. We see how we've turned away from ourselves, rejected ourselves, shamed ourselves. In not turning away, we generate that connection within. We invoke and deliver the energies of connectivity. We're connected to everything, so in deep presence with Self, we bring in the ultimate seeing, the energy of pure consciousness, inviting energy to enter and dissolve all the parts that are hiding and have been pushed into the dark. We learn to invite the energy of acceptance in, in a new way, at all levels of our beings. That is the unabandoning. That is the healing. That is the waking up from separation.

Chapter VI

Consciousness Delivery Systems

C onsciousness delivery systems are processes, people, and things that deliver energy. They deliver higher frequencies and increased quantities of energies. We want to incorporate some or all of these systems in our lives in order to deliver healing energy to all our 3D parts—the pain, the stories, the trauma, the ego infrastructure—that experience disconnection. We want to explore and experiment with resources that will serve our work. These are resources we find within and without that are best able to penetrate the 3D densities. And our delivery systems may change depending on the time of day, or a time in our life. They may differ depending on geography, our body type, or depending on the story that comes into view, that we are ready to work on, on any given day, year, or decade.

Consciousness is allowed to penetrate into our beings when we relax the agendas of the 3rd dimension—the ego and the masculine; the clenching, bracing, and avoiding—and allow it all just to flow. When presence enfolds the agendas of the 3rd dimension, consciousness penetrates the densities of pain. Processes, technologies, and rituals that deliver consciousness into the calcified pain imprints in our body raise our vibration, raise our energies, and feed our expansion.

Through growing awareness of the mind, we can see the extent to which the mind impedes our efforts to direct consciousness, awareness, and the healing energy of the Collective deep into the 3D wounds. In our goal to access the densities in our body, bypassing the mind—getting under it, over it, or around it—needs to be part of our strategy.

Meditation

Meditation is a central player on this journey. It was explored in depth as one of the 5 Pillars in Chapter V, but I would also consider it the most basic and foundational consciousness delivery system. While we won't be going over meditation again, please revisit the section on meditation as we now explore it as a consciousness delivery mechanism and know that it stands alone and as an opening practice in this chapter as well. It is the foundation in consistently delivering the energies of silence to our beings. We get out of our own way in meditation, letting consciousness permeate our entire beings bit by bit. What serves our practice of meditation is an increasing capacity to surrender in the silence.

Surrender

We may need to feel the agony of our resistance to achieve the gift of our surrender.

In the space of surrender, we soften, collapse, and hypnotize ourselves into sinking into the depths of the universe that are in our heart, in our core, and allow the energy that emerges to run the show for a while. We surrender to get below all parts of our egoic mind that tell us there's something to solve, something to fix, something to resolve, something to win, something to change, or something from which to flee. If we can *feel* our way into that space, into that grace, that's where both the ecosystem of the body and the metaphysical parts of Self can take over. Our immune system activates, and the physical, emotional, and energetic bodies purge unwanted toxicities.

We infuse our meditations with surrender. We surrender into our hearts, into our inner beings, knowing there's no truth, no wisdom, no healing beyond the heart, nothing beyond the consciousness that sits within the heart. We surrender into the universal wisdom that sits within our bodies. We find it, explore it, and have fun going deeper into it.

Because we have lots of practice resisting the healing process, and avoiding our discomfort, surrender can be challenging, even frightening. When we ask ourselves to move into the pain instead of expending our energy running from it, we defy the rules of ego. We develop trust and a knowing that healing is happening even when (and especially when) the mind is not there.

The more we sit in the feeling that there's nothing there, the more we deliver that reality into our beings, meaning we make it our reality. We have to take this body and mind "into" consciousness to give it room to heal the delusion that there is so much going on. It's like walking a child into a doctor's office. They don't know that they'll heal, and will feel better when it's over, but we do. We have to let go so the Self can take that lead.

When you feel your way into a space of surrender, you practice embodying pure love and pure acceptance.

We have multiple systems of consciousness delivery to discuss in this chapter, and with all of them we get out of the way of the energy that the system is there to deliver. When we try to let go, the egoic mind can push back. If we have constructed safe circumstances around us, then our response is to surrender even more. The journey is surrender. There is nothing to do. We move through our density, our pain, and arrive at the knowing that we hand everything over to nothingness. Source, pure awareness, knows what to do with the pain.

Exercise:
Meditation on Surrender

Find a comfortable spot. I prefer lying down for this exercise.

Set an intention. Maybe your intention is to deepen your experience of surrender.

Take a few minutes to breathe. Watch your breath move in. Watch it move out.

Know there is a current running within you, underneath all that you think you know and believe. It runs underneath all the stress, tension, fear, denial, and avoidance. It runs underneath all of the clenching and holding. It runs underneath all of the attachments, goals, objectives, desires, and beliefs. It flows easily and completely underneath all of the activities of your physical, emotional, and mental life.

This current is your anchor to surrender. Your connection to everything and nothing.

As you breathe in and out, invite your entire being to fall into that current. The flow of everything underneath.

Watch your body. Witness any shifts or changes. Sometimes the breath will shift. Sometimes things will slow down.

Practice feeling like every cell in your body has accepted everything.

If you find any part of you that is clenched, resisting, thinking, or wanting, notice it. Observe it, if just for a second or two, and then let go and fall into that current that is the center of you. Notice the resistance in the obvious ways and eventually in the more subtle ways.

It may take time to find that current and to connect to it. It may take time to see the subtle ways that you hold and resist. Surrender beneath any expectations you have about doing it right or wrong. Know that the place of surrender is your place of connection, truth, potential, and healing. Even if your mind doesn't quite know it yet.

Remain here for five or ten minutes. The more we surrender, the more we free up consciousness to do the work for us.

One of my favorite places to practice and assist others in experiencing surrender is on extended silent/meditation retreat. After a few days of leading the mind and body into a quieter, more pliable, and less resistant space, that is where the experience of surrender can be most available to us, especially if we are guided by someone we know and trust.

While moving toward surrender is so much a part of this journey, for you practitioners/healers/facilitators out there, I offer a few reflections while working with your clients. We may need to be aware of the fine line we are walking between bringing in safety and encouraging surrender. Telling someone who is working on a big-T trauma during a session (therapy, plant medicine, energetic healing, etc.) to surrender and let go when they're experiencing great discomfort or even terror can re-entrench a trauma and deepen the state of fear and separation. As journeyers out of the 3rd dimension, we need to be mindful if our actions deepen the story of aloneness and abandonment in another. We accompany people's journeys into their own power. While they step into their own stories, we hold their hands (metaphorically). They will let go of your hand and surrender into themselves when they're ready, when they feel bigger, more present than the fear. It's our job to ask and to respond to cues that inform us of their readiness to fall into a pain story on their own. We need to honor their process so as not to project our expectations and our egoic stories onto our clients.

Positive Feelings: Upping the Vibration

Many of us understand that everything is vibration. Everything is energy, and so everything vibrates at its own frequency. Including feelings. Author Masaru Emoto describes this in his work on the effects of feelings and emotions on the crystal formation of water.[44]

Our cells are not just workers; they're receptors. They're there to receive signals from the body, signals showing if it's time to work or time to relax, time to laugh or time to cry. The signals alert us to whether we're safe or in danger. When we receive a message of love in the body, it activates cellular activity that behaves in a state of order, a higher state of consciousness. By engaging in positive feelings, we bring the vibration of love, kindness, and safety into ourselves. We deliver messages to the body that these positive thoughts and feelings are part of our reality, at all levels. When

---

[44] Masaru Emoto, *The Hidden Messages of Water* (New York: Atria Books, 2005).

we activate feelings of higher frequency in our heart space, we infuse ourselves with drops of consciousness.

When we bring in gratitude, compassion, and joy, we deliver higher frequencies, which heal the body on all levels. This is not thinking. Writing down all the things we are grateful for without activating a feeling of gratitude in our hearts does not generate much energy. But when we activate the feeling of appreciation, we create a field of positive energy, radiating high vibrations from the inside out. When we meditate on love, we not only bring in light, but we also ready the body for more light. It's an iterative process—light creates light, which brings in more light and creates more space for light.

So, check your attitude and the underlying feeling. Are you a victim? If so, your body will radiate that energy. Are you owning everything with love and compassion? Are you creating energies of appreciation? Curiosity? Respect? If so, your body will feel the transmission of those energies. At the end of every meditation, I like to include five minutes of positive reflection. My body/mind recalls something for which I'm appreciative so I create a glow of gratitude throughout my being. If there's something I'm hoping to feel in the future, I bring that feeling in to prepare my body for that feeling. Higher vibrations help clean out lower vibrations that prohibit manifesting high-energy reality. Joe Dispenza is a well-known leader in this practice, and I recommend either finding or reminding yourself of his wisdom at some time on your journey.[45]

It's interesting how many people understand the logic of the positive impact of feeling good on our mood, our physiology, and our energy body. However, to make this a habit seems difficult, just like meditation itself. I find the human resistance to feeling good fascinating. When I suggest to clients a practice of just feeling good, they believe it in principle, but do they incorporate it into their lives? Usually, no. Does our inability to feel good reflect

---

[45] Joe Dispenza, *Breaking the Habit of Being Yourself* (Carlsbad: Hay House, 2012).

our ego's fight against knowing that we can create our own love and joy? Ego doesn't want us to see that we can create a sense of feeling good, independent of the tribe. There's resistance to accepting that feeling good is an internal creation, and not about what the external world tells us.

I invite you to be a little bit fascinated, perhaps amused, at how difficult it is to sit in an internally created feeling of joy for five minutes a day. But from my personal experience, sitting in feelings of love and joy are the big jumper cables of awakening—this lovely jumpstart allows higher frequencies into our reality. We can also use positive feelings to avoid our stories. I invite you *not* to use positive feelings to suppress the uncomfortable ones. That is just more oppression, denial, and rejection. We want to allow room for both to exist but know that only the love is real.

Ayurveda

Ayurveda is a three-thousand-year-old healing arts tradition that connects our healing to the rhythms of nature. Healing is premised upon directing the frequencies of consciousness by delivering the wisdom of nature through food, herbs, healing touch, fragrances, breath, etc. Yoga moves energy in the energy body. Tantra moves energy in the mind. Ayurveda moves energy in the physical body. The trifecta of these Vedic wisdoms is there for our holistic evolutionary journey.

For me, Ayurveda is powerful poetry. It reminds me we are part of the spectacular intelligence of this earth. It shows us our way back to ourselves, past the delusions of the mind, the sufferings recorded in the emotional body, and the imbalance in the tissues. In the West, we've been rooted in the separation of mind and body. We've disregarded and scoffed at the world of prana and the movement of subtle energies. Many years ago, Ayurveda reminded me I have a body that requires love and attention if I am to connect it to natural intelligence and allow consciousness to flow into my being and release contractions and delusions.

There are many beautiful things that stand out about Ayurveda, in particular from my viewpoint as a psychotherapist. Ayurveda says each one of us is unique, and therefore, what we need to be healthy and in balance will differ for everyone. My path toward wholeness is unique to me. So, my job may be to do the opposite of what everyone else is doing. In fact, Ayurveda gives me direct permission to *not* listen to everyone else's perception of right and wrong, or healthy and unhealthy, but to find my way into listening to what my body/mind needs. This aligns with our understanding that we all carry unique stories, have a unique path, and therefore our journey toward wholeness will be unique.

Ayurveda reminds us that there is no bad; there's just imbalance. There are degrees to which we have fallen out of step with our true nature. That paradigm challenges the egoic urge to judge. For example, instead of criticizing ourselves for being anxious, we reframe it—"My Vata is too high." Or, instead of labeling ourselves with depression, we need to get our Kapha moving. In Ayurveda, we're just balancing the elements in our body. If something doesn't feel right, it's because we have moved out of balance.

Ayurveda gives you the tools and training to take the journey inward, to listen to your body, and tune into your body's sensations as it communicates its needs. It also says you may need to find an excellent practitioner who knows how to see and listen to your body in ways Western medicine practitioners are not trained to do.

Being in balance is moving closer to a state of natural intelligence. Our true nature connects to the silence and the flow of consciousness. The body (physical, mental, emotional, energetic) is a record, a revealer, of where we are holding densities that throw us out of balance. It tells us where we hold too much or too little of something. It tells us in subtle (and not-so-subtle) ways where we need to bring our awareness. Ayurveda is a guide into silence. An imbalance—a pain, a discomfort—is where we have a density stuck, where we have an ego loop showing up in the physical tissues, and where the cells of the body have rearranged themselves as they follow our repressed stories in thought and feeling. That's all ego noise. Discomfort in the body is an indicator of where we host stories of separation. Ayurveda is a grand connector. The more we bring the body into balance, the more we bring natural order into our body, the quieter we are, and the more we connect to our being underneath the 3D mental, emotional, and physical noise. We release egoic patterns and move into flow. The body reveals the next layer of imbalance needing our attention. It tells us where something is talking (or screaming) for help, so we can come in with love and intelligence to return it to flow. Consciousness and inspiration move in that natural flow. They bring us closer to our magnificent metaphysical Self. Our authentic Self. Our connected Self.

Nature

Few people today would deny the healing power of nature. Almost every client ignited on this journey expresses their desire to get into nature more. They see it as a necessary part of their healing, grounding, and connection to themselves.

To surround yourself with nature is to drink in the signals of the natural intelligence of this planet. Through the sun, moon, water, earth, mountains, sand, forest, and foliage, you receive a transmission that invites you to step away from chaos and step into order. Nature is our teacher and healer, leading us to trust and surrender in the knowing that we're part of a rhythm that carries us along our path. This luscious planet gives us her countless treasures as a profound instrument of healing and consciousness for our journey out of the 3rd dimension. I have experienced altered states, both in and out of plant medicine, where the communications from nature were clear, telling me she's our ally and guide on our challenging journey through this reality. Plant medicines are the most powerful and extreme example of nature's medicines of consciousness. I wonder if they've been tailor-made for our collective journey!

Your body is connected to the wisdoms in the rhythms of nature. Find your way into the natural ebbs and flows, births and deaths, rising and falling of this planet. For example, walking in the woods at sunrise is healing. Let nature talk to you. Be in it. Preserve it. Adore it—it's a gift to you in your awakening. It is your medicine guide. Let the magic happen. Let the messages come through. Watch for her arrows and signs, directing you back to you.

Yoga or Meditative Movement

Yoga has so many gifts, is studied widely, and is infused into the movement culture around the world. It's where you practice presence, self-compassion, and connection to feelings/sensations. A regular practice facilitates deep levels of decompression of the 3D.

I tell my clients who are resisting getting their movement practice going that when I'm feeling something big coming to the surface to be released, it becomes obvious because that is when I circle my yoga mat, arms crossed, defiant, resentful, and a little terrified. I stare at the mat, walk around it, snarl at it. That's because my nervous system—with ego whispering in its ear—already knows if I get down there and start moving my body, the toxins are going to come to the surface and soon I'll be very uncomfortable.

As someone who is releasing all the time, I found yoga (and especially hot yoga) an essential part of my detox routine. Yogic movement and static poses access the body's energy channels, moving and flushing stuck energies and encouraging easier flow of intelligent energies in the body. While hot yoga is not recommended for everyone, for someone who detoxes regularly, deep sweating can release energetic, physical, and emotional residues that get stuck in the channels and tissues. I don't believe I would've survived these last years without yoga as my constant companion.

I go to a beautiful yoga studio with glorious teachers who are willing and able to hold space while I release and shift and cry my way through a class. Find your community and bring in that safe space to facilitate your surrender.

Breathwork

My brilliant yoga teacher once said in class that today, on average, we breathe between twelve and twenty-two cycles a minute, and that we *should* breathe around six. That tells me we are all hyperventilating! Normalized rapid and shallow breathing sends persistent signals to the body that we're under attack, in danger, and need to be ready at all times to fight or flee. Regulating our breath delivers messages of safety. Easy peasy healing. Breathwork is a wonderful way of getting prana, life-force energy, circulating in the body, bringing consciousness to the sticky places. At a more fundamental level, it is a profound tool for delivering the message of safety to the body.

Pranayama, a technique of controlling the breath to raise and circulate energy in the body, is an ancient practice that's becoming more common in yoga studios. I recommend a few pranayama techniques such as Nadi Shodhana (alternate nostril breathing) or three-part breath in order to assist clients in regulating an anxious nervous system.

Exercise:
Pranayama Practice – Three-Part Breath

You can do this for 10 breaths or 10 minutes, depending on what your body needs that day. This practice is great for cleaning out stale air and bringing in new energy as well as releasing tensions we hold throughout our torso, especially our lungs. It helps regulate our nervous system. If we feel anxiety as a stickiness in our heart space, over time this practice can assist in releasing that stuck fear. We bring in the lightening and clearing prana to clean out old perspectives and make space for higher frequencies. As with all breathwork, it brings us into the present moment.

Find a quiet place. Sitting up straight or lying on your back, bring your attention to your breath. Observe if it is fast or slow, deep or shallow.

After a few minutes of just observing, attempt to deepen your inhale and exhale so that you feel your lower belly expand and contract. After practicing that for a few minutes, upon your next inhale, expand your lower belly, pause a second, and then breathe into your solar plexus/mid belly. And then exhale. Practice that breath for a few minutes.

Upon your next inhale breathe deep into your lower belly. Pause. Mid belly. Pause. Now breathe into your chest, expanding your upper ribcage. Pause, and then exhale all the air out.

Now, put it all together. Inhale into lower belly. Pause. Mid belly. Pause. Chest. Pause. Big, long, slow exhale. Pause. Inhale lower belly. Pause. Mid belly. Pause. Chest. Pause. Exhale.

Rinse and repeat.

Holotropic breathwork is another profound use of breathing techniques to access non-ordinary states of consciousness. Many describe the altered states they achieve as being similar to plant medicine journeys.

Our bodies are primed to assist us in our path to expansion. We don't need big money, an enormous space, or special tools to access this wisdom, nor do we need to leave our own living room. We can revisit the healing power of our breath anywhere.

Energetic Therapies

I recommend getting familiar with the subtle energy bodies within you. There's a growing library of resources and wisdom about our subtle body.[46] Many people who awaken are drawn to exploring energetic healing modalities. As we release density in the physical body, we deepen our relationship with the energetic parts of ourselves. They're both there and will reveal themselves in a way and time that is right for you. Just as we hold toxins and blockages in the physical self, we hold toxic imprints in our subtle bodies.

Acupuncture, acupressure, other hands-on healing therapies, and sound therapy have all been essential in my journey. I've brought a select number of wonderful people into my reality that each bring their own vibrations at the right time in the right way, helping me activate and move the intelligence within. Energetic therapies have been fundamental in moving into places my conscious mind resists going. When the discomfort is too much for my mind to tolerate, I often need someone to hold my hand and walk with me into the dark. They are also there when I'm so fatigued by the work that I have crawled to their offices in need of a jumpstart. I am grateful for all the boosts.

Working with a potent energetic healer can feel like we've hit the jackpot. It feels like we can get someone to do the hard lifting for us. But on this path we come to realize that we are in charge of our own healing. Because of the pain infrastructure and its addiction to being a victim, most people engage the services of a "healer/facilitator" in order to be cured, healed, fixed, and to have their pain taken away. But this intention is part of the pain infrastructure. It's a 3D-ego loop. It perpetuates the notion that you're powerless, that you're at the mercy of someone else, that you need rescuing, that you require fixing, that there's something wrong, and that you're not whole. All of those are

---

[46] Cyndi Dale, *The Subtle Body: An Encyclopedia of Your Energetic Anatomy* (Louisville: Sounds True, 2009).

pain cues. Because no matter how good the "healer" is, if you live in victimhood and in a reality of denial, in not knowing that everything is in you, you'll reassert the pain reality; it will rebuild itself, and the pain will come back. It's your job to witness the story (not continue to be the story) and to own your journey. Faced with that ownership, all a good "healer" is doing is adding consciousness to your process.

Those who are here to raise the frequency are here to share that energy, to add energy to the process. We're here, each sharing energy and raising the frequency in our own unique ways. And with your awareness, we can transmit that energy in the way your highest Self requests it, needs it, and wants to receive it. Your agenda is your own, your path is your own, your timeline is your own, your process is your own. We so-called healers give you a boost when you're aware enough to ask for it, aware enough to integrate it, and aware enough to join us.

Many people who come to me feeling there's something going on beyond the five senses want to explore more for themselves but don't know where to begin. I say, "Begin anywhere." I started with Ayurveda and marma therapy, which led me to try Reiki and then sound therapy. All of that was enough for me to see and validate my journey into my subtle body. But you take your journey with energetic practices where you need it to go, and you go where your soul leads you. There are so many modalities out there: polarity therapy, acupuncture, acupressure, chakra healing, shamanic healing, crystal healing, qi gong, etc. Enjoy the exploration and the communities you find along the way.

Good Therapy

In the last ten years of my career, I have seen an increase in psychotherapists who incorporate an energetic component into their practice. I see this more in hands-on practitioners such as massage therapists, osteopaths, chiropractors, etc. They connect with the subtle vibrations and work skillfully with emotional trauma imprints. I believe there will continue to be a dramatic rise in the blending of psychotherapeutic and energetic therapies, as the two modalities are natural allies in facilitating safety and boundaries, working with pain, and integrating it into our metaphysical path of expansion. Two psychotherapeutic modalities that are compatible with this work are Internal Family Systems and Somatic Experiencing. They both recognize the centrality of the Self and integrating trauma imprints into the whole.

Plant Medicine

On our journey out of the 3rd dimension, we work with knowing (or developing the knowledge) that we are not who we think we are. Of all the consciousness delivery systems, plant medicine feels like a deep soul commitment. Plant medicine reveals how little we know about ourselves, the function of our reality, the purpose of our existence, etc. It sees/reveals who we really are. Or what we really are not. It's often the catalyst for our dismantling journey. The medicine can show us our hidden pain stories to us quickly, revealing what's been sequestered below consciousness.

I experience psychedelic medicines as a giant distracter, in a good way. I take the medicine, then off I go on a little stroll, "Look! Over there! Shiny thing!" And while I look away, the medicine dives deep into my 3D trauma(s) and takes the highest energy with it.

After we use plant medicines, we feel disorientated as we figure out how our inner furniture just got rearranged, followed by the bliss of the new, higher frequency flowing through our bodies. Often, we see/feel some of that trauma as it leaves our beings, and the body experiences the purge of egoic toxicity (hence why it can be uncomfortable). Our pain story surfaces. We experience fresh energies and the transformational potential of the wisdom, and we take a step toward a new reality.

Opportunities for sustained expansion lie in the medicine integration process. The medicine's potential works on our realities well after the ceremony has finished. It flows through the channels of consciousness within our beings for weeks, months, even years. We want to pay attention and incorporate the wisdom into our lives. We support ourselves and our work with a mindful process, merging new, higher frequencies into our reality through mindful practices, reflections, silence; times when we allow the deeper workings of the medicine to float into awareness, where we can make choices. I recommend finding support after a medicine to integrate the healing. There are an increasing number of psychotherapists working with plant-medicine travelers. Seek plant medicine opportunities with practitioners trained in plant-medicine integration or have your plant-medicine facilitator connect you to an integration therapist.

Many people who engage in plant medicine journeys do so frequently. Of course, it depends on the medicine, but I suggest that when incorporating these big energies, less is more. Ego thinks its job is to push back, return us to the status quo. When we engage with a lot of medicine, we can also face a lot of push back, and that can disorient, confront, even be traumatic. Forcing our minds and bodies to alter their view of reality at a sped-up pace can destabilize instead of inspire, making integrating new frequencies difficult. We need to feel safe to change. Too much change too soon is the perfect recipe for trauma imprinting. Take your time with plant medicine. Build silence and space into your life to allow the medicines to continue communicating and teaching.

For every new plant medicine practitioner you consider working with, I recommend they have a thorough process of assessment and screening. There are people not suited or not ready to incorporate plant medicine into their journey. Ensure you're with a facilitator who sees you and is comfortable saying "No." Your sense of safety is paramount. As with all things in this reality, there are people holding pain stories that lead them to exploit or abuse another in ceremony. We are vulnerable. Do your research. Go by trusted referrals. Ensure facilitators have answered all your safety and security concerns and that you feel comfortable and seen in the space. When you facilitate such a deep surrender, your boundaries are paramount. You co-create a container for surrender. Know that plant medicine is not for everyone. If you're not comfortable or it doesn't feel safe, that's not the place to do your work. There are so many other magical avenues to bring in big energies. Explore, discover, and find what resonates with you.

People often describe being called to do medicine. They get a coherent message, an intuitive hit, telling them this is where they are supposed to be. When I was first invited to take part in an Ayahuasca ceremony, for example, weeks before the actual event, I sat across from the host as she spoke the word "Ayahuasca" to me. What felt like an electric shock exploded in my body. The person inviting me felt it, looked at me with eyes wide, and said, "Well, I think you're supposed to be there!" And the dance between me and the sacred medicines began.

Temazcal or Sweat Lodge

A deep, guided sweat from a competent shaman is as powerful as plant medicine in purging the 3D from the body. The Temazcal (Mexican tradition) or sweat-lodge ceremony (North American indigenous tradition) are centuries-old medicines. The intensity of heat digs deep into our programs, metabolizing pain at all levels. Sitting in the dark, enveloped by glowing rocks and the penetrating energies of your healing facilitators, transports you and connects you to hidden parts of yourself. It's a 3D purge at all levels. For many people, it can overwhelm the senses. Temazcal always leaves me weeping, trembling, sometimes with purging seizures, as toxins are released from my body and the energy surges.

It's a wonderful teacher in the profound practice of surrender. This kind of heat is not recommended for everyone. Consult your doctor to determine if you have any contraindications.

Exercise:
Create Consistent Consciousness/Remembering

○ Create time every day in a routine that includes silence and surrender.

○ Make time every day to meditate. This could be guided or not. An hour a day with intentional presence creates shifts.

○ Make time daily or throughout the week to engage in meditative movement such as yoga, tai chi, or qi gong.

○ Once a week or once a month, join your communities in generating the energy of silence or reflection. Try a meditation group at your local yoga studio or connect to a group online.

○ Once a year, dive into a deep pool of consciousness at a silent meditation or plant medicine retreat.

Continue to nurture the new paradigm within, and it will nurture the global remembering.

We will forget. Often. We'll get lost in our stories and believe our stories and invest in our stories. Our dramas carry us away, and our pain takes hold, and we feel we'll never get to the other side. But we do. In this migration, we always do. So, if you get lost, don't harm yourself. Don't judge yourself. When you're ready, you'll reconnect to your quiet. There are many of us here to hold the space until you remember again.

We Heal Each Other

In the therapeutic dance between my clients and me, I may bring them into the present moment, where higher frequencies of consciousness are invited to heal the dense vibrations that come into focus during a session. But because the client and I are reflections of each other, because they and their pain are just an aspect of me and my programs, my karma, and my trauma, we're engaging in the bigger project of healing each other, engaged in a subconscious contract to reveal that pain, that density to me, facilitating the healing of both of us. The teacher is the student. The healer is the patient. The partnership in evolution is a perfect mirror. Know that people who come into your life reflect you and your relationship with yourself. Let them reveal you to you. Even (and especially) the parts that ego does not want you to see.

When Consciousness Flows

As a therapist, when you're working with a client and they wake up—see the loop they've been living in, see the lies their mind has been telling them, see the higher intelligence at work—you can feel the energy in the room shift. It's a frequency change. It feels lighter. Often, my ears ring, the air feels like it is crackling, my heart opens, and I can't help but smile.

When I'm working with someone and we experience a higher truth, they feel a swoosh of energy move through. When they've allowed themselves to receive the vibration of the "truth," their bodies, their energetic bodies, will tell them they've arrived. The shift can be tremendous. Clients become dizzy, things spin, they feel tingling in their arms and legs. There's a lightness, a dream-like state. Can anything but truth feel that good, that liberating, that grounding, and that loving? As you integrate and release the toxicity of the egoic delusions from your body, you become receptive to receiving the vibrations of love and consciousness, and they will shift you easily and readily.

Summary: A Life of Bringing in Light

There are so many paths we can take to invite the energies of consciousness into our dense reality and use them to decompress and expand. Many of you have explored some of the above practices and services that deliver higher vibrations into your pain stories. And there are more I've not touched upon. It's not uncommon for someone to share that they tried something once (for example, Reiki or plant medicine) and report they felt nothing. Or they tried therapy but didn't connect with the therapist, so they gave up. Or they tried meditating, but after a few times, they felt they could never do it because their mind is too busy. Some practices will work for you; some won't. But if you're on a journey of expansion, then however it unfolds, keep going. You might need to cut through one story to find one big energy that is going to finally find its way in there. Your path may require you to bring in a hundred different energies to break through a hundred different stories or a hundred layers of one story. Whatever it is, the journey is finding your way to you, so keep searching, trying, and exploring. You are worth it.

Chapter VII
_____

Conclusion –
Dismantling Nothing

I f it isn't already obvious: *We are not actually dismantling any-thing.* Because there is *nothing to dismantle.* How can we dis-mantle what is non-existent? If none of this is real, what are we dismantling? We're in the process of pure creation. We are exploding into pure potential. There is nothing breaking down, only expanding. The word *dismantling* is a little trick, a seduction, for our busy minds—the minds that want to do something, want a process, a strategy, a direction. *Dismantling* provides the feeling, a little fix, and gives us something to do.

I have needed the idea of a *process* to allow my thoughts to organize around all of that discomfort, to feel some sense of control while everything felt so out of control. But as the need for control releases, so does the notion that there's anything to do. We've landed here in our dense selves and are opening them up to their higher expressions. And we do that with a lot of expressions of nothing—silence, space, surrender, observing, and being. So, keep dismantling—until your mind understands that there's nothing to dismantle.

I've shared something antithetical to how human beings have operated for thousands of years—I'm going right into the pain. I'm going right into the childhood wound. I'm asking you to fall directly into the unknown, inarticulable karmic pain. I know this may not be a popular prescription for our evolutionary path, but it's time to take on the big stuff and take care of ourselves and each other in this next era of expansion.

We're zooming out. We're stepping away from this existence. The more we zoom out, the more we can see the stories of pain that make up this reality. When we zoom out, we see how we've been lost in a fog of our own pain. We've been stumbling, blind, believing everything our pain has told us and believing that nothing is more important than our pain. Now we imbibe the healing power of surrender and let the feminine cradle us while we free-fall into awareness. She has taught me I'm here to see all and transform all. What your unique role is on this collective journey is beyond my awareness, but if you're reading this, you're taking part in what I believe to be a creative apex for this space/time. To wake up is to arrive at a moment of clarity and quickening for yourself and what your creative journey is about. Many people feel that there's something bigger happening, even if we can't quite define it, see it, or hear it. But we know it. At some level, we know there is more going on than our families, our lovers, our governments, our influencers, our economy, or our minds have told us.

There are still a lot of us engaged in the doing. And for many of us in service, it doesn't yet feel right to disengage from all the suffering we see. We want to heal others and be of help. So, let's do so, but more mindfully. Let's be aware of the part of us that feels trapped in the pain or the powerlessness that we witness in others. See the stories come up and use your doing as an opportunity to bring light to your own pain. Let us remember that if we serve from a place of pain—disappointment, anger, fear—we are contributing to the 3D versus healing our Selves and others of it.

Expect to get discouraged. Expect to feel conflicted. Expect to feel like your mind is always hijacking you. Expect it to feel insurmountable. It's going to happen. Allow it. These are opportunities to deepen your witness, to deepen your surrender, to deepen your detachment from the drama. The practice is trusting and surrendering past these ego stories into the journey of this lifetime. Know that all these feelings need to show up. Because we all have them; they're all part of our collective unconscious/conscious. We need to witness them before they can feed our expansion. These are densities our ancestors have carried around for thousands of years and you have signed up to bring them into the whole. Feel the discomfort...then find your way into the inspiration. The inspiration is there, and it always will be, because you are steeped in it. It's everywhere and growing.

Allow what you are learning about yourself and the world and the universe to evolve. Accept the limitations of your mind; what you think you know will shift and change. While we're here, the mind will continue to put itself between you and consciousness. It will filter and interpret from its own lens. It will try to remain in states of contraction. Be aware if you are attaching to any thought or drawing any hard conclusions. See the attachment and feel it dissolve like vapor. Stay open and practice staying anchored in love. Make yourself malleable to your own experience. Allow it to shift and change and step outside of your expectations and intentions. This is going to be easy for some and harder for others, depending on what your ego tells you is the route to safety. Know that anything you become attached to you'll be asked to let go of, so practice loosening your grip. That means don't attach to anything you have learned here, either. Make it like water. It will soak and pool where it needs to, but someday it will turn into vapor. Who needs to work on safety if you know you are safe? Who needs to meditate when you know you are presence? Who needs to work on boundaries when nothing but love comes near you? Who needs to heal when you know you are already perfection? Who needs to practice self-compassion when you know you are nothing but love? So be in the work, but know it too is a delusion; a righteous one, but no less a delusion.

Nothing has any meaning but the meaning we give it. Our repressed emotions may want to give it one meaning, but as we accept, move into, and see the world through consciousness and love, we allow ourselves to heal and give it new meaning. Or we give it new meaning and allow ourselves to heal. Examine what part of you is making meaning at any moment. If that meaning is not love, then it is the creation of the 3rd dimension. It is asleep in the density. What meaning will consciousness give it? What meaning will love give it?

This is not a simple path, as I remind myself, and many of my clients and fellow travelers continue to remark. However, there's an unlimited amount of joy that seems to pull us through as we traverse our inner landmines of pain. We feel the deepening of connection and presence every time we integrate and let go of an element of suffering. For me, it can feel like an ongoing reunion, where I'm walking the path to myself and feeling great joy every time I'm reunited with an unseen, abandoned part of myself. And with every reconnection to Self, I'm more connected to those around me, more connected to Mother Earth. I see the hearts of my fellow human beings. I see the vibrancy in the moon and the water and the wind.

While this journey has defined the very meaning of life for me, it's not the journey for everyone. Honor others' paths with love. Do not judge their paths with ego. The wisdom of universal consciousness knows what it's doing and the role of everyone in it. We're simply different moving parts of the same whole. Make this your most intimate journey inward. Make it about you. All about you. If it's about you, it's about the universe. It's about the Collective.

This is just an offering. A sharing. It's up to you and your highest Self to discern what works for you and what doesn't. You are planting seeds that germinate in their own time. Reserve the right to be in your process, walking your path in your way. There may be elements and energies in these writings that feed and nurture your path at this moment and in a way that speaks to you. Your healing is tied to my healing. Your expansion is tied to my expansion. As I deliver energy to you, I receive energy for my evolution. I'm part of the Collective and so I send an energy out there knowing it comes right back to me. Let's give each other permission to be fluid, malleable, and always learning...and always unlearning.

Keep remembering. Keep knowing. Keep loving your way toward surrender. Because she's there to remind you that there's nothing going on. Nothing is everything. The masculine has dominated our understanding of the world to such a degree that many of us don't see it anymore. The masculine has inhabited our inner infrastructure and our outer infrastructure. It inhabits our language and our culture. It has defined good, bad, success, and failure and reflected a desire for efficiency, speed, dominance— be the best, be the meanest, be the strongest. It infuses our work, how we relate to our partners and our children, how we talk to ourselves. It's embedded within all parts of us. We need to see all those parts and reclaim them. We're reclaiming the feminine and giving her space to create, knowing that her guiding principles, her energies, are fundamental to this stage of our journey. We can see without prejudice the need to bring in the feminine, to transition out of survival-based masculine living and shift into a bigger journey, guided by compassion and consciousness.

We are decompressing from the pain of existing in an ancient state of separation. There are denser 3D energies committed to fighting for survival on this planet that may not be ready to receive the love you bring. They're not ready to see. But know that every meditation and kind word, every practice of acceptance, forgiveness, or expression of gratitude feeds the deeper penetration of consciousness. It integrates all those forgotten parts of you into the greater whole.

I offer this sharing with great gratitude and great humility.

Chapter VIII

Addendum –
Extra Chapter

At the time of publication, there was an additional chapter that I had not yet completed. This chapter shares some challenges that I went through as a physical being purging the 3D trauma from my body for sixteen-plus years. It outlines the weird and wild things the body will experience when it is shedding pain stories and adjusting to new energy levels. I was going through it myself and I could hardly believe they were happening. I will also share some tips that helped me through this uncomfortable process.

In particular, this chapter speaks to many of us who are emerging with big energies and are living in very dense areas on the planet where things do not move easily. I have often felt like I'm trying to cram Niagara Falls through a straw. There's an increasing amount of energy coming through, and I believe the discomfort, at all levels of our being, can become heightened when we are adjusting to the new reality. You can access the addendum by visiting the book page on my website at: https://www.tribetocollective.com/the-book

Glossary

Acupressure
Acupressure is a hands-on therapy in which pressure is applied to certain points in order to remove energetic blockages, release muscular tension, and encourage a healthy flow of energy. https://www.yogapedia.com/definition/11614/acupressure

Acupuncture
Acupuncture stimulates the balance and flow of Qi energy, which in traditional Chinese medicine is considered essential to health. Acupuncture stimulates the release of endorphins—the body's natural pain-relieving neurohormones—through the insertion of needles into specific anatomical points (acupuncture points) to encourage natural healing. https://acupuncturecanada.org/acupuncture-101/what-is-acupuncture/

Chakra Healing
Chakra healing is a treatment of the energy body. This modality channels energy into the seven-plus chakras, or energy centers, that run along the midline of the body.

Consciousness
Dr. David R. Hawkins defines consciousness as the energy that connects us to everything. It flows through everything and is

everything. However, there are measurable levels of consciousness, or 'energy fields' that are "calibrated to measurable effect. With each progressive rise in the level of consciousness, the 'frequency' or 'vibration' of the energy increases. Thus, higher consciousness radiates a beneficial and healing effect on the world, verifiable in the human muscle response, which stays strong in the presence of love and truth."[47]

Consciousness Delivery Systems
These are varying practices that facilitate an increasing flow of consciousness directed toward the self.

Crystal Healing
The crystal healing technique uses precisely placed crystals either on and/or around the physical body. Crystals may also be laid in precise geometric patterns (grids) within the environment. Crystals absorb, focus, direct, detoxify, shift, and diffuse energy as they interact with the electromagnetic forces and subtle vibrations within the subtle human or environmental energy field.
https://www.schoolofhealth.com/be-better/natural-health-definitions/crystal-healing

Ego
Ego is the manifestation of this dimension in the body. Ego is the drive within that believes the body is the only relevant part of our beings. It sees its role as keeping the physical body alive and sees all negative feelings as a threat to survival.

Feedback Loop
A feedback loop, in the context of this book, is an impulse outside of conscious thought, whereby emotional imprints inform the mind and mind validates the emotional imprint. This results in having thoughts, behaviors, and beliefs, which become

---

[47] Hawkins, *Power vs. Force*, xxxvi.

pain-driven reflexes that don't actually serve us but exist as self-serving patterns.

Frequency

Frequency is the rate at which a vibration occurs. As argued by Dr. David R. Hawkins, everything in the universe vibrates, including emotions and feelings. Feelings such as compassion and gratitude vibrate at a higher frequency. Higher frequencies facilitate higher consciousness and result in healing and states of increased order. Rage and shame vibrate as low frequencies and result in destruction and disconnection.

Marma Therapy

Marma therapy is an Ayurvedic healing treatment that facilitates the movement of subtle energies through physical massage. Marma points are similar to acupressure points, which are points on the surface of the body where the subtle energy bodies and physical bodies converge. Practices of acupuncture and acupressure emerged out of the teachings of marma therapy.

Metaphysical

This term is used in this text to define those things that exist beyond the realm of the physical. These are often described as things detected outside of our five senses.

Mind

Mind is the part of us responsible for mental phenomena. In this text, we look at the mind's construction of thought.

Pain Story

A thought, behavior, or belief that makes up a pain-defined reality, versus a 'truth.' We hold pain stories at various levels of our bodies, including at the emotional, physical, mental, and energetic levels.

Polarity Therapy
Polarity therapy is the art and science of stimulating and balancing the flow of life energy within the human being. The term polarity relates to one of the fundamental laws of nature, namely the attraction and union of opposites through a balanced middle point.
https://polaritycenter.org/what-is-polarity/Transmutation

Qi Gong
Qi gong is a combination of "Qi" (life force, bioenergy, creativity, consciousness, breath, function) and "gong" (cultivation or practice over time). It is a self-initiated health and wellness practice consisting of a combination of movement, meditation, and breathing. It also includes self-massage. Researchers describe Qi gong as meditative movement that has the following characteristics: "(a) some form of movement or body positioning, (b) a focus on breathing, and (c) a cleared or calm state of mind with a goal of (d) deep states of relaxation."

Pure Awareness
Pure awareness is the practice of being fully conscious of oneself, but without thought, perception, or belief.

Reiki
This healing technique is based on the principle that a practitioner can channel energy through their hands, directed to the client for healing and stress reduction.

Self versus self
In this text, I refer to the being we are below the 3rd dimension, our eternal beings, as Self. All other references to human beings use the lowercase presentation, self.

Shamanic Healing

While there are many definitions of shamanism and shamanic healing, for the purposes of this reading, I will refer to a couple of elements in shamanic healing.

Some methods include Soul Retrieval and the healing of ancestral patterns.

1. The healer enters an altered state of consciousness, thereby merging physical and metaphysical realities; and
2. Supports a person's return to wholeness through the transformation of illness at all levels, including disordered states at the 'spiritual' or metaphysical level.

Sound Therapy

Sound therapy is a therapeutic technique that uses varying sound frequencies to enhance wellbeing. It is known to facilitate energy flow that may elicit various positive emotional states as well as the healing of organs and tissues.

Trauma

Trauma is the emotional, energetic, and physical imprint of a painful event that happens in the past but leaves a feeling of helplessness and terror in the present.

Vibration

Vibration is oscillation of waves created by all things, including feelings.

Reading List to Raise Your Frequency

Tara Brach	*Radical Self-Acceptance: Embracing Your Life With the Heart of a Buddha*
Dr. Henry Cloud and Dr. John Townsend	*Boundaries Updated and Expanded Edition: When to Say Yes, How to Say No to Take Control of Your Life.*
Cyndi Dale	*The Subtle Body: An Encyclopedia of Your Energetic Anatomy*
Joe Dispenza	*Breaking the Habit of Being Yourself*
David Hawkins	*Power vs. Force: The Hidden Determinants of Human Behavior*
Jack Kornfield	*A Path with Heart: A Guide Through the Perils and Promises of Spiritual Life*
Lynne McTaggart	*The Field: The Quest for the Secret Force of the Universe*
Kristen Neff	*Self-Compassion: The Proven Power of Being Kind to Yourself*
Penny Pierce	*Frequency: The Power of Personal Vibration (Transformation Series)*
Jane Roberts	*The Seth Materials*
Richard Rudd	*The Gene Keys: Embracing Your Higher Purpose*
Michael Singer	*The Untethered Soul: The Journey Beyond Yourself*
Eckhart Tolle	*The Power of Now: A Guide to Spiritual Enlightenment* and *A New Earth: Awakening to Your Life's Purpose*
John Wellwood	*Conscious Relationships: Where Is Your Relationship Going?*
Gary Zukav	*The Seat of the Soul*

Bibliography

Atlas, Galit. *Emotional Inheritance: A Therapist, Her Patients, and the Legacy of Trauma*. Boston: Little, Brown and Company, 2022.

Brach, Tara. *Radical Self-Acceptance: Embracing Your Life With the Heart of a Buddha*. Louisville: Sounds True: Audio, 2008.

Cloud, Henry and John Townsend. *Boundaries Updated and Expanded Edition: When to Say Yes, How to Say No to Take Control of Your Life*. Grand Rapids: Zondervan, 2017.

Dale, Cyndi. *The Subtle Body: An Encyclopedia of Your Energetic Anatomy*. Louisville: Sounds True, 2009.

Dispenza, Joe. *Breaking the Habit of Being Yourself*. Carlsbad: Hay House, 2012.

Emoto, Masaru. *The Hidden Messages of Water*. New York: Atria Books, 2005.

Frances, Richard C. *Epigenetics: How Environment Shapes Our Genes.* New York: WW Norton, 2012.

Grace, Fran, ed. in Hawkins, David R. *Power vs. Force: The Hidden Determinants of Human Behavior.* Carlsbad, California: Hay House, 2012.

Hawkins, David R. *Power vs. Force.* Carlsbad, California: Hay House, 2012.

Hobbes, Thomas. *Leviathan.* New York: McMillan Publishing Company, 1962.

Levine, Amir and Rachel Heller. *Attached: The New Science of Adult Attachment and How It Can Help You Find - and Keep - Love.* New York: Penguin Publishing Group, 2010.

Levine, Peter. *In an Unspoken Voice: How the Body Releases Trauma and Restores Goodness.* Berkeley, California: North Atlantic Books, 2012.

Linden, Anné. *Boundaries in Human Relationships: How to Be Separate and Connected.* Bancyfelin, Wales: Crown House Publishing, 2008.

McTaggart, Lynne. *The Field: The Quest for the Secret Force of the Universe.* New York: Harper Collins, 2008.

Neff, Kristin. *Self-Compassion: The Proven Power of Being Kind to Yourself.* New York: William Morrow Publishing, 2015.

Oren, Nurit. *The Feminine Principle: The Key to Awakening for Men and Women.* Budapest: Gabor Arsanyi, 2018.

Pert, Candace. *Molecules of Emotion: The Science Behind Mind-Body Medicine.* University of Michigan: Scribner, 1997.

Pierce, Penny. *Frequency: The Power of Personal Vibration (Transformation Series).* New York: Atria Books, 2009.

Poole Heller, Diane and Peter Levine. *The Power of Attachment: How to Create Deep and Lasting Intimate Relationships.* Louisville: Sounds True, 2019.

Rudd, Richard. *The Gene Keys: Embracing Your Higher Purpose.* London: Gene Keys Publishing, 2015.

Singer, Michael. *The Untethered Soul: The Journey Beyond Yourself.* Oakland: New Harbinger Productions, 2007.

Tolle, Eckhart. *The Power of Now: A Guide to Spiritual Enlightenment.* Novato, California: New World Library, 2004.

—. *A New Earth: Awakening to Your Life's Purpose.* New York: Penguin Group Publishing, 2006.

Wellwood, John. *Conscious Relationships: Where Is Your Relationship Going?* Louisville: Sounds True, 2015. Audio Book.

Weisstub, E.B. "Self as the Feminine Principle." J Anal Psychol. 1997 Jul;42(3):425-52; discussion 453-8. doi: 10.1111/j.1465-5922.1997.

Wolynn, Mark. *It Didn't Start with You: How Inherited Family Trauma Shapes Who We Are and How to End the Cycle.* London: Penguin Life, 2017.

URLs (except where noted, all URLs accessed March 29, 2023)
Acupuncture Canada
https://acupuncturecanada.org/acupuncture-101/what-is-acupuncture/.

Antonia
Episode: "Who Took the Zen out of My Zen?"
https://podcasts.apple.com/ca/podcast/who-took-the-zen-out-of-my-zen/id1588908885?i=1000538224610.

Merriam-Webster.com
https://www.merriam-webster.com/dictionary/tribe, Accessed 3 Aug. 2022.

Mooji
https://mooji.org/.

Nalanda Translation
https://www.nalandatranslation.org/offerings/translations-and-commentaries/the-wisdom-of-the-feminine/.

New York Times
https://www.nytimes.com/2018/01/31/science/dutch-famine-genes.html.

The Polarity Centre
https://polaritycenter.org/what-is-polarity/Transmutation.

The Qi Gong Institute
https://www.qigonginstitute.org/category/5/what-is-qigong.

The School of Health
https://www.schoolofhealth.com/be-better/natural-health-definitions/crystal-healing.

Tribe to Collective

www.tribetocollective.com.

Wikipedia

https://en.wikipedia.org/wiki/Social_technology.

Yogapedia

https://www.yogapedia.com/definition/11614/acupressure.

About Antonia

Antonia's mission is to Activate, Enable, and Expedite your journey into the next reality.

Antonia's accelerated transformation started in 2006 when she discovered her capacity to dissolve lifetimes of pain in her own body through a harrowing journey inward. As her reality shifted, her energies increased, and she was soon assisting clients in activating their process of expansion. Raising the vibration by inviting a deep seeing of the truth of pain, she enables their process of dissolution of ancient trauma stories. As her expansion continues, she shares the energy and awareness it reveals.

Antonia spent her early decades collecting degrees at prestigious institutions of higher learning. She graduated from OISE, the University of Toronto, with a Masters of Education in Counseling Psychology. In addition, she has a Masters of Arts in International Development from St. Mary's University in Halifax. She graduated from the Center for Ayurveda and Indian Systems of Healing (CAISH), where she became a certified Ayurvedic Counselor, and studied Women's Herbal Remedies at the Ayurvedic Institute in New Mexico and Ayurvedic Psychotherapy at Renaissance Yoga and Ayurveda in Toronto.

She built up knowledge, intellect, data, and credibility. Now, she is learning to unlearn. To expand awareness, she disassembles the infrastructure of the mind and surrenders it to the heart. Because she is here to let it all go—all but the love.

Like many on this journey, the work—the psychotherapy, the energetics, and now the podcast and healing modules—were compulsive in nature. She is pulled by the need to contribute to the collective sharing of our visions in the next phase of our global evolution.

In this life, Antonia plays the roles of Registered Psychotherapist, Plant Medicine Integration Counselor, Transmuter/Facilitator, Ayurvedic Counselor, Yoga and Meditation Teacher, and Retreat Facilitator and is now in training for Plant Medicine Facilitation. As an integrative therapist, she blends Western modalities of a therapeutic relationship with the metaphysical transmutation of the trauma of separation. Antonia helps people see the pain as a signal, a signpost, and an opportunity for expansion; to bring awareness to pain and integrate our hidden suffering into the greater whole.

Antonia takes you to deeper levels of knowing and being through her one-on-one healing sessions, online modules, workshops, and retreats. She anchors you in her presence to direct the energies of consciousness and healing into sights unseen. To truly see the 3D in your body transforms it into a higher Self. She invites the power of awareness to raise the vibration, detoxing layers of 3D pain you hold in your body. Her goal is to assist healers, seekers, and psychonauts in preparation for a wave of healing as our collective, ancient traumas surface more rapidly and readily on our path to the next reality.

This is her passion. This is her destiny. This is her Collective.

In her non-professional life, her favorite pastimes are kayaking, reading, painting, meditating, and playing in her sacred garden. She is originally from the Western Provinces of Alberta, and B.C.

Keep walking with me on an often uncomfortable but magical journey into your next reality. It's not an easy path because we must see our pain for what it really is. This is the alchemy of awareness. This is the transmutation of pain into love and dark into light. This is the next dimension.

Visit TribeToCollective.com and get firsthand access to the Tribe to Collective Video Modules, retreat dates, events, blogs, podcast interviews, and much more.

If Dismantling the 3rd Dimension ignited or fed your journey in any way, please do take a couple of minutes to leave an honest review with the retailer you purchased from. Your feedback and support is greatly appreciated.

~ Antonia

Made in the USA
Las Vegas, NV
27 July 2023

75324363R00155